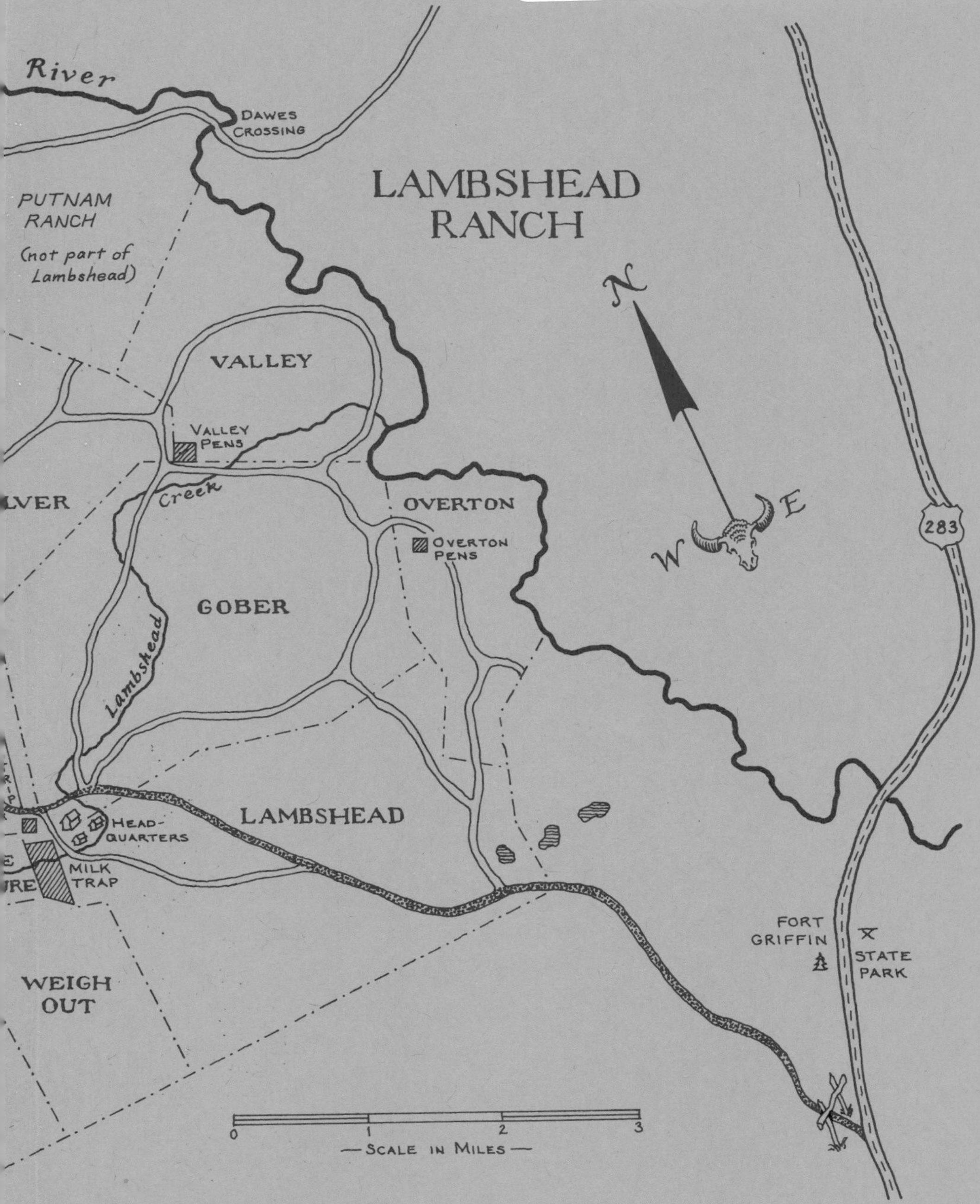
River
DAWES CROSSING
LAMBSHEAD RANCH
PUTNAM RANCH
(not part of Lambshead)
N
E
W
VALLEY
VALLEY PENS
Creek
OVERTON
OVERTON PENS
283
GOBER
Lambshead
LAMBSHEAD
HEAD-QUARTERS
MILK TRAP
WEIGH OUT
FORT GRIFFIN
STATE PARK
0
1
2
3
SCALE IN MILES

LAMBSHEAD LEGACY

NUMBER SIXTY-SIX:
The Centennial Series of the Association of Former Students, Texas A&M University

Watt R. Matthews at Headquarters, Lambshead Ranch, 1965.
Photograph, Guy Gillette. Courtesy Guy Gillette

LAMBSHEAD LEGACY

The Ranch Diary of Watt R. Matthews

EDITED BY JANET M. NEUGEBAUER

INTRODUCTION BY FRANCES MAYHUGH HOLDEN

Texas A&M University Press
College Station

04 03 02 01 00 99 98 97 5 4 3 2 1

Map of Lambshead Ranch drawn by Amy Troyansky.

The paper used in this book meets the minimum requirements of the American National Standard for Permanence of Paper for Printed Library Materials, Z39.48-1984. Binding materials have been chosen for durability.

Library of Congress Cataloging-in-Publication Data

Matthews, Watt.
Lambshead legacy : the ranch diary of Watt R. Matthews / edited by Janet M. Neugebauer ; introduction by Frances Mayhugh Holden.
p. cm. — (The Centennial series of the Association of Former Students, Texas A&M University ; no. 66)
Includes bibliographical references (p.) and index.
ISBN 0-89096-738-5
1. Matthews, Watt—Diaries. 2. Ranchers—Texas—Brazos River Region—Diaries. 3. Ranch life—Texas—Brazos River Region. 4. Lambshead Ranch (Tex.)—Biography. 5. Brazos River Region (Tex.)—Biography. I. Neugebauer, Janet M., 1935- . II. Title. III. Series.
F392.B842M38 1997
976.4'06'092—dc20 96-41415
CIP

For Watt R. Matthews,
gentleman rancher

CONTENTS

ILLUSTRATIONS

MAP

PREFACE

Watkins Reynolds "Watt" Matthews is highly regarded locally in Clear Fork country, throughout Texas, and beyond. He is considered to be a man of vision with sound judgment and an experienced, successful rancher. This he has proven to be in his contacts with those involved with the creation of this book, which focuses on Watt and the ranch called Lambshead.

Watt Matthews made his ranch diary, dated January 1, 1951, through December 31, 1980, available to historians and authors William Curry Holden and Frances Mayhugh Holden for copying. The Holdens convinced him that the diary was not "dull as dishwater," as he often had claimed. He modestly agreed that the daily record of the cow-calf operation of their family-owned ranch would accurately portray Lambshead, which has often been described as one of the finest ranches in Texas and the American West.

Watt earlier had been most helpful with Frances Mayhugh Holden's research for a volume entitled *Lambshead before Interwoven*, published by Texas A&M University Press in 1982. He had confidence that the Holdens would handle with care the little leatherbound books, thirty volumes vital to him as references of carefully recorded ranch work and other events of importance.

Janet Neugebauer, upon seeing the copy of the diary, asked if she might edit it, having completed a similar editing of *Plains Farmer: The Diary of William G. DeLoach, 1914–1964*, published by Texas A&M University Press in 1991. After Watt R. Matthews agreed that Janet Neugebauer could edit the diary and Frances M. Holden write an introduction to it, an agreement to this effect was properly signed.

Lambshead Legacy focuses on the ranch, Watt R. Matthews and his extraordinary achievements at Lambshead Ranch. The reader of this book may then judge if Janet Neugebauer has interpreted and enlivened Watt's diary and if Frances Mayhugh Holden has properly introduced you to Watt Matthews, gentleman-rancher, as well as Lambshead Ranch.

INTRODUCER'S ACKNOWLEDGMENTS

The person who most inspired this Introduction to *Lambshead Legacy: The Ranch Diary of Watt R. Matthews* is the gentleman-rancher who wrote the diary. The other person who inspired and encouraged me is my late husband and mentor, William Curry Holden. We both realized the rarity and historic value of Watt's record of the day-to-day cattle work and other events on this family-owned working ranch in northwest Texas.

Watt's interpretation of his mother, Sallie Reynolds Matthews's frontier classic *Interwoven* was of special benefit. He aided in our understanding of his two families and Lambshead Ranch. He also took great pains to show us the land, its pastures, pens, and varied aspects of ranch work and to explain the ranch operation. He then showed us the cattle, the wildlife, and his faithfully restored historic family homes.

My enduring thanks go to Watt for my introduction to four of his sisters, Susan (Susette) Matthews Burns and her family, Ethel Matthews Casey and her family, Lucile Matthews Brittingham and her family, Sallie Matthews Reynolds Judd and her family, and his one brother Joseph Beck (Joe B.) Matthews and his one child, a son. I am in turn indebted to all of these generations for their assistance with my two books about their ranch of Lambshead. This association also developed into friendships and sharing of recollections of their own family experiences, their photographs, and many hours of valuable taped information.

My warm thanks to all Reynolds and Matthews family members and friends who have helped in the Introduction of Watt R. Matthews and the Lambshead Ranch. Glenn Reynolds, Susan Hughes, and Mary Fru Reynolds Pealer also shared Reynolds and Matthews genealogy, documents and photographs, along with family stories, especially those about George and William D. Reynolds. Joseph E. (Joe) Blanton and other members of his family have made available Matthews family and other rare photographs to illustrate this Introduction.

I especially wish to give grateful appreciation to John Brittingham who has generously given his valuable time and personal knowledge to enrich the Introduction.

Watt's numerous friends in the Albany area and a variety of ranchers and other persons throughout Texas and even in New York City readily gave their pertinent recollections of Watt and Lambshead Ranch. I am not only indebted to these friends of Watt, but also I am ever more deeply in debt to the capable, dependable, and experienced men and women who are vital to keeping the ranch in such good working order. There were Terry Moberly, ranch foreman, and dependable Bill and Doris Cauble. Carrol Martin guided me through pastures and pens and created a map to accurately interpret them for readers of Watt's diary. For their patient sharing of their experiences and knowledge of the ranch and its operation, I extend to all these people a grateful "thank you."

Watt has been considerate in introducing to me talented, professional people. His guests included photographers, researchers, journalists, and, among others, his Princeton University "Class of '21," who held their reunion at Lambshead. Their suggestions and expertise have been most helpful in describing interests and events of consequence to Watt, his family, the ranch, and the people of the Albany area. Without the help of Watt and all of these people this Introduction could never have been put together nor written.

I keenly appreciate every person who has had a part in the creation of an honest Introduction to Watt R. Matthews and the Matthews family ranch. I sincerely thank Albany area friends; Joan Farmer for her assistance as archivist of the Old Jail Art Center in Albany; Mildred Diller for her personal recollections; Robert (Bob) and wife Nancy Green and Clifton (Cliff) and wife Shirley Caldwell who furnished documents and the benefit of their long-time association with Watt, his family, and Lambshead Ranch. To all the ranchers who have helped out I give special thanks, especially to Jim Humphreys, retired manager of the Pitchfork Ranch. I am grateful to my associate and editor-author, Janet Neugebauer, who, as archivist of the Southwest Collection of Texas Tech University, also assisted with required photographs. Photographers and friends of Watt have contributed their talents to illustrate this book. The Gillettes, father Guy of New York City and son Pipp, a Texas rancher, have made available definitive photographs of Watt as rancher and historical preservationist.

I wish to thank the staff of Texas A&M University Press. I sincerely appreciate their interest, expertise, and encouragement throughout my part in the development of this book. I am indebted to my talented and faithful typists, Elizabeth Pass, TyAnna Herrington, and Richard Mason, and my brother Roger P. Mayhugh, who also contributed to the completion of this work.

To my supportive family and friends and to all the special people who have contributed to the writing of this Introduction to Watt and Lambshead Ranch, I give my warm and sincere thanks.

Frances Mayhugh Holden

EDITOR'S ACKNOWLEDGMENTS

Editing Watt Matthews's diary provided a wonderful opportunity to know this man and to learn how ranchers live and work. I am grateful to Frances Holden for sharing this opportunity with me. It has opened a whole new world. I could not, however, have done my part alone. Many people helped.

Watt gave me many tours of Lambshead Ranch, explaining the various aspects of ranching as we went. His friends and relatives also helped with explanations when I was confused. Frances Holden and Carrol Martin carefully compiled the map of Lambshead Ranch that cartographer Amy Troyansky drew for this book. John Brittingham read my manuscript of the edited diary. Because he was a part of so many of the events Watt recorded, his comments were invaluable. Their patience and attention to detail are greatly appreciated. They all corrected many of my mistakes. Any that remain are my own.

Family members generously allowed me to reproduce photographs from many albums at Lambshead Ranch and they helped with identification. Over the years these were sent to Watt. My thanks to these creative photographers whose identity is now unknown. I take no credit for their work.

Most of all, I am grateful to Watt Matthews for the hours he spent recording each day's activities and for allowing me to edit his diary. He wrote conscientiously for more than forty years and his first-hand account of life on a Texas family ranch is, indeed, a legacy that he left for future generations.

Janet M. Neugebauer

EDITORIAL POLICIES AND PROCEDURES

Selected entries from the diary of Watt R. Matthews form the basis of this story of the day-to-day operations of a Texas family ranch during the last half of the twentieth century. Because ranching is the story of cattle, weather, grass, markets, and the people who know how to combine these factors profitably, emphasis has been given to those entries offering insight into Watt's combination of these factors and the recognition he has received for his management of Lambshead Ranch.

Family activities are one thread that holds this story together; however, most entries about the social life of "Albany's most eligible bachelor" are repetitious and so have been excluded. Often Watt's day ended at a friend's house for a toddy and supper, or he hosted friends at Lambshead Ranch for toddies and supper. He treasured these friendships, but, because of space limitations, this brief comment about the warm hospitality of cattle people will have to suffice.

Annotations place Watt and his ranching operation in the larger context of the beef cattle industry. Nothing else would be appropriate. He was equally at home in the branding pens, in the winner's circle at a stock show, in a board meeting of a national breed association, or with fellow rancher, U.S. President Lyndon B. Johnson.

Watt made entries not at the end of each day, but the following morning. Thus his entries lack the feeling about the day's experiences that is captured when a diarist writes each evening, before any part fades during a night's sleep. In fact, often several days passed before Watt brought his diary up to date, which may be the reason strong feelings were seldom expressed.

Abbreviations were common in the cryptic entries that Watt intended only for his own reference, not for publication. Because the abbreviations have no special significance, the words have been spelled out to facilitate reading. Punctuation often was lacking, but the spelling and grammar generally were in good shape; thus corrections were seldom made. Editor's additions and annotations are bracketed and italicized.

The diary is really a big tally book of Watt's life after 1950. After working the cattle in a particular pasture, he recorded the number, the kind of animal (calves, steers, etc.), the work that was done, the pasture they were moved to, or the sale price. Likewise, he recorded the weather at Lambshead Ranch each day, the names of visitors, all the places he went, and each person he saw. When he attended a party, he recorded the number of people and listed their names. He referred to the diary often to refresh his memory or settle disputes.

Watt contended that he deserved no credit for his accomplishments—he merely did what he enjoyed doing. That contentment with his life's work was quite obvious during my visits to Lambshead Ranch. Always the gracious host, he went about business as usual, never in a hurry or under stress. He seemed to savor each task and each moment, especially the time he spent taking visitors on "tour." Every visitor got a tour of the ranch. I asked how he could do that so often with such interest and enthusiasm. He responded that it was easy to be interested, because he was just checking on his cattle while enjoying the company of his friends. Perhaps readers will find Watt Matthews's enjoyment of ranch life as contagious as I did.

Janet M. Neugebauer

PART I

Introduction:

Watkins Reynolds "Watt" Matthews and Lambshead Ranch

BY FRANCES M. HOLDEN

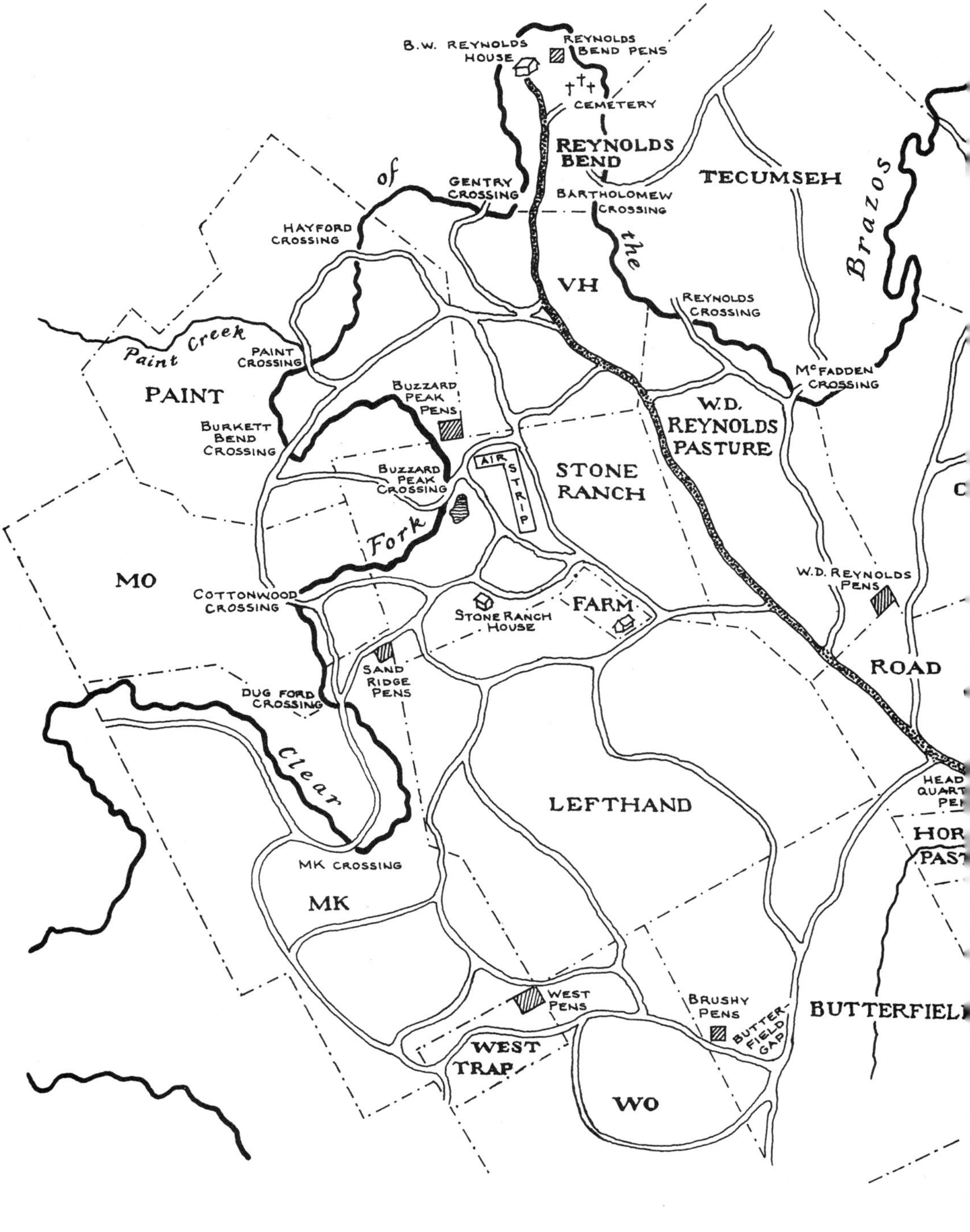

B.W. REYNOLDS HOUSE
REYNOLDS BEND PENS
CEMETERY
REYNOLDS BEND
TECUMSEH
Brazos
of
GENTRY CROSSING
BARTHOLOMEW CROSSING
the
HAYFORD CROSSING
VH
REYNOLDS CROSSING
Paint Creek
PAINT CROSSING
McFADDEN CROSSING
PAINT
BUZZARD PEAK PENS
W.D. REYNOLDS PASTURE
BURKETT BEND CROSSING
AIR STRIP
STONE RANCH
BUZZARD PEAK CROSSING
Fork
MO
W.D. REYNOLDS PENS
COTTONWOOD CROSSING
STONE RANCH HOUSE
FARM
ROAD
SAND RIDGE PENS
DUG FORD CROSSING
Clear
LEFTHAND
MK CROSSING
MK
WEST PENS
BRUSHY PENS
BUTTERFIELD GAP
BUTTERFIEL
WEST TRAP
WO

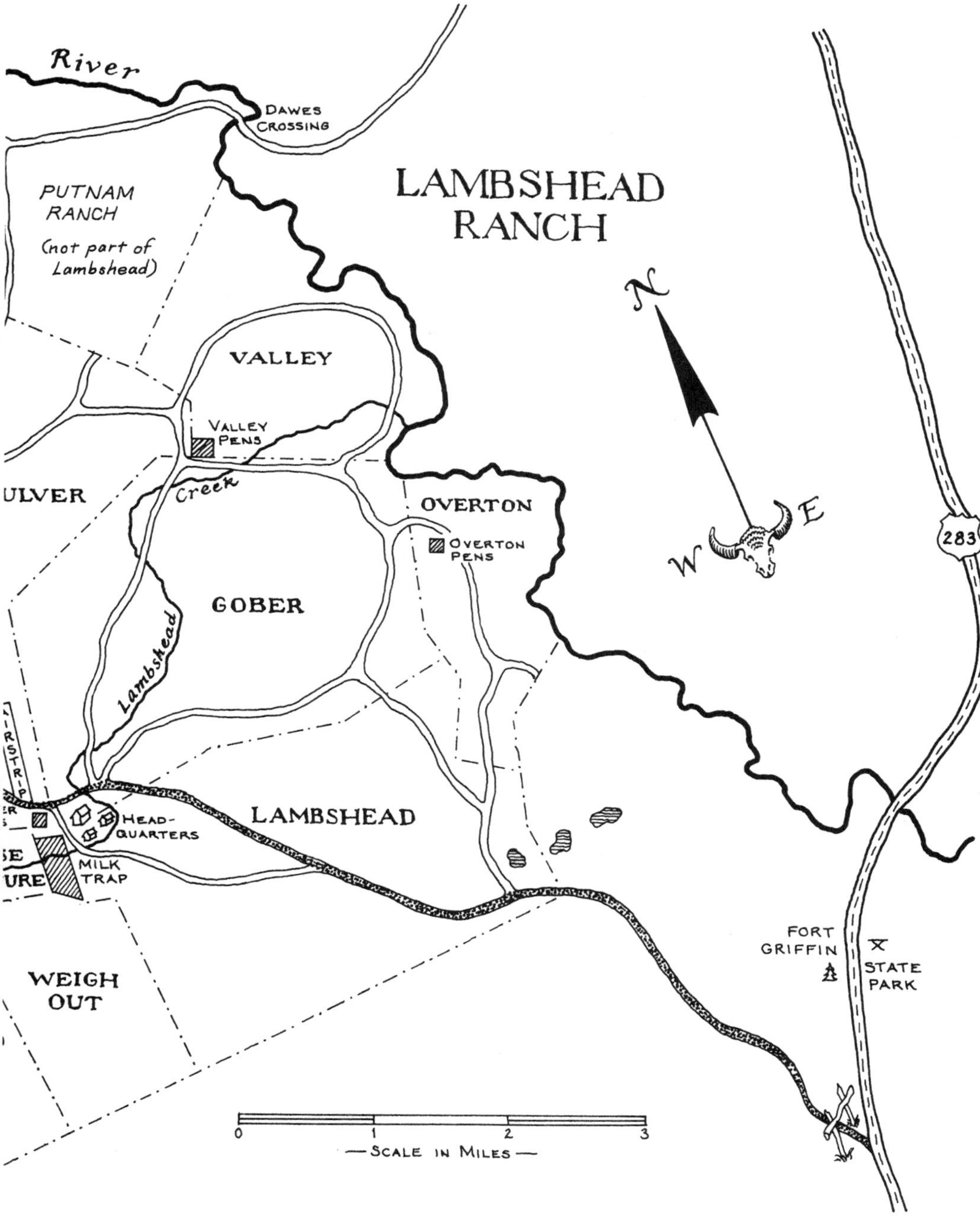
River
DAWES CROSSING
PUTNAM RANCH
(not part of Lambshead)
LAMBSHEAD RANCH
N
E
W
VALLEY
VALLEY PENS
Creek
ULVER
OVERTON
OVERTON PENS
283
GOBER
Lambshead
AIRSTRIP
HEAD-QUARTERS
LAMBSHEAD
MILK TRAP
FORT GRIFFIN STATE PARK
WEIGH OUT
0
1
2
3
SCALE IN MILES

Watt and Lambshead

Born on February 1, 1899, Watt R. Matthews was the eighth and last child of a frontier lady, Sallie Reynolds Matthews, and a trail driver and rancher, John Alexander Matthews. In 1885, the couple—assisted by Sallie's two older brothers, George Thomas Reynolds and William D. ("Will") Reynolds—began putting together the fifty thousand acres that would become Lambshead Ranch. The "Reynolds boys" and John A. Matthews had been in the cattle business together, but in 1885 Sallie and John A. decided to go it alone. They had a dream; by 1909, they had realized it. That year they finally were able to purchase the Lambshead Valley and complete the assembly of their remarkably productive ranch. This ranch, of all those they knew about, was the most historic and the most generously endowed by nature.

For twenty-seven miles, Lambshead is encircled by a river; it has good water, grass, and foliage for cattle, horses, and a plenitude of wildlife. No minerals came to light in a 1913 digging, but eventually oil was discovered—handy security for droughty years.

Lambshead Ranch was named for Thomas Lambshead, a farmer from Devon, England, who, in the 1850s, came with his wife and little daughter to the ranch's present Lambshead Valley. The family located at the confluence of a stream and the Clear Fork Branch of the Brazos River. The Clear Fork, with its ever-flowing clear waters, encircles nearly the entire ranch. The smaller stream became known as Lambshead Creek. Upon that creek, John A. Matthews located a camp in 1907. Expanded in 1919, the camp became headquarters for Lambshead Ranch. As was cus-

Watt R. Matthews as a young schoolboy in Fort Worth, 1909.
Courtesy Joe E. Blanton Collection

tomary, the ranch took the name of the well-known creek, a geographical feature on the ranch property.

A portion of Lambshead lay in Throckmorton County; the remainder was in Shackelford County. The ranch was well located near cattle markets, being 120 miles west of Fort Worth, Texas, and seventeen miles northwest of the lively, historic little town of Albany, county seat of Shackelford County. This town is where Watt was born.

Family-owned ranches are not uncommon in Texas. Such a ranch may operate as a corporation, a trust, or a one-man enterprise. The most famous such "spreads" were founded a century ago. A key to their longevity has been experienced managers, especially ones who know how to work well both with third-generation owners and with the extra edge that oil production has added to ranch operation. Oil income offers a ranch

Lambshead Ranch Headquarters. The house, enlarged and refurbished, was completed in 1919. Courtesy Watt R. Matthews

protection against a long drought, the vagaries of the cattle market, devastating fires, floods, and other unpredictable events.

The Pitchfork Ranch in Northwest Texas has been very successful since the original owners, who were experienced businessmen in St. Louis, Missouri, established it in 1880. Several other historic ranches are located within a hundred-mile radius of Lambshead. These include Burk Burnett's 6666, the Waggoner DDD, and the Swenson SMS, all of which have been operated successfully for over a hundred years. The 6666, DDD, and SMS had no sons in the family to operate their properties; therefore, managers were chosen with grave concern.

Lambshead Ranch, their historic neighbor to the south, stands in contrast to these other ranches, as it always has been managed by family members. "Converting grass into beef cattle at a profit" has been the objective of the Matthews men, their supportive wives, and other family members since John A. Matthews and Sallie Reynolds Matthews began putting Lambshead Ranch together in 1885.

Joseph Beck "Uncle Joe" Matthews, Watt's grandfather, from whom he inherited his tradition as "Host of Clear Fork country." Courtesy Watt R. Matthews

John A. Matthews and wife Sallie Reynolds Matthews at their Albany residence, 1936. Courtesy Joe. E. Blanton Collection

For generations, the Matthews have displayed a special talent for ranching. John A. Matthews entered the cattle business soon after he returned from an early trail drive with Ben Reynolds (another of Sallie's brothers) from Colorado to Nevada in 1872. John A.'s father, Joseph Beck ("Uncle Joe") Matthews, introduced barbed wire to the Clear Fork country in 1880. Over the next few years, the newly formed Reynolds Brothers and John A. Matthews partnership fenced in the open range, enclosing the first pastures in what is now Lambshead Ranch. John A. demonstrated as much aptitude for running a large enclosed pasture ranch as his brother-in-law, George T. Reynolds, had shown in the era of the open trail drive.

After the deaths of Sallie in 1938 and John A. in 1941, the ranch passed into the hands of their two living sons and five daughters. Watt and his older brother, Joe B. Matthews, assumed responsibility for managing this successful ranch and caring for their five sisters, as they had promised their parents. Joe B. Matthews died in 1977, and at that time the responsibility for maintaining Lambshead as a model of ranching conservation, preservation, and management fell entirely to Watt.

WATT THE RANCHER, WATT THE MAN

Watt R. Matthews, the master of Lambshead Ranch, is also a master of simplicity. Simplicity is his keynote; it is evident in his speech, his dress, his bunkhouse, and the family homes he has restored on Lambshead Ranch. The architecture is simple and sparse. The interior furnishings are simple and honest, evoking the lives of Watt's ancestors who lived there on the frontier.

Watt's speech is simple, direct, and amusingly pithy. When he "throws in" a delightful "Wattism"—a simple phrase or word characteristic of his flow of speech, such as "Pay no tench"—it seems to come straight out of the frontier era epitomized by his ranch.

On a typical weekday, Watt can be found wearing his work clothes, out in the pastures or wherever his cow-calf ranching operation takes him. Watt enjoys continuing the daily and yearly work schedule established by his two grandfathers, his father, his Uncle George T. Reynolds, and other Reynolds and Matthews men.

On the first day of a spring roundup, for example, Watt starts the day before dawn at the cookshack, which is ablaze with light and with warmth from large stone fireplaces at either end of the long room. Assembled for this annual event is a small crowd of men and a few women—assorted members of the Matthews and Reynolds clan, ranch hands, and a few faithful friends who seldom miss spring roundup at Lambshead. Watt, with his quirky smile, welcomes and shakes the hand of each person there except the cook, who gets an encouraging slap on the back.

Dawn has not yet broken, but the horses, saddled for the cowhands to use in rounding up the cows and their calves, have been loaded into a large red cattle truck parked by the big red barn across from the cookshack. The hands and Watt's guests wash down a hearty breakfast with steaming

Oliver Jackson at the steam table ready for hungry hands or Watt's guests.
Courtesy Joe E. Blanton Collection

cups of strong black coffee. With breakfast finished, Watt steps up onto the raised stone hearth of the north fireplace.

Watt's responsibility in the Matthews Family Ranch partnership is to operate the ranch and to be in charge of the work. This morning, he is ready to lay out the day's work for the hands. Included are cowboys from neighboring ranches who have come to help out, as is the custom among ranchers. All wear similar outfits. Each wide-brimmed hat has been crushed to conform comfortably to a particular head; each has its own individual "bash" to crown and brim. Blue denim jeans and heavy denim jackets top high- or medium-heeled leather boots, spurs, and well-worn leather chaps slung low on hips. The men are of several heights, but most are nearly six feet tall or taller.

At five feet six ("plus two" with his medium-heeled boots on), Watt was born to be a little man; but this day there is no doubt as to who is in charge. He stands straight in well-washed, crisply ironed blue denim jeans, their cuffs brushing the tops of good leather boots handmade by Abilene's James Luskey. Watt's shirt of fine cotton has a pattern of small red checks. His "Spanish Gourd" brand has been embroidered, by a neighbor lady, on the left cuff. He cinches his shirt into jeans with a slim leather belt. Watt usually wears a small navy or black silk kerchief knotted inside his shirt collar with the points hanging down. Watt is not a smoker, as his flat shirt pocket reveals; however, he goes ready for any emergency, with work gloves stuck in his right hip pocket.

Watt also knows how to dress up. He has his "Sunday best" pants and jackets or suits of fine British woolens or tweeds, which he and friends from his days as a Fort Worth schoolboy select from samples brought over by a London tailor. Out of this cloth, a Fort Worth tailor then makes up suits for each customer. Watt selects fabric for his tuxedos from the same source. His white shirts are made to order. Handsome black dress boots, too, are made to order by his favorite boot maker; and his latest hat, properly "bashed," is on for dress occasions, funerals, and weddings. In cold weather, he sometimes wears a handsome wool overcoat that he purchased in New York during his years at Princeton University.

But Watt usually wears his "trademark" hat of fawn-colored felt, encircled by a brown-and-gray twisted wool cord. The three-inch brim and medium crown are crushed by the owner's strong hands into his own comfortable, individual shape, "so the branches won't knock it off my head when I ride," Watt says.

Now Watt's bright blue eyes, set into his weathered face, look directly at the men. He gives his orders for the day in a soft but firm drawl: "I will meet you at the West Pens to start branding at ten o'clock."

The Lefthand, MK, and WO pastures are served by the West Pens. These three pastures to the west of Headquarters hold about three hundred head of three-year-old cows, most of which have calved since being placed there in October after the fall roundup. Selected Hereford bulls then were turned in with the cows. Watt, his brother Joe B., and their foreman expect a fine calf crop, as all signs so far have been good.

The cookshack crowd roars out of Headquarters shortly after nine o'clock, with Watt's pickup truck in the lead. On this warm April morn-

Joe B. (left) *and Watt R. Matthews inspect pastures of the ranch after taking over responsibilities in 1941 after the deaths of both of their parents.*
Courtesy Watt R. Matthews

ing, cowboys wrestle a bawling calf onto a branding table under Watt's watchful eye. The hands vaccinate, dehorn if necessary, and, if male, castrate the animal. "Mr. Watt"—so called to differentiate him from his paternal grandfather, who was called "Uncle Watt"—dons a pair of cotton gloves, grabs the heavy steel handle of his gray-hot branding iron, and sears the Matthews family's "open A–Lazy V" brand into the hides of the heifers and the "newly made" steers. Watt walks over to the folks leaning on the high wooden fence. The men have questions. Some of the women turn away; they hear the low moaning response of the cow mothers to their babies' bawling.

Branding has a long tradition, having been carried to Spain by the Moors and subsequently brought to the Americas. By 1640, Spanish settlers had brought cattle and their large, heavy marking irons, first to

John A. Matthews's AV cattle before herd was improved by use of registered Hereford and other breeds of bulls. Courtesy Joe E. Blanton Collection

Mexico and then to Texas. Watt and his family predecessors have been putting hot iron to hide in these same pastures for over a century.

In the 1880s, calves were branded in the pastures, as there were no pens. Whenever John A. Matthews found a five- to six-month-old calf, it was roped and thrown, and its hind legs were held down by a helper. At the same time, John A. was heating his iron over a quickly made fire. When it grew gray-hot, he applied his "open A–Lazy V" brand to the calf's upper left side. Branding moved from the ground to the "table" in the 1940s.

After Watt brands the Hereford steers and heifers, he also brands the heifers with the last digit of the year, which is placed on the left shoulder. Watt Matthews also burns his own Spanish Gourd brand on the left thigh of his Longhorn bulls and steers. He ear marks the heifers with a crop and underbit creating an open v-cut out of the bottom of the ear. Watt, ranch hands, and members of the Matthews family know how to "read" these marks.

Watt inherited the Spanish Gourd brand from his maternal grandfather, Barber Watkins Reynolds. Lambshead's Spanish Gourd dates to 1858, when Reynolds was on the move from Shelby County, Texas, with his family. They were leaving the monotony of a cotton farm for excitement on the frontier they found at Palo Pinto, Texas. Somewhere along the way, Reynolds met up with the owner of a small herd of cattle with the Spanish Gourd brand and traded for them.

CYCLES OF WORK

Lambshead is a cow-calf operation, breeding heifers and cows each year and selling their progeny. The ranch's history spans the various stages of the development of the cattle industry in the United States, from cow-hunting on the open range of the Texas frontier to breeding in the enclosed or fenced pasture common in American ranching today. In the 1940s, cattle trucks replaced the "drive" to market, simplifying the entire marketing process, from ranch to feed lots. Through the years, with the introduction of new breeds, the cattle themselves have changed, too.

Lambshead operates on a yearly cycle tied to the seasons. Cattle are moved through different ranch pastures during each season, depending on their stage of growth, their age, and market conditions. Watt's diaries show how the work moves over the ranch, from pasture to pasture, on a regular schedule. Roundups and brandings are placed on the work schedule for the ranch.

The modern story of Lambshead Ranch is one of seasonal work simplified. Branding begins in February and continues well into May, sometimes June, if the calf crop is good. After the new crop is branded, calves are weaned and separated from their mothers in October and November. As summer wanes, in August, open cows (cows without calves) are sold, along with other "nonkeepers." "The best place to keep an old cow is in the bank," Watt's older brother Joe B. Matthews, president of the bank, used to say. Steers and heifers are shaped up and sold in late May or early June. Steers are sold according to the market, as is every animal the rancher (Watt) does not want. Selected bulls usually are cut out and put in the W. D. Reynolds Pasture with the cows in February and taken out during the summer, generally in July. The animals are fed intensively during the winter, until springtime rains cause the grass to green up. In the summer, the bulls are taken to the Bull Pasture. Then the seasonal cycle begins again, with the branding of a new calf crop, the ranch's main economic product. (Sometimes, in a good year, native pecans also can be sold at a profit.)

PASTURES AND PENS

The ranch is composed of two operating areas—the pastures and Headquarters. Lambshead's fine pastures, along with the water in the Clear Fork branch of the Brazos River, are its greatest basic resources. The pastures were judiciously thought through, planned, and laid out like a giant checkerboard to provide access to the ingredients that would ensure a successful cow-calf operation: good land and grass, and plenty of clear water.

Ordinarily, all cattle, horses, and other animals deemed necessary for the ranch are trucked in and unloaded in the pens of the pastures allotted to them. Here animals encounter varied grasses and edible weeds, as well as good water. There are attractive thickets where a cow can hide herself and her calf so effectively that no plane, helicopter, or sharp-eyed cowhand can discover them. Therefore, spring and fall roundups always are a challenge to the men in charge of moving the cattle into the corrals, traps, and pens for calf branding. Other drives from one pasture to another follow the branding. Selected livestock are cut out to be loaded into trucks and driven to feed lots or other market centers.

John A. Matthews and the Reynolds brothers, and later Watt and Joe B. Matthews, understood these requirements of successful cattle ranching. Thus Lambshead was developed to facilitate the production of calves. Cows would be placed near good water and grass so that they would be content; in consequence, they would produce healthier calves, and these in turn would yield a healthier profit for the ranch. Still, for more than a century, the layout of Lambshead pastures gradually has been revised. Pastures have been reduced in size, as Watt has proven that smaller pastures yield a better product.

At the time this book was written, Lambshead's forty thousand acres (at one time the ranch had been 50,000 acres) were laid out strategically in sixteen inviting pastures. In 1951, when Watt began writing his diaries, two other pastures, Tecumseh and Long, existed, making eighteen. The pastures were divided so that cattle could be moved easily from one area to another, according to seasonal demands and the marketing strategy developed at Headquarters.

Each pasture is focused on a set of corner pens. The ideal is to have four pastures around one large set of pens, which handles cattle from all those pastures. The pens are designed to be functional and to serve various purposes. They must hold market-tabbed animals for loading into trucks. They must handle mother cows and calves—and sometimes mares and their colts, as well as buffalo and Longhorn steers—for the branding process. They can serve as a stage for "showing off" by hands who are handy with a rope and enjoy subduing broncs and frisky ponies.

The owner-manager usually designs the pens of wood planks or, more recently, iron pipes. At Lambshead the layout and design of pens, corrals, and traps show a master's hand at work in arranging these elements to the mutual advantage of men, their horses, and the animals. Among the pens on the ranch are very old ones put up by Watt's father, John A. Matthews, a hundred years ago. They are of wood and are still used. A memorable early day foreman, whose son succeeded him, created sets of functional pens. The newer iron pens have turned out to be true works of art, as well as excellent working pens. Watt has designed several handsome, functional sets, the Valley Pens among them. His last set, made of heavy iron pipes, will hold huge Longhorn steers and big buffalo.

Optimal location of the branding pens is vital to successful spring and fall work. This work has become easier as pens have come to be located at either end of the pastures and as the pastures' sizes have been reduced. Now the hands can do better work in a shorter time. The great expense of a helicopter to help round up the cows and calves has been eliminated. Now a pickup truck, with a horn that signals "feed" to the animals, is used. Cowhands on horseback urge the calves into the pens. The calves are put on the branding table. There, every man has a job to do and the experience to do it well.

The Pastures and Their Names

Each pasture occupies its own historic position on the larger Lambshead map. Tecumseh and Long Pastures, the first pastures acquired by John A. Matthews, have been part of the Comanche Indian reservation and was named for a notable Comanche, Chief Katumse. (Scholars use various spellings; John A. chose to use the Tecumseh spelling so it would relate to the spelling on the professional maps.) In 1856, the chief officially greeted Lt. Col. Robert E. Lee, who had come to take command of the U.S. Army post, Camp Cooper, which had been created out of the reservation lands. Later, in 1878, Camp Cooper became available for purchase by John A. Matthews. It made a valuable combination with the Stone Ranch pasture, which he and associates George T. Reynolds and W. D. Reynolds located in the 1880s. Butterfield Pens and Pasture received this name from the Butterfield Stage Trail, which in 1858 crossed the area.

Pens and pastures often have been named for the original settlers of the land: Culver; Gober; Overton; the Reynolds family—W. D., Ben, and their father, Barber Watkins Reynolds—of Reynolds Bend; Martin Van Buren Hoover, who married John A.'s sister Mattie; and Lambshead.

Some pens and pastures are named after cattle brands. The MO is the brand John A. Matthews brought to the ranch in 1885, upon amicably dissolving his association with George T. Reynolds and W. D. Reynolds in the cattle and trail driving business. The WO brand came to the ranch pastures on the hide of a stubborn old cow. When the pasture now called WO became the property of the Matthews family, this cow was on it. Whether driven or trucked away, she would be discovered again, contentedly grazing or drinking water on her old "stomping grounds." Her persistence merited reward. This dowager cow ruled "her pasture" for many contented years, dying there of old age. The MK brand was on a bull that stayed in one canyon. Both the canyon and the pasture were named MK after the bull.

Other pens and pastures carry names descriptive of geographical features: Sandridge, Valley, Buzzard Peak, Brushy, West, Lefthand, Road, and Paint. This last name reflects the reddened water carried by Paint

Creek along the banks of this pasture. Paint Creek is an ever-running stream which originates above Round Mountain and flows through red clay beds. Lefthand Pens and Pasture take their name from Lefthand Canyon.

The well-maintained main road that runs through Lambshead Ranch justifiably gives its name to the pasture it runs through the middle of. The name at Headquarters indicates that this place is the core of work on Lambshead Ranch. The names of Milk Trap and Weigh Out Pens announce their original utilitarian functions—for milk cows; and for holding, adjacent to the Headquarters, livestock being weighed out on scales for shipment to markets or elsewhere.

The Pens and Their Associated Pastures

1. Tecumseh and Long Pens Serve Tecumseh and Long Pastures: While at the time of this writing the Tecumseh and Long Pastures weren't a part of the ranch, at the time Watt wrote his diaries they were an integral part of Lambshead Ranch. Tecumseh and Long Pastures are strategically located on the far northeastern corner of Lambshead Ranch. Their good grass is well watered by Tecumseh Creek. Established in 1872, these pastures' 2,400 acres are separated by Tecumseh Creek into two large pastures of equal size. One, Tecumseh Pasture, runs north and south; the other, Long Pasture, runs east and west. Each has an identical pen, named for its respective pasture. The pens are located west of the fences.
2. Valley Pens Serve the Valley, Culver, and Gober Pastures: The Valley Pens and Pasture lie northeast of Lambshead's Headquarters. Valley Pasture is the ranch's best pasture; it has the best grasses, is well watered by the river, and is very well protected, being surrounded by high stone bluffs. This valley is abundantly rich: in grass and water, in human and animal life, in ancient history, and, more recently, in oil, as giant pump jacks there attest. Here Chief Katumse welcomed Lt. Col. Robert E. Lee to the Comanche reservation in the years after the Civil War. This pasture houses the Valley Pens, which also serve Culver and Gober Pastures.

3. Overton Pens Serve Overton Pasture:
   This excellent pasture adjoins the Gober Pasture on the east. It once was owned by the J. D. Overton family, who were neighbors and good friends of the Matthews and supplied them with fresh fruit and vegetables in the early 1900s. Sallie Matthews and John A. Matthews purchased this fine piece of property from the Overtons.
4. Reynolds Bend Pens Serve the Bend Pasture:
   Reynolds Bend is a fine protected valley contained within the bend of the Clear Fork River, which later circles around the foot of a rugged bluff on the north to make a very attractive setting for a home and ranch headquarters. The Bend Pens always have been part of the original pasture. The main road of Lambshead Ranch leads to the Bend, which lies north of Lambshead's Headquarters.
5. W. D. Reynolds Pens Serve William Reynolds, Culver, and Road Pastures:
   These pastures and pens, among the finest on the ranch, spread to the south of Reynolds Bend.
6. Brushy Pens Serve Butterfield and WO Pastures:
   This good pasture land lies on the south and southwest line of the ranch. Running across it, ruts of the historic Butterfield Stage Trail still may be glimpsed. The trail passes north, then veers toward the southwest to pass west of Headquarters. Sometimes Lambshead Hereford bulls will challenge small vehicles for right-of-way.
7. Buzzard Peak Pens Serve Stone Ranch, VH, and Paint Pastures:
   Stone Ranch Pasture was the first pasture located when the Reynolds brothers and John A. and Sallie Matthews began putting together the future Lambshead Ranch. As a little girl, Sallie had lived in the old Stone Ranch House, built in 1856, with her family, the B. W. Reynolds. The restoration of Stone Ranch House and its giant stone corrals, sheds, and lots was Watt Matthews's most ambitious historical restoration project. Work was completed in 1983. The VH Pasture was named for Watt's uncle on the Matthews side, Martin Van Buren Hoover.

Near the old Stone Ranch House are the original roundup

Watt at Stone Ranch House with restoration in progress, 1982. Dedicated by descendants of William D. Reynolds, 1983. Courtesy Watt R. Matthews

grounds of the 1880s. Each spring, scores of ranchers came here, from as far as the Rio Grande Valley and the Davis Mountains, hoping to find and brand their lost cattle. Severe storms would push cattle great distances from their range. The roundups also were enjoyed as social gatherings by ranching families. The old Roundup Grounds have become the Lambshead landing field, being large enough to accommodate DC-3s.

8. Sandridge Pens Serve Lefthand, MK, MO, and Stone Ranch Pastures:
   The Sandridge branding pens epitomize one of the best possible arrangements of pastures and pens. Here four adjoining pastures—Stone Ranch, Lefthand, MK, and MO—have pens together in one corner. This spatial arrangement makes it practical to synchronize work in these pastures, making the cow-calf drives easier for both animals and men.

These four enormous pastures cover a large part of the north western part of the ranch, enclosing varied terrain. Lefthand Canyon, a major geographical feature, is a valuable asset to the ranch for cattle work; its rich protected valley is ideal for pens and pastures.

9. West Pens Serve the Lefthand, MK, and WO Pastures:
These three pastures, located west of Lambshead Ranch Headquarters, together are almost one-third the size of Manhattan Island. Here the heifer yearlings are put after fall roundup. The bulls then are turned in with them.

10. Headquarters Pens and Corrals Serve Lambshead, Milk Trap, Weigh Out, Road, and Culver Pastures:
The Headquarters area, described in more detail later, is the focal point of ranch operation. Until the 1920s, Milk Trap Pasture held the milk cows which furnished milk and its products to Sallie's kitchen in Headquarters House. There were traps for horses, sheep, and sometimes Longhorn and orphaned calves. In the Hog Pens, feral hogs were held for butchering.

Weigh Out Pasture is where the Longhorn cattle are kept. These Watt has "restored" as the original cattle of the ranch. He also uses Longhorn bulls with first-calf Hereford heifers to make calving easier for the heifers and hence more profitable for the ranch.

Lambshead Pens are named for the ranch and are located adjacent to Headquarters. To the northwest of the Headquarters is the Road Pasture. Because it is adjacent to the Headquarters facilities, this pasture is used to hold cattle for shipping.

Recreational Use of Pastures

The William D. Reynolds crossing of the Clear Fork has a delightful picnic area adjacent to Reynolds Bend. William D. Reynolds and Susan Matthews Reynolds's lumber home was built just across the river. This is a favorite entertainment spot for fish-fries, birthday celebrations, and convivial gatherings for Watt's family and friends.

Watt's "tours" sometimes end up at one of his favorite locations on the river. Invited ranch neighbors and other friends gather there for toddies, tall stories, singing, and some of the best catfish guests have ever enjoyed. Here Watt often makes his famous hushpuppies, building a perfect fire and cooking them upon it in a heavy iron skillet. He performs this ceremoniously while his friends look on with gustatory anticipation.

Lambshead pastures thus serve dual purposes: their good grass and water are processed through the cattle to furnish profit, and they also afford pleasurable experiences for the Matthews family and their friends.

AT HEADQUARTERS

I feel sorry for any person who spends their life doing something they don't enjoy doing.
—*Watt R. Matthews*

No matter how good the grass, water, and cattle are, another ingredient is imperative to produce a good working ranch—the human element. At the top of the ranch hierarchy is the man (or, very rarely, the woman) who is an experienced manager or owner. Best of all is the ranch owner who knows how to run a ranch and has good judgment. If the ranch has a foreman, working under a manager or owner-manager, he must earn the respect of the hands under his direction, so they can work as a team. He also must merit the confidence of the owner or manager. The foreman then is able to perform his duties with confidence.

This rare combination of qualities was available at Lambshead Ranch. Watt's mother died in 1938 and his father in 1941. At that time, Watt, along with his older brother, Joe B. Matthews, shouldered management responsibilities. The two men shared ownership of the ranch with their five sisters. Joe B. had his own fine ranch, however, and Watt lived at Lambshead.

Watt proved adept in both areas required of a ranch owner-manager: the cattle work in the pastures and the Headquarters business office. As we shall see, Watt's expertise in ranch business affairs had been proven to the satisfaction of his very demanding father upon his return from Princeton University in 1921. He also displayed a talent for planning that seems almost hereditary, however. Gifted with good judgment, Watt appears to have worked out a phased "masterplan" for the work he would implement over many decades to improve Lambshead Ranch.

The Headquarters area holds the old Headquarters House, the Matthews family's bunkhouse containing individual rooms for Watt and three of his sisters. Later, Watt, a sister, and a nephew built separate houses to complete the Headquarters Quadrangle. Within the Quadrangle are the cookshack, Watt's bunkhouse and picket house, the big red barn, the tool shed, a very large truck shed, and, on the north end, quarters for hands, gardeners, and workers and their families. Other sheds house the ranch vehicles, service vehicles, very large machinery, old family cars and trucks, and Watt's car and his other vehicles. Watt's bunkhouse is to the north. His bedroom windows and sleeping porch overlook the entire Quadrangle. Nothing can escape his watchful eye.

Headquarters is the place, above all, where the office of the ranch's owner-manager is located. Here operational planning is done and financial decisions are made to keep the ranch functioning advantageously. Watt set up his office in the southwestern corner of the cookshack, with telephone and filing cabinets handy. Only the large stone south fireplace separates the office from the cookshack's front door. Watt easily keeps tabs on who comes and goes at the ranch, and he is easy to find for business or other matters.

Each morning for many years, Watt, before settling down to work at his cookshack desk, flipped on the radio for the 6 A.M. weather report and received temperature, relative humidity, precipitation, wind velocity, and other information important to Shackelford and Throckmorton counties. He listened carefully for news of grass or brush fires and heard the weather forecast for the week. Weather is the favorable or unfavorable force at work on the ranch, which experiences drought four years in ten.

Before 6 A.M. each day, Watt also picked up the phone and called Joe B. at his ranch about twelve miles away. Watt was in charge of daily ranch operations, but he and Joe B. would discuss long-range ranch policy, the cattle market, the details of ranch operations, and upcoming events. They would exchange the latest news—good, bad, or merely amusing—of family, friends, and others, producing loud chuckles on both ends of the line. They would agree on travel arrangements to livestock shows, cattle or horse sales, organization meetings (where Watt usually was on the board of directors), and social events. They usually would end the conversation as they opened it, with a discussion of the weather, having heard the early radio report. This routine continued until Joe B.'s death in 1977.

At his desk, Watt prepared profit-and-loss reports on ranch operations, as well as the annual report for the Internal Revenue Service. Yearly reports always showed a profit. There never was an audit.

Each day Watt carefully read the *Wall Street Journal,* especially the financial pages; he perused livestock journals and opened the mail when it was brought out from the Albany post office. He always read his *Princeton Alumni Weekly* and also kept close at hand a copy of *Principles and Problems of Estate Planning.* He handled correspondence, usually answering with a phone call or, if necessary, taking something into Albany for secretarial service. He devoted time each morning to his daily diaries, carefully recording the cattle work in the ranch pastures and other pertinent events.

WATT'S SCHOOLING

As soon as he could stand alone, Watt R. Matthews put his feet on Lambshead Ranch soil. In that soil he put down roots for life. Soon afterward, he was joined by his older sister May's two young sons, the Blanton boys. Watt's nephew Tom was a year younger than Watt, and Matt was three years younger. The three boys were as close as brothers and were raised as such. Joe B., Watt's one actual brother, was seventeen years older than he and left for college the year Watt was born. After a few months, Joe abandoned college and came home. His father opened the door one morning to find Joe sitting on the front steps. He said he had come home to go to ranching. Very shortly, his father found him a good ranch, and Joe B. happily went to work.

John A. Matthews trained his two sons and two grandsons, Tom and Matt Blanton, in the same way his brother-in-law, George T. Reynolds, had trained him. When quite young, Watt, Tom, and Matt were educated in "the school of experience." As they grew, the three boys learned to ride and manage horses. Watt practiced riding bareback. His ambition was to become a bareback rider in a circus. Instead, his father put him in charge of gentling and training the ranch horses.

Watt and the boys got into the branding pen as soon as Watt's father found they could wrestle a small calf to the ground. Watt wanted to brand it but had to begin with a "cold" iron, to practice placing the "open A–Lazy V" Matthews brand exactly where his father wanted it. Watt later refined this "art" in the branding pens. Watt's diminutive size never hurt him on the ranch. Watt's father told him that he always liked the way a little man handled cattle, especially in the branding pen, and that smaller men were lighter on horses.

Watt's father was well qualified to school the boys. As trail drivers at nineteen years of age, John A. and a friend (and later brother-in-law), Ben Reynolds, took a cattle herd from Colorado to Nevada and then traveled on to San Francisco. They returned "not richer, but wiser." John A. understood cattle, horses, men, land, water, sometimes weather, and what it takes to put together and run a successful ranch. The J. A. Matthews Cattle Company and Lambshead Ranch were two good examples. With John A. Matthews as guide and stern task master in mastering ranch work, Lambshead's pastures would impart their secrets to the boys. It did not take many "lessons" before Watt and his Blanton "brothers," though they were younger and taller than he was, made a fine working team. All three became successful ranchers.

Sallie Reynolds Matthews had nine children. Not all lived beyond the frontier era, but all who did were schooled at her behest. Her greatest influence on her children was cultural. Under her guidance, school and church became important to her children. Watt recalled that he, like all her other children, learned his catechism through recitation on the eighteen-mile buggy ride to Sunday church in the early 1900s.

Early in their marriage, in 1884, Sallie and John A. moved their family from the Hoover Ranch into Albany, Texas, to be close to schools and church. In the late 1890s, Albany was a vibrant community. Rev. French McAfee, a fine young Presbyterian minister educated at Harvard University and Princeton Theological Seminary, injected excitement into local cultural life. Under his leadership, other church members joined the

Reynolds and Matthews families in building the Matthews Memorial Presbyterian Church. It was dedicated to the memory of John A.'s father, Joseph Beck ("Uncle Joe") Matthews on April 1, 1898; the Reynolds Presbyterian Academy, named for Sallie's father, Barber Watkins Reynolds, was dedicated on January 10, 1898. Sallie always was an avid reader. Because she was likely inspired by the summer Chautauqua programs in Boulder, Colorado, she assisted in the creation of cultural and literary clubs in Albany.

Watt's early education took place in the Albany public school. In 1907, the family moved to Austin, where the daughters attended high school and the University of Texas. Lucile and Watt attended the private Whitis School there. The family returned to the Camp Cooper ranch in the summers. In the fall of 1909, the family moved to Fort Worth for schooling for Watt and Sallie, while the other girls attended the University of Texas in Austin. From 1910 to 1912, as the general financial climate worsened, Sallie, John A., Lucile, and Watt returned to Lambshead Ranch. His mother and some of his sisters acted as tutors for young Watt. In the fall of 1912, the family moved back to Fort Worth, where Watt attended the seventh grade at the Eleventh Ward School, with Mrs. Mina Wright as his teacher. Watt recalled her as his most memorable and talented teacher. He attended Central Ward High School in 1913 and 1914. He was invited to ride with a friend, Anne Burnett, daughter of Burk Burnett, owner of the 6666 Ranch and an associate of Watt's family. In 1915, Watt attended San Antonio Academy, where his oldest sister, May, and his brother, Joe B., previously had graduated. Watt graduated from the academy with a good record, in 1917.

When it came time to send Watt to college, Sallie chose Princeton University, due to the sterling example set by the Reverend McAfee. Watt was admitted to Princeton in the fall of 1917 and was followed by Tom, and Matt Blanton, along with another Albany friend, Robert E. "Bob" Nail.

While at Princeton, Watt Matthews registered for courses which he believed would help him in the ranching business. His lists of courses included constitutional government, Spanish, biology, economics, and accounting. This list was included in his own early diaries from the pe-

Watt in army uniform at Princeton University, 1921.
Courtesy Watt R. Matthews

riod. Watt learned to ice skate on the deeply frozen ponds and learned to take pleasure in "bickering" talk sessions with classmates in the dormitory. He religiously attended church services and took advantage of cultural events and speakers visiting at Princeton.

Watt's mother's cultural influence came to the forefront at Princeton. He frequently took the train into New York City to attend the theater or to take the visiting daughters of Texas ranch families to tea at the Ritz and for carriage rides in Central Park. Watt did well at Princeton. His proud mother and father, with sister Lucile, attended his graduation in August 1921. Interestingly, Princeton has educated one son, five grandsons, and one great-grandson of Sallie and John A. Matthews.

The fundamentals needed to cope with his future challenges as a rancher and a businessman Watt to a large degree learned at Princeton. Upon Watt's return from Princeton, his father expected to see practical evidence of Watt's "schooling." Accounting stood Watt in good stead. That year of 1921, Watt figured the ranch's deficit on the failure of the pecan crop (from native trees on the river) and made a case that it be tax deductible. He sent in the report, carefully annotated, to the Internal Revenue Service. It was returned. Watt argued his case so soundly that the IRS finally accepted his figures, and Watt "won." From that time on, Watt's pragmatic father had a somewhat better opinion of Watt's four years at Princeton and of his ability to contribute to the ranch and its future.

This event proved a turning point in Watt's life. In what had been a rather strained father-son relationship, John A. had been unconscionably severe, demanding that Watt work on the ranch's farm (which Watt hated) from dawn to dark during school vacations when he was at Lambshead. Now John A. turned over the financial operation and tax work of the ranch to his youngest son. In his success with the finances and tax work of Lambshead Ranch operation, Watt "won his spurs" with his father. Of course, his mother was extremely proud of her well-educated son.

Watt continues ranch work, doing it the way he was taught by his father from the time he was a young boy. In the ranching industry, even nationally and internationally, today he is known for having one of the best managed and thriftiest of cattle operations.

MATTHEWS-REYNOLDS FAMILY

As the youngest child of Sallie Ann Reynolds Matthews and John Alexander Matthews, Watt was born into an intricate web of Matthews and Reynolds kin. John A. was the only son of Caroline Spears Matthews and Joseph Beck ("Uncle Joe") Matthews, while Sallie was the last child and youngest daughter of Barber Watkins Reynolds and Anne Maria Campbell Reynolds.

The coming of barbed wire brought an end to both open-range cattle raising and the frontier era. Generations of Reynolds and Matthews witnessed these transitions as neighbors who developed deep and lasting friendships. Some of those relationships resulted in marriage.

Marriage, on the frontier and in the twentieth century, strengthened bonds among families and neighbors. For at least three decades, wedding bells kept ringing for sons, daughters, cousins, and other Matthews and Reynolds relatives. Each wedding brought the two extended families closer. Four of Sallie's brothers married four Matthews girls (two sets of sisters who were first cousins); Sallie herself wed the only Matthews son. Sallie describes her life in *Interwoven*, her frontier chronicle of the Reynolds and the Matthews, published in 1936, two years before her death in 1938. This book, which tells of two families who intermarried as the frontier came to a close in Shackelford and Throckmorton counties, eventually was designated one of the best books on Texas frontier history.

Frontier marriages were festive occasions. Sallie recalls the marriage of her sister, attractive fourteen-year-old Susan Reynolds, to her popular teacher, Sam Newcomb, in November 1862. The entire region was invited to this frontier wedding; the entire region and a few passing strangers came. The house and yard were filled to overflowing with family, friends, and anyone else who heard about the wedding.

Bettie Matthews, Joseph Beck Matthews's oldest daughter, was Susan's bridesmaid. After vows were exchanged, "there was not only feasting and dancing, but a candy pull to add to the festivities," Sallie recalls in *Interwoven.* "Susan was too young entirely," Sallie confides, although Sallie herself married at age fifteen. Sallie explains: "There were reasons for this. Pioneer life tends to mature boys and girls earlier—and the high ratio of unattached young men, seeking their fortunes on the frontier, to girls, who are not so plentiful and therefore are much sought after."

The second marriage between the Barber Watkins Reynolds and Joe Beck Matthews clans took place in 1867, when seventeen-year-old Bettie Matthews married the dashing George Thomas Reynolds. According to Sallie in *Interwoven,* Bettie's husband was twenty-four and was the first of the Reynolds's sons to wed. Bettie and George's honeymoon began with a trail drive to Colorado, where they sold the herd and ended with a long stay in San Francisco, California.

Sallie's brothers were to figure prominently in the future of the cattle industry. George T., the entrepreneur, was the oldest, and next came William D. ("Will") Reynolds, later a famous rancher-financier. In the cattle world, George T. was known for making money in the cattle business and William D. for taking care of it. Throughout his life, Watt picked up valuable "tips" on the cow business from the "Reynolds boys," Will Reynolds's sons, as he was a non-voting member of the Reynolds Cattle Company.

Two weddings were celebrated in the summer of 1872, before Barber Watkins Reynolds sold his Parker County farm and moved the family to Point of Rocks Ranch in Colorado. In the only double wedding among either the Reynolds or the Matthews, Will Reynolds married Mary Byrd, a lovely frontier Texas girl. At the same time, his younger sister, Susan Reynolds Newcomb, widow of Sam Newcomb, married Nathan Bartholomew. Will Reynolds took Mary Byrd to the Reynolds families' Point of Rocks Ranch, where, tragically, she died within a few months. The Bartholomews went to Eastland County and established a small ranch.

John A., George T., and Will worked in tandem assembling pastures for their cattle operations. The Reynolds family moved back from Colorado to Clear Fork country. If Will's brother, Ben Reynolds, had searched through several counties and up and down the Clear Fork, he could have discovered no more promising place for a ranch than Reynolds Bend. The Barber Watkins Reynolds family agreed with Ben's high opinion of his "discovery" and, on January 2, 1876, began work on an L-shaped one-and-a-half-story rock house there. Adding urgency to this work was the fact that youngest daughter Sallie was to be married on Christmas Day, 1876, to John Alexander Matthews.

Will Reynolds married again in 1879, seven years after Mary Byrd died, taking Susan Alice Matthews as his bride. She was the sister of Bettie Matthews Reynolds and John A. Matthews. As usual, Joseph Beck ("Uncle Joe") Matthews, father of the bride, invited everyone in the area to the wedding. Everyone came, filling the yard in front of his picket house.

Another wedding took place five months later, uniting Ben Reynolds and Florence Matthews, a niece of Joseph Beck Matthews. The "infare" was held on May 6, 1879, in the new stone home of George T. Reynolds and Bettie Reynolds. Not quite so many guests were invited to this wedding, but everyone who was invited came.

A fifth link between the Reynolds and Matthews families was created when the last Reynolds brother, Phin, married Rosa Matthews, another of Joseph Beck Matthews's nieces and Florence Matthews's sister, in 1883. Thus was formed the final link in the chain of marriages between the two families. As Sallie put it, "Two pairs of sisters, first cousins to each other, married to Sallie's four brothers and she married to the only brother of one pair of sisters—surely we were being interwoven."

Watt never has been married, nor has he ever been engaged. His family consisted of his one living brother, Joe B., married with one son; and his five sisters, all married with children. His five sisters were Mary Louise ("May") Matthews Blanton, Susan Elizabeth ("Susette") Matthews Burns, Ethel Matthews Casey, Lucile Matthews Brittingham, and Sallie Reynolds Matthews Judd. Watt's close associates and ranching friends say, "Watt Matthews is married to the land and Lambshead Ranch."

NEW ERA IN RANCHING

Although Albany, Texas, was several hundred miles from the nearest major rail point, George T. Reynolds and Bettie Matthews Reynolds managed to attend the Centennial Celebration of Independence for the United States of America. It was held in Philadelphia, Pennsylvania, in 1876. The Reynolds couple, by then married for some nine years, invited John A. Matthews and his bride-to-be, Sallie Reynolds, to join them by marrying in time to make the outing to Philadelphia their "honeymoon trip." Sallie declined, and the couple waited at home for the agreed-upon wedding date, Christmas Day, December 25, 1876.

Upon arrival at the Centennial Celebration, George, a born entrepreneur, undoubtedly followed his custom of inquiring about financial and other affairs that would affect his banking and livestock interests. The Morrill, Homestead, and U.S. Department of Agriculture Acts had been passed by Congress in 1862. Now George discovered details concerning the government's plan to use the provisions of these acts to revolutionize what it called "animal agriculture." This information would prove useful to him, the Reynolds and Matthews families, and selected friends.

He likely compared notes with other stockmen about the present status of the Chicago Stockyards and their reliability and success in marketing cattle.

The Chicago Stockyards had "done right by" the Reynolds brothers (George and Will) with the cattle herd George had sent there in 1874, with Will in charge. Earlier, in 1871, George had sent his younger brother Glenn, then seventeen, to deliver a herd to a railhead in Kansas. In Texas, cattle had been worth four dollars a head; in Abilene, Kansas, the price was double that. The cattle were sent on by rail to Chicago, where the beef was sold at twenty to forty dollars a carcass to industrial workers in steel mills and other new industries springing up in the East. It had taken Glenn three months to reach the market in Abilene, but the drive of a thousand head of cattle had resulted in a profit of eight thousand dollars.

In 1885, the family group, plus friends, journeyed to New Orleans to see the Cotton Exposition. The men gathered useful information, and the women enjoyed seeing the sights and visiting with women from other parts of the country.

In 1889, George and Bettie Matthews arranged an informative and enjoyable Matthews-Reynolds family visit to the World's Columbian Exposition in Chicago. This large family group stayed in Chicago for a month. While there, the men went out to inspect the Reynolds brothers' North Dakota ranches and traveled elsewhere on cattle business. Undoubtedly they visited the Chicago Stockyards.

Watt's mother's two oldest brothers, George T. Reynolds and William D. Reynolds, helped John A. and Sallie locate and assemble Lambshead Ranch. The land all had been located by 1885, and the last pasture, the Valley Pasture, was acquired in 1909. The Reynolds helped fence the early pastures, using barbed wire first introduced into the area by John A.'s father, Joseph Beck ("Uncle Joe") Matthews.

Watt's father, John A. Matthews, was variously called "John A.," "J. A.," "Bud," and "the Judge." The latter title reflected his election to the judiciary in 1894 in Throckmorton County.

Beginning in 1891, John A. started using registered Hereford and Shorthorn bulls and cows to improve his herd. At this time, the cattle industry also was seeking ways to improve the quality and character of its product. Progress moved forward slowly, one breeding cycle at a time. Not all methods worked. Shorthorns had trouble on the Texas range, and Herefords gradually came to dominate in Central Texas by 1920.

According to a 1909 report by the U.S. Bureau of Animal Industry, South Texas rancher Shanghai Pierce by then had acquired his first Brahman cattle from India. He had observed for some time that the Brahman cattle did not harbor the cattle tick, so he incorporated that breed into his herd. Word of his success spread throughout Texas, and many Texas ranchers along the Gulf Coast and elsewhere followed suit, incorporating Brahman cattle into their herds. Another breed of cattle introduced to Texas at this time was the Angus.

Later, John A. led the movement to eradicate ticks (the cause of Texas fever). Interestingly, the connection between the tick and Texas fever was discovered by the Rockefeller Institute at Princeton University, where Watt Matthews was to graduate in 1921. Prior to 1915, John A. became a pioneer in building dipping vats for controlling ticks. Then he led a concerted effort to eradicate the tick in Throckmorton and Shackelford counties. He made many trips to Austin to share his ideas with the Texas Legislature. Those efforts resulted in legislation requiring Texas ranchers to clean up the tick problem. The plan involved zoning. As ranchers in each zone completed the required dipping, their zone was put above the quarantine line. The plan worked.

Like the Reynolds brothers, John A. led his family in acquiring a great cattle empire in Texas. Over the years, that empire expanded to include other fine ranches in the Albany region, in some ways the heartland of Texas cattle country. Although the holdings included a ranch in Colorado, Lambshead Ranch always remained the headquarters.

In 1929, John A. and Sallie moved into a new red-brick two-story home in Albany. For John A. Matthews, the ranch remained a daily concern. Until 1939, he was riding out to the ranch daily with his grandsons or other drivers to supervise ranch operations.

Having published *Interwoven,* her autobiographical account of life on the frontier, in 1936, Sallie died in 1938. Thereafter John A.'s health began to decline rapidly, and Watt and Joe B. shouldered more of the ranching responsibilities at Lambshead.

John A. Matthews was a product of the frontier generation. One can imagine him, as ranch owner, tying up the final loose ends of his business affairs as time grew short. Ultimately John A. sold all his properties other than the home ranch. His wise management created a family empire that has stretched into four generations. With his death four decades into the twentieth century, an era was coming to a close.

NEW GENERATIONS

My feeling is that there is nothing in life but refraining from hurting others and consoling those that are sad.

—Olive Schriner, South African author (1855–1920), quoted as his motto by Watt R. Matthews

Upon graduation from Princeton in 1921, Watt returned to Lambshead Ranch. He has remained there ever since.

After John A. Matthews died in 1941, Watt and Joe B. continued their father's cattle operation according to their father's custom. Their first innovation was to begin purchasing even better top-ranking registered Hereford bulls than their father had done. Watt follows his father's example of breeding nationally recognized purebred Hereford bulls to his Hereford cows, except for first-time heifers. He began using Longhorn bulls with those Hereford heifers to produce a smaller calf.

For years, the highlight of the summer for Watt and Joe B. often was a train trip out to visit their double cousins, the Reynolds brothers, on their Long X Ranch in the Davis Mountains in far West Texas. Watt was a nonvoting member of the board of directors of the Reynolds Cattle Company, and he usually attended board meetings with his cousin and close friend, Watkins "Wattie" Matthews Reynolds.

The legacy of John A. Matthews's management was recognized in 1960, when Lambshead Ranch celebrated its seventy-fifth anniversary. The innovations of the sons were noted that same year, when they won national awards for two truckloads of Hereford calves entered at the American Royal Show in Kansas City, Missouri. Cattle industry awards have continued to come (see appendix A).

The Matthews earned an international reputation for raising good

Hereford cattle. One shipment of yearlings was sent to Portugal in 1967. Two more were sent to Hungary, including one by air in April, 1972. The American Hereford Association was instrumental in arranging these sales of Lambshead heifers. Watt is pleased when longtime buyers continue to order their cattle from Lambshead with a simple phone call to him.

Watt's sister, Lucile Matthews Brittingham, although nine years older than he, became closely associated with her younger brother after the death of her husband, Dr. Harold Hixon Brittingham. He died in 1937, leaving Lucile with a family to raise. At the Brittingham home in Fort Worth, Watt always was welcomed as part of the family. Lucile had accompanied Watt's father and mother to Princeton for his graduation in 1921. Lucile and Watt joined forces in ranching and other business interests in the Albany area. It was natural, too, for Lucile to join Watt in his interest in restoring their family homes. Lucile and Watt together restored the Bartholomew House, a rock house at the Bend. It had been the home of Susan Reynolds Newcomb Bartholomew, their mother's sister, and her husband Nathan Bartholomew.

Watt took seriously his charge to look after the ranch and the family. He kept up with all his sisters and their children, making visits to Lambshead by the latter a time for learning as well as pleasure. Like his father before him, he taught all the young people to ride the ranch horses well. He saw to it that Lucile's children, and any other children who were interested, learned about ranch operations.

Watt is respected by friends and family for always attending funerals, graduations, and weddings, regardless of distance, weather, or other circumstances. He often is consulted for advice by men and women of all ages, but especially younger people. As adults, nieces, and nephews often return to Lambshead, bringing children and spouses with them. Watt has insured that they and their children enjoy the pleasures and advantages they desire.

Back when John A.'s health failed, Watt had replaced him in the Matthews Memorial Presbyterian Church in Albany. Watt has been one of the most faithful and supportive parishioners and deacons. If he is at home on the ranch, he is faithfully in his pew every Sunday. His easily recognized hat will be in its accustomed place on the hat shelf in the entrance hall. And he can be counted on to support and attend Christmas, Easter, and other special events. With modest pride, Watt shows visitors this architecturally significant cut-stone edifice as a central aspect of his family's heritage.

LAND AND WILDLIFE CONSERVATION

Lambshead's cow-calf operation is based upon a self-replenishing crop of nourishing grasses. Efforts at range preservation have lasted more than a century. As one who had spent long decades assembling his ranch, John A. Matthews became a devotee of range conservation practices. He eradicated prairie dogs and began grubbing the troublesome prickly-pear cactus. The appearance of bitterweed grieved him, so he hired crews of workers to pull the plants up by their roots. Watt's lifelong goal has been to return the Lambshead range to its original condition, that described by his mother in her book, *Interwoven.* The century-long battle to salvage the range has been successful.

Watt seldom hesitates to describe his two greatest enemies in that battle. The first is the mesquite tree, which surreptitiously steals precious nourishment from the soil. A tap root from a two-foot tree can reach sixty feet to the water table. In a dry year, mesquite endangers the water supply of cattle, horses, and people. Mesquite thorns are bothersome to cowhands, cow ponies, and cows. This enemy, peculiarly adapted to cow country, plagues ranches from Texas to Chile and Argentina. The trees were brought north with the trail drives from South Texas. The Longhorns dropped seeds from the mesquite's edible beans, along with a little fertilizer to help them grow. Watt Matthews wages the mesquite battle all year long. Like his neighbors and his father, Watt tackles mesquite with fire and destructive spraying, followed by bulldozing.

Watt's second enemy is one that also troubled his father, the prickly-pear cactus. Each spring the pear blooms with exquisite yellow flowers, which accentuate the beauty of the pastures and ravines. Cattle, horses, and unaccompanied people, however, discover that the picturesque cactus patches harbor sharp needles or, often, the sharp fangs of a camouflaged rattlesnake. While fire works against mesquite, prickly pear must be grubbed out of the ground.

Knowledgeable visitors comment that Lambshead Ranch is one of the finest ranches they have ever visited. They applaud Watt for continuing his father's war on mesquite and prickly pear. Today those pastures where mesquite and prickly pear have been eliminated are grass-covered parks with occasional islands of oak or pecan trees.

Weather governs life, cycles of work, and the future of Lambshead Ranch. Man, beast, and the land depend on weather for survival. All residents on the ranch respect the vagaries of weather. In Clear Fork country, it is the opener for most conversations between friends or strangers. Other vital topics are water (always too much or too little) and the dangers of floods or droughts.

Equally devastating to the range, only faster, is a grass fire with a high wind behind it. Fire is a traveling holocaust, and the work of stamping out a range fire separates the men from the boys. Women form a support team for the firefighters, furnishing food, drinking water, coffee, medical aid, and other necessities. Lambshead keeps good firefighting equipment on the ranch and delivers it to burning range—their own or a neighbor's—as soon as possible. (Clear Fork ranchers help each other when faced with adversity, a legacy from the frontier tradition of neighborly assistance.) Fire does have one beneficial effect—it makes the grass green up faster and better in the spring.

Watt has implemented long-range preservation programs permanently to restore both native plants and original wildlife to the land (see appendix B). Among the latter are white-tailed deer, wild turkey, buffalo, and Longhorns. The restoration of the white-tailed deer began with the release of twenty animals, which have multiplied to full carrying capacity, creating a profitable hunting season for family and friends. Buffalo were brought back from the Reynolds's Long X Ranch in the Davis Mountains. Wild turkeys not only multiplied to carrying capacity, but also provided one hundred or more for experimental restocking on other ranches throughout Texas and the western United States.

Watt began using Longhorn bulls to make first calving easier and more profitable. He once was asked how they got all those Longhorn steers "made" ready for the trail drives. "Anyone's guess will do," was the reply. Watt's visitors usually are surprised to see his herd of Longhorns in the Butterfield Pasture, running there with their progeny, great steers with horn spreads six feet wide.

Watt has sustained his father's conservation efforts and, in addition, has reintroduced species of wildlife originally found on the property. Lambshead frequently has been recognized for its role as a natural preserve. The ranch's wilder spots support fish, fowl (even eagles), and untamed creatures who live in the valleys of the Clear Fork. The variety of terrain makes for wildlife diversity. The result is a natural setting very similar in many respects to the open range the Matthews and Reynolds families first encountered in North Central Texas before the Civil War.

HISTORICAL RESTORATION

The descriptions of Reynolds Bend by Watt's parents appear to have lingered brightly in Watt's memory. He decided that he would restore the historic family homes to their original condition (see appendix B). The buildings range in age from the Stone Ranch (built in 1856) to the schoolhouse (1888).

In 1943, Watt was able to purchase the land of Reynolds Bend, upon which the headquarters house of the Barber Watkins Reynolds family stood. This purchase allowed him to begin the first of his restoration efforts. Between 1943 and 1983, Watt implemented the restoration of the historic buildings on Lambshead. The Barber Watkins Reynolds House at Reynolds Bend, built in 1876, was restored by Watt in 1943. That same year, he began supervising and caring for the Matthews Family Cemetery, created in 1881. In 1951, Watt's sister Lucile Brittingham, under his supervision, began restoring the Nathan L. Bartholomew House, built at the Bend in 1876. Watt then accurately replicated the schoolhouse, built in 1888 at Reynolds Bend, and the House Dugout, built in 1890 and named for an early settler named House.

In 1976, Watt marked with upright native limestone slabs the Butterfield Trail at Butterfield Gap and the Relay Station located at Old Clear Fork Crossing. Then, in 1982, Watt began the restoration of the Old Stone Ranch House in Stone Ranch Pasture, as well as two large stone corrals and another corral with pens. These had been built in 1856 by Capt. Newton C. Givens, who was stationed at Camp Cooper, and were used by the Barber Watkins Reynolds's extended family from April 1, 1866, to 1867, the year that George T. Reynolds married Bettie Matthews. In the summer of 1983, the restored Old Stone Ranch was dedicated with a Matthews-Reynolds family celebration.

Over the years, Watt has restored more than a dozen properties. Those structures help to give Lambshead Ranch its special character. They are what visitors most remember. Some of those restored buildings serve as guest quarters and contain early family furnishings and memorabilia. They reveal the history of the Reynolds, the Matthews, and the North Texas frontier. Usually restorations are undertaken by local, state, or national organizations dedicated to historic preservation, but here the work was undertaken at Watt's own expense and at his own initiative. In carrying out these projects, he has preserved the stage upon which the salient events of this part of the Texas frontier took place.

CIRCLE TOUR

Watt enjoys giving guests, friends, and family members tours. They allow him to sketch the patterns of work on a ranch of this size, along with its challenges. Giving tours also allows him to honor and explicate the frontier history of the Reynolds and Matthews families, as well as the beauty and the varied resources of Lambshead Ranch.

Customarily, Watt tours the ranch every day in the late afternoon; usually he is at the wheel of his favorite tour vehicle, with a crowd aboard. He wheels out of the Headquarters compound, passes through the gate crowned with a bleached-white Longhorn skull, veers left, and passes the grassy entrance area. It is a picturesque site. The trunks of scattered mesquite trees are encased by cones of wooden fence posts. They appear to be a tiny teepee village.

Traveling the well-maintained principal ranch road leading to Reynolds Bend, one can see to the right a landing field for small airplanes. Moving along the road, Watt glides left up a hill, swerves to the right, and stops at Lookout Point. Directly below are the ruins of the Martin Van Buren Hoover House, where Joe B. was born. To the right are the rock walls of the George T. Reynolds Headquarters, which sadly was gutted by fire.

At Lookout Point, the visitor has two beautiful vistas. A breathtaking view across the Bend of Clear Fork River stretches for miles up the green valley to the rim of the horizon, upon which Round Mountain can be seen. At the mountain's base are the headquarters buildings of one of the finest ranches in the region, Round Mountain Ranch. This extraordinary ranch property was early located and owned by Thomas Lambshead. Only Lambshead Ranch exceeded it in desirability. Beyond and to the right, within the Bend of the Clear Fork, lies Reynolds Bend, a gem of a ranch headquarters. It is named for its founders, Watt's grandparents and his Uncle Ben.

The other beautiful vista is the colorful carpet of Texas spring wildflowers. Like a great Joseph's coat, the exquisitely melded colors spread over the meadow pasture of the Bend. This dazzling display is broken only by the contrast of dark, slowly moving forms, as heifers graze on the nourishing green grasses. Particularly in a favorable spring, the fields of wildflowers for which Texas is famous impresses native Texans and visitors alike. Many groups come from afar to enjoy their beauty. On Lambshead alone, more than sixty species of wildflowers have been identified.

Watt's mother was especially fond of wildflowers. Other appreciative eyes will see the orange-reds of Indian paintbrush blooming vibrant among bluestem, bluebonnets, black-eyed Susans, blue salvia, bright pink California filaree, lavender verbena, golden corydalis, Mexican buckeye, yellow daisies, purple thistle, and the white blooms of snow-on-the-mountain. The beautiful but dangerous prickly-pear cactus holds lush yellow blooms.

A rock home of one and a half stories, built by Watt's Reynolds grandparents in 1876, the year John A. and Sallie married, charms guests as they admire the conveniences of the frontier. The women are surprised to see built-in cupboards containing Sallie Reynolds Matthews's wedding gifts of china and glassware. Men are intrigued by the twisting staircase leading to the large bedroom and bathroom, the hidden closets, the practical bucket well enclosed on the back porch, and the ample stone fireplace in the parlor. Here also are Sallie's tiny Esty organ, which still plays, and the Barber Watkins Reynolds's marriage certificate hanging over the fireplace mantel.

Performers in the Fort Griffin Fandangle. *Courtesy Donnie Lucas,* Albany News.

Leaving this comfortable home, visitors view the large green meadow to their left. Encircled by a low rock wall, it was used as an amphitheater for the first *Fandangle Sampler,* which Watt created for his first annual "Party at the Bend." Watt built a shed for the historic vehicles used for this production and the Fort Griffin *Fandangle.* Watt, who has owned the Bend since 1943, also constructed a large cookshack and other buildings there.

The group moves on to the Matthews Family Cemetery. This beautiful cemetery lies above the Headquarters on a gently sloping hilltop. The date 1880 is engraved upon the ornamental stone marking the grave of Watt's youngest sister. Two decades separated the births of these oldest and youngest of the John A. and Sallie Matthews children. Scattered mesquites wave their fronds among the grass-covered graves of Watt's family. He restored the cemetery in 1943 and continues to maintain it.

On a slope across from the cemetery stands a one-room schoolhouse, built in 1888. Watt's parents were determined to see that their first two children, as well as other children living up and down the Clear Fork, received schooling. Watt rebuilt the structure and furnished it with appropriate desks and a blackboard.

A short distance down the slope toward the river, visitors enter the charming rock home of Watt's aunt, Susan Reynolds Newcomb Bartholomew, and her husband Nathan Bartholomew. The Bartholomew House, built in 1876, shows the architectural influence of Bartholomew's native New England. Watt assisted his sister Lucile with this restoration. Lucile selected simple but handsomely crafted furniture to fill this one-and-a-half-story home. Furnishings, uncrowded and comfortable, date from the 1870s and 1880s. Lucile and her children use this delightful place as their home on the ranch. Another two-room modern stone house of similar architecture and a cedar bunkhouse accommodate the overflow of Lucile's large family and guests.

An antique wrought-iron weather vane charms the visitors as they climb back in the vehicle and swing down a lane lined with stacked-stone walls bordering a field to the left. There Longhorn steers with enormous horns graze, and white-tail deer can be seen. A big feral, or wild, sow and her five piglets scoot onto the road, running across in front of Watt and his startled but delighted guests.

Glimpses of bends in the river reveal the places where John A. and Sallie located "camps." Generally their purpose was purely social, as family and friends came and stayed a week or more at a time. Although the camps were well chaperoned, several marriages came about as a result of them. Joe B. Matthews courted and later married Louise Webb after getting acquainted with her at such a summer camp. Their one child, a son, carries on the Matthews ranching tradition.

One camp popular with the men was both convivial and practical in aim—to kill and dress feral hogs like the one just encountered. These are the descendants of hogs remaining on the land of Camp Cooper's Comanche Indian reservation. Fattened on native pecans, these animals yielded flavorful meat which the participants carried home, making these unusual gatherings popular with their families, too. Sallie Matthews and her children always welcomed this wild pork at their table.

Lambshead wildlife—deer, coyotes, colorful game birds, quail, turkey—plays hide-and-seek as Watt passes by the animals' favorite thickets. From one such place, songbirds entertain the party with their trills and warbles.

On down the road, Watt pauses at the primitive, stone-walled, half-dugout dwelling of an early family who homesteaded and tried to make a living at farming. Like many others who tried to farm instead of raising livestock in Clear Fork Country, they failed and moved on to New Mexico or elsewhere to try to make a living. Watt calls it, after the family's name, the House Dugout. He has faithfully restored and furnished the structure.

With this frank restoration, Watt completes a historic sequence—a story of families and the dwellings in which they lived for half a century, from 1856 to 1906, on what became Lambshead Ranch.

It is nearly twilight as Watt stops at the legendary Stone Ranch House, Bunkhouse, Meat House, and Spring House. These are masterfully built of tremendous stones removed from ledges in a nearby hill. They were stacked and cut by nature as for a mason's trowel. Behind the large house are the famous stacked-stone corrals, built in 1856, along with the other structures, by Capt. Newton C. Givens. He also added sheds with smaller corrals. All were constructed of enormous stones. Rumor had it that he built this layout as a hunting lodge, but others wondered where and how he would find cattle, horses, or other animals to fill these giant stone corrals.

Watt's mother and her family lived in the Stone Ranch House after the Civil War ended. In *Interwoven*, Sallie describes Indian raids, her brother George's meaningful, near fatal encounter with a Comanche chief, and his and Bettie Matthews's "infare" wedding celebration. The interior is furnished as Watt's mother describes it. Handcrafted heirloom quilts and rugs are in place in the large room, which is furnished as a bedroom-kitchen. A long table, covered with a white linen cloth, is set with china, silver, and glassware, as if the petite frontier lady, Anne Maria Reynolds, had just left the room.

This house was the last building travelers encountered on the far western frontier before the Spanish villages on the Rio Grande, in New

Mexico, hundreds of miles to the west. Watt takes his guests to the two stone slab monuments upon which he has placed bronze plaques telling the history of this impressive landmark and his own Reynolds family history. These monumental stone slabs remind these guests of ancient Stonehenge in England.

Dusk deepens, and Watt, with his guests, heads back to Headquarters. Lambshead's wildlife is emerging. Deer leap, coyotes slink into bushes, turkey and quail flutter and fly as the headlights spotlight them.

Watt unloads his guests at his picket house, modeled after the one his grandfather Matthews built in 1874. He proudly leads them past a newly installed bronze sculpture, *Texas Gold,* then into the cookshack.

There, having served assorted beverages, their host makes room so that all can see his detailed aerial map of Lambshead Ranch. One of Watt's "kissin' kin" relatives on the Reynolds side, who knows the ranch intimately, offers to show the tourists where they have been that day, using Watt's map. Sitting comfortably on benches, guests are intrigued to see where they have been "toured."

First, the relative points out the circuitous trail along which the Lambshead story and its associated landscapes have been revealed. Headquarters compound is where the tour began. Next came the Road Pasture, up hill and down dale; then the W. D. Reynolds Pasture, with the Lefthand Pasture on the left. She points out the Farm, where one lone buffalo showed up to greet the crowd. Then comes Stone Ranch and its pasture, where they saw contented three-year-old heifers at a water tank, awaiting the birth of healthy calves. Up the map is the VH Pasture. Moving left, the relative notes Lookout Point, with its view up the long green valley to Round Mountain Ranch on the rim of the horizon. There Watt pointed out the Hoover House across the river, presently being restored. Ruins of the George Reynolds house remains. Next the guide indicates the location of Reynolds Bend.

Watt's guests prove perceptive observers, as they recollect their most vivid "tour-scapes" of the day. A bird fancier speaks of the large flock of wild turkey hens that appeared to flow gracefully up the sloping road ahead. Their feathers glistened in the late sunlight, recalling the spread of a giant peacock's tail. One visiting rancher remarks on his impression of a black chasm they stopped to view. It was located in the Lefthand Pasture, above the Clear Fork River valley; at its center stood a small, round, grass-covered knoll. The mysterious view of the deep ravine across the valley struck this man as a good place for a cattle rustler and horse thief to hide his stolen herd. The men, including Watt, agree.

The quick "map tour" has been enjoyable, and so is the hot supper on the steam table, to which host Watt leads his guests.

HOST OF CLEAR FORK COUNTRY

It was from his grandfather, Joseph Beck Matthews, that Watt inherited his well-deserved reputation as the leading host of Clear Fork country. These two men, of different generations, both were known for their cordial and generous hospitality.

Joseph Beck ("Uncle Joe") Matthews, as he was respectfully called, became famous for the celebrations he gave to mark the weddings of his children and other kin, including Watt's father and mother, John A. and Sallie. These festivities, with dancing and grand spreads of food, lasted through the night. Sometimes they went on for two days and nights.

Epitomizing Watt's hospitality is his annual spring "Party at the Bend," also called "Watt's Party at Reynolds Bend." With this festive gathering, Watt has established his own personal tradition. This annual event grew out of a need to develop a modified version of the *Fort Griffin Fandangle* that could travel and be performed on an indoor stage. Now called the *Fandangle Sampler,* the condensed version always is performed at Watt's party—which has turned out to be the best possible advertising for the main production of the *Fort Griffin Fandangle.* The full show is performed on the outdoor Fandangle Stage in Albany during the third weekend in June.

Watt's Party at the Bend is held in a beautiful grassy park dotted with a few selected mesquite trees. Long tables covered with red-checked cloths and surrounded by chairs are scattered between a chuckwagon and a dance platform. Guests at this now-famous event typically include countless ranchers, their wives, and their families. Many are members of noted old ranch families of Texas, New Mexico, or other western states. Some guests, who represent other professions, come from as far away as New York. As many as eight hundred guests may be invited, and most come.

The menu includes tender, flavorful prime rib, baked potato, *frijoles*, vegetable salad, and desert. Watt always has the best "chuck" to be had in the area.

As the long tables in front of the dancing platform fill up, Watt's favorite western band strikes up music for the "Texas Trail" or the "Varsouviana" ("Put Your Little Foot"), traditional dances from Clear Fork country's frontier days. Some exuberant couples begin dancing even before they go to the chuckwagon.

At his party in 1990, Watt was surprised at being presented a National Honor Award from the National Trust for Historic Preservation, in recognition of his achievements in historic preservation, particularly in restoring the large family rock houses (see appendix B). While the guests stood to honor him, this modest man accepted the honor with his usual simple "Many thanks" and a wry smile. Then the crowd followed as he led the way through a gate in the stone wall around his meadow amphitheater below the Reynolds family home. It was nearly dusk, and the clouds looked somewhat threatening. Guests scurried to their seats as the organist struck up the stirring theme song. Watt took his accustomed seat in the rock niche beside Alice Reynolds, the original organist. High klieg lights flooded the meadow amphitheater. Expert cowboys on swift, well-trained horses, carrying the *Fandangle* banner and the six flags of Texas, furiously crisscrossed one another to open the show.

Each year, for more than an hour, the audience is entertained by the lively songs, dances, and "showing-off" frontier style of the *Fandangle Sampler.* A grand finale closes this superb production, which Watt's old friend and Princeton classmate, Bob Nail, adapted from Sallie Reynolds Matthews's book, *Interwoven,* the story of her two frontier families in Clear Fork country.

Asked how and why he began his remarkable historic preservation projects, Watt answered simply:

Maybe sometimes we're too quick to change. At Lambshead Ranch we're preserving the physical signs of our history and the memory of those who set us on our course. No matter what changes come, I told the family, there's no memorial they could ever build that would match holding this place together. I guess in some ways I kind of resist change. . . . I was Class of 1921 at Princeton, and my listing in the class directory has never changed. It's always been: "Rancher, Box 636, Albany, Texas."

The year Watt received the National Trust award, Bob Nail included in his show at Lambshead a new number that had been created especially for Lady Bird Johnson, wife of former U.S. President Lyndon B. Johnson and founder of the National Wildflower Research Center in Austin, Texas. She had invited Watt to bring the *Fandangle Sampler* to the LBJ Ranch the following week to entertain a special group of the former president's guests. Lady Bird said of Watt:

To describe Watt Matthews, the words "quintessential Texan" spring to mind. I have always felt that he could have leapt off the pages of a stirring western novel or a book of Texas history.

Watt and his Lambshead Ranch are a part of the lore of this state, and he possesses the great heart of its legendary heroes. The citizens of Albany have long known him as a driving force and benefactor of the annual Fandangle presented there and, on occasion, at the LBJ Ranch (with a much smaller cast!). It tells an epic, spirit-raising story of frontier life.

A renowned and beloved figure in his community and to a wide circle of friends beyond these boundaries—Watt is a good neighbor and a thoroughly good human being. I feel privileged to have known him.

Watt restored the historic family homes to preserve and interpret the family's heritage from the past. He has tended and preserved the land of Lambshead Ranch as his and the Matthews-Reynolds families' legacy for the future. He considers conservation of wildlife and restoration of the land to its original condition as part of that legacy. These achievements also have made it possible for Watt to realize his most fervent ambition. "Lambshead restored" is being shared with fourth- and fifth-generation descendants of the Matthews and Reynolds families. Due to Watt's foresight and family pride, Lambshead Ranch remains for present and future generations to enjoy, appreciate, share, and—above all—preserve intact.

PART II

Daily Diary of Watkins Reynolds "Watt" Matthews, 1951–80

1951

[By mid-century, the United States was a nation of meat eaters. A growing population and rising average income encouraged a trend toward eating beef; that trend was to make the hamburger a national institution. While cattle sold for record-breaking prices, rising production costs and the threat of federal controls made this period of prosperity one of the most frustrating in the history of livestock raising. Like most ranchers, Watt Matthews had more on his mind than a tally book would hold, so he started this diary.]

JANUARY

Fri 19: Warm. Nearly hot. More big grass fires. North bluff & Hendricks. [*These are locations on an adjoining ranch.*]

Sat 27: . . . I went to Ft. Worth, reaching there about noon. Shopped for fire fighting equipment. Went to rodeo & stock show . . .

Wed 31: Temp 12°. Fire fighters meeting. Below 32° all day. Snowed a little. (water) .03.

[*Cattlemen organized to get the best use of firefighting equipment during one of the worst outbreaks of grassfires in history. See "Grass Fires out After 100 Sections Burn,"* Albany News, *January 25, 1951, p. 1.*]

FEBRUARY

Thur 1: Temp 0°. Cookshack –3°. Lot of ice cutting for cattle.

[*Water is essential to increasing the weight of beef cattle. They consume at least five gallons per head daily and as much as twenty gallons in hot weather. See Minish and Fox,* Beef Production and Management *(2d ed.), 182.*]

Fri 23: Mild, cloudy & damp. Has misted quite a bit up to 4:30 & is still doing so. Hard on heel flies. . . .

[*Cattle grubs, the larvae of heel flies, cost cattlemen millions of dollars in damaged hides and inferior meat. Heel flies become active with the first warm days of spring. By the mid-1950s, Dow's ET-57 systemic insecticide was being used to control the problem. See "Soon—A Livestock Systemic,"* Cattleman *43, no. 8 (January, 1957): 60–62.*]

Wed 28: Warm (about 60°) & cloudy early. Mild norther came up about 9. Shorthorn looking red eyed cow took best red eyed bull while we were feeding. Changed bulls in Overton pasture & brought 2 in from Lambshead & turned out 3 with C on left shoulder. Put one C right shoulder in Road. . . .

[*Cancer of the eye is common to Hereford (whiteface) cattle. Herefords having a small red rim of segmented skin around the eyelid are relatively immune to this affliction; therefore it was a desirable characteristic in selecting breeding animals for a herd. See Dykstra,* Animal Sanitation and Disease Control, *432–33.*]

MARCH

Sat 3: . . . Worked on books & income reports all day and part of night.

Sun 4: . . . I worked on figures again all day & until nearly one in night. Finally got M & B [*a partnership between Watt and his sister, Lucile Matthews Brittingham*] books balanced.

Tue 20: Temp about 30°. Worked Culver . . . Mighty dry and the steer years [*year-old steers*] show the effects of the drought. Was windy & dusty in the pens & my eyes are feeling poorly tonight.

Sat 24: . . . Lucile [*Brittingham*], Sallie [*Judd*], R. B. [*Judd*] [*Watt's sisters and a nephew*] & I went up to Throckmorton for Marianne Brown's wedding & reception which was quite a blow out and no doubt produced the most excitement up there since the coming of the railroad. . . .

APRIL

Wed 18: Warm, windy & partly cloudy. There has probably never been a spring with less green stuff than as of the present. The mesquites are not even green yet, even though the young ones are putting out. . . .

Thur 19: . . . Went to Bend [*Reynolds Bend, where the Barber Watkins Reynolds home has been restored*]. Listened to MacArthur's speech to Congress which was grand.

[*Gen. Douglas A. MacArthur was dismissed from command after he openly criticized President Harry S. Truman's orders to limit the war in Korea. Upon returning to the United States, he addressed a joint session of Congress, ending with the now-famous line, "Old soldiers never die, they just fade away." This controversy highlighted the dilemma of limited war.*]

MAY

Mon 14: . . . Went in to Mesquite control meeting after lunch. We went out to Ray Elliott's & looked at some he had sprayed last year with good results. Came back and looked at sprouts on Phin Reynolds Ranch which Fisher said are ready to spray. Ate birthday dinner at Ethel [*Casey*]'s for sister May [*Blanton*].

[*Watt is referring to C. E. Fisher, a recognized authority on mesquite control, who recommended spraying with 2,4,5-T. Noxious brush is eradicated from range land to conserve water for grasses. A mesquite three feet tall can transpire as much as six gallons of water a day. A limited amount of government money—eighteen thousand dollars—was available in Shackelford County to defray the cost. Early applicants received $1.75 per acre. See Vernon A. Young, Fisher, Darrow, McGully, and D. W. Young,* Recent Developments in the Chemical Control of Brush on Texas Ranges.]

JUNE

Fri 1: Was clear pleasant morning. Starting June with fine green grass & the range in excellent shape except for water as most tanks haven't caught much water. Rained .14 just before noon. . . .

Tue 5: . . . Cool, damp. Great grass growing weather. . . .

Sat 9: . . . First plane off ground at 6:10 [*spraying mesquite*]. Got in full day[,] each plane pulling 38 loads (45 acres per load except 1st 2 loads which were 40 acres). . . .

Mon 11: . . . Went to Throckmorton for Grand Jury service. We were through for the time being at 11:30; however, we are on call for 4 months.

Fri 15: . . . worked on my tally book all morning.

[*When cattle are worked, the ranch foreman gives Watt a count of the cows, calves, steers, and bulls in that pasture. This information is recorded in his tally book when each pasture is worked. Watt Matthews, interview by Janet Neugebauer, September 19, 1991.*]

Wed 20: . . . Went in town just in time to get to barber shop before 5:30 by driving too fast.

Tue 26: . . . Buck [*a horse*] threw R. B. [*nephew*] high & hard & I am mighty thankful he was not hurt. It happened in front of Overton house on smooth grassy ground & was R. B's own fault. It should be a good lesson to him as I have been ding-donging at him for years about being careless. . . .

JULY

Tue 3: . . . checked on my windows & finally ordered two Philco coolers which I believe will cool the whole house.

Fri 27: . . . Carrol [*Martin, Watt's bookkeeper*] & I went to town[,] then over to Abilene. He to get piece for tractor & I to have an old beam out of Stone Ranch house (built 1856) planed for a mantle. . . .

[*Watt's mother, Sallie Reynolds Matthews, lived in the Stone Ranch house when she was a young girl. According to her account in* Interwoven, *the place was so named because it was built entirely of native stone, even the large corrals. It is believed to have been built by U.S. Army Capt. Newton C. Given, who was stationed at nearby Camp Cooper. Wooden material probably was freighted in from San Antonio along with the material to build Camp Cooper. In 1983, Watt completed restoration of the buildings and corrals. He placed a marker on the site in 1984. These structures are located in the pasture Watt refers to in his diary as Stone Ranch.*]

AUGUST

[*By the first of August, the cattle industry finally had won an uphill battle against price controls. In May, the Office of Price Stabilization ordered a 10 percent rollback of live beef prices that was intended to return retail beef prices to pre–Korean War levels. All segments of the beef industry objected, pointing to Bureau of Labor statistics indicating that industrial workers could buy more beef with an hour's wages in April 1951 than in 1929. Cattlemen believed that price controls would give rise to shortages and black markets. Congress agreed and prohibited the rollback. See "Control Powers Curbed,"* American Cattle Producer *33, no. 3 (August, 1951): 7.*]

Mon 6: . . . O scorching hot day. . . .

SEPTEMBER

Sat 15: . . . to Olney where I went to a meeting at 2:30 to nominate directors of the REA.

Fri 28: Went down to Overton . . . saw some of the little bulls down there and they then looked at those in the Weigh Out. They were covered with horn flies. . . .

[*Hornflies are tiny, grayish-black flies that multiply very rapidly and annoy cattle to the point of reducing their gain as much as twenty pounds per month. Spraying or dipping with a solution of DDT controlled the flies. See "Treat Early for Hornflies,"* Weekly Livestock Reporter, *May 3, 1951, p. 3.*]

OCTOBER

Wed 3: Warm morning after a very warm day (102°) & night. Did desk work during morning then went to town after lunch. Put wages to men's credit [*at the bank*], paid grocery bills, etc. . . . another hot day. Maximum 104°.

Fri 5: . . . Boys hauled two loads hay from Hayford to Lambshead. Had to quit & go to fire along fence at Swag & Round Valleys, etc. Part of us came in about 3 A.M. Jack & White boy stayed there to watch.

Sat 6: Norther blew in before four. This increased the danger of the fire breaking out again. Oscar, Weaver, Carrol & I went up & relieved the other boys who were pretty chilly. We didn't lose over a section of grass or many posts which is lucky. No more than a section burned in Wolf Creek either, if that. . . .

Sun 7: Cool (big thermo 38°) . . . Jack going to ride west fence & check the damage. There were only 40 posts burned out. . . .

[*According to a diary entry on February 7, 1952, Watt bought eight hundred fence posts at sixty cents each. Even though his loss from this fire was small, grass fires can be costly when a large number of posts and the labor to install them are involved.*]

Fri 12: 6:05—about ready to start to Salina. Had a good trip up with no trouble & a strong tail wind. Ate lunch at Enid & reached Salina about 5:30. Ran into Kirk Edwards after supper & had a visit with him. Also, a man from North Platte.

Sat 13: After breakfast Joe [*B. Matthews, Watt's brother*], Kirk, & I drove out to the Jo Mar & I looked at the Denver load of bulls, then back by the hotel where we picked up Frazier Biggs & Kirk got his car. We went out to ranch & looked over the calves & Townsend took us to a pasture & showed us a calf (full brother to Cascade 28th) which we bought. He has a wonderful dam & sire. After the sale we had supper at the Vanier's ranch house.

[*Upgrading commercial herds is achieved by breeding purebred bulls to common cows. The best heifer calves are saved as replacements for the less desirable cows, which then are culled from the herd. The first generation of offspring carries 50 percent of the desired hereditary material from the purebred bull, and the next generation carries 75 percent. In just a few generations of continued use, purebred bulls can bring a herd to the point of having the practical value of purebreds. The success of this system, however, depends on the use of truly outstanding sires. Beginning in 1950, Watt and Joe Matthews bought all their bulls from the CK Ranch of Brookville, Kansas. John J. Vanier, owner of the CK Ranch, was one of the best-known registered Hereford breeders in the nation. Among the prizes it won at shows, the CK Ranch had the champion carload of bulls at the National Western Livestock Show in 1951, 1952, and 1953.*

John J. Vanier and Watt Matthews. Vanier, owner of the CK Ranch, sold Watt and Joe Matthews many purebred Hereford bulls that were used on Lambshead Ranch. Courtesy Watt R. Matthews

Over the years the Matthews bought bulls that had been set aside by the ranch for possible entry in the Denver show. Watt Matthews to Janet Neugebauer, September 19, 1991. See also Fowler, Beef Production in the South, *rev. ed., 164.*]

Sat 20: We worked Lambshead . . . The calves averaged 487, which was mighty good considering how long it has been dry. They would probably have weighed over 500 a month ago. The cows are also in fine shape & they are a wonderful set. One cow weighed 1370 & her outstanding heifer calf 530. She is a dandy.

[*Working a pasture in the fall involved spraying the cattle and weaning the calves before sending them to winter pastures or selling them to a feed lot. Watt Matthews, interview by Janet Neugebauer, November 11, 1988.]*

Wed 24: Temp 34° by thermometer at shack. First frost of year. [*November 11 is the average date of the first frost in Shackelford County.*]

NOVEMBER

Fri 2: Snow (.04 on ground white with water) & temp below freezing which is an early start on winter . . . Went to town late in afternoon at which time the snow was practically all gone. . . .

1952

[Ranchers wear their rugged individualism with pride, but they are keenly aware of the benefits of mutual support. Although they comprise only a small percentage of the national population, they exert considerable political strength, because they are informed, articulate, and united on issues facing their industry. When a problem arises, state and national livestock associations quickly can bring heavy influence to bear upon elected officials.]

JANUARY

Tue 1: Norther blew up in early morning and is down near freezing. Uncle Phin [*Phin Reynolds*] died around 5 o'clock (94 yrs old). . . .

Mon 7: Went in early & Tom [*Blanton*] & I left for Ft. Worth before 8. Went straight to American National [*Cattlemen's Association*] meeting & got there early enough to hear what we wanted to. Harold Arney & Mr. Erch of Parkman, Wyoming, Fred Hobart, Tom [*Blanton*], Will [*Reynolds*], Joe [*Reynolds*] & Watt [*Reynolds*] came by our room (Joe [*Matthews*] & mine) then the Reynolds boys took us to Ft. Worth Club for lunch. We had a lot of fun. Went to party given by Texas & Southwestern Cattle Raisers Association in evening which was nice. Weather good.

[The annual meeting of the American National Cattlemen's Association was held in Fort Worth, Texas. During the three-day convention, approximately fifteen hundred members from twenty-two states reaffirmed their opposition to government price controls, quotas, and subsidies. Most of

the previous year's activities had consisted of fighting government control of the industry. Among the resolutions passed, members voted to support a presidential candidate in the next election who actively would defend free enterprise. The National CowBelles Association, a women's auxiliary, was officially organized at the meeting. See "Lone Star Meeting," American Cattle Producer *33, no. 8 (January, 1952): 11–13; and Frank Reeves, "Cowmen Reaffirm Views at Fort Worth,"* American Hereford Journal *42, no. 18 (January 15, 1952): 14–15.*]

Wed 9: Went down for part of meeting. Heard Joe Clarke thank the American National. Tom & Edna [*Blanton*] picked up Chan Sweet [*Watt's classmate at Princeton*] & Fred Hobart & brought them out to Albany. I brought the Monahans [*Earl Monahan was a rancher from Hyannis, Nebraska*] out to Lucile's & we came out to Albany with Ethel in her car. After taking them (the northern visitors) down to see the heifers at Joe's & back by Edna's for a while we came out here for supper. Matt & Patty [*Blanton*] also came out for supper. Weather fine but windy.

Thur 10: Temp 20°. We got a fairly early start. Saw the steer years while being fed then thru the Overton, the Culver, W. D. Reynolds, Long, Tecumseh, back by Bartholomew, Reynolds, Hayford where we saw the young bulls thru Paint & by the farm to see older CK's. Saw a lot of cattle of all classes & a lot of turkeys and deer. We got in a little after one for lunch. They were impressed with the cattle & the country . . . Carrol drove us to Vernon where we took the train (5:22).

Fri 11: Got to Denver about 2 hrs late. Joe & I went to yards soon after getting located in hotel. The CK's had a wonderful load of bulls & a dandy calf by Cascade 28th on the hill. . . .

[*For a week in January each year, the National Western Livestock Show, in Denver, Colorado, becomes the crossroads of the range livestock industry. Having originated in 1906, this show is one of the nation's outstanding livestock events. Competition in stock shows has been a major force behind the improvement from Longhorns to modern beef cattle. See Henry Biederman, "Livestock Shows,"* Cattleman *38, no. 8 (January, 1951):*

18–19 and 43; and Willard Simms, "National Western Livestock Show," Cattleman *43, no. 8 (January, 1957): 34–36.*]

Sat 12: We took in the year car lot bull judging which started at 1 P.M. (Judges—Earl Monahan, Albert Mitchell, & McClelland). The CK's got first which pleased us. The judges worked hard & had most pleasant weather to do it in. We went to Albert Mitchell's cocktail party. The Joe B's & Blantons went to the rodeo with the John Swartz & I went to bed early.

[*All three judges were well-known and highly respected Hereford breeders. They have been recognized for their contributions to the progress of the Hereford breed with a place in the Honor Gallery of the American Hereford Association's Hereford Heritage Hall.*]

Sun 13: We went out for the car lots of bull calves judging & the finals which the CK load won after much checking in allies, etc. Wyoming Hereford Ranch won reserve on their serial calf load which was very nice . . . Tom, Edna & I went by Angus party then to Gov Dan Thornton's [*governor of Colorado and a well-known Hereford breeder*] party after I got Toni at the airport. Then to dinner with Swartz. . . .

[*A carlot usually consists of twelve animals. Uniformity was the strong point of these grand champion carlot bulls. All sold at substantial prices, the top being $15,000.*]

Mon 14: Jim & Frances ate breakfast with me. Jim, Joe, Tom & I left for yards in a cab & had a little wreck which didn't amount to much. Another cab picked us up & took us on. We watched bull judging which Milky Way Ranch won & CK Ranch got reserve with CK Crusty 46. The Cascade calf won his class & a Crusty took second (A full bro to 11 & 46). We had dinner with Chan Sweet, Shart & his daughter Sweet Skinner & her husband, Tim. Earl Guitar [*of the Hardy Grissom Hereford Ranch, Abilene, Texas*] also with us. He had won a class with a bull calf. [*Guitar also exhibited EG Royal Lady 253rd, the champion female calf at the show.*]

Tue 15: We went out to see the 46th [*Crusty 46th from the CK Ranch*] sell & he brought $41,500. The Dudley Bros. from Comanche got $33,250 for a calf which won 1st in his class yesterday & another also won first which made a dandy showing by the Texas cattle. We saw the Dudleys later at the Sidley & Anderson cocktail party. Bill Sidley bought the $33,250 bull for his Chicago people. After that Toni & I went to dinner with the Joe B's, Blantons, Craigs & McKenzies in the Emerald room.

Thur 17: Weather still warm & fine. In fact the entire time has been excellent. I trust the Ft. Worth show can do half as well weather wise . . . We left for 12:00 train about 11:20. . . .

[*The Southwestern Exposition and Fat Stock Show in Fort Worth is one of the oldest livestock shows in the nation. It started in 1896 with only a few animals under trees on a creek bank; by 1955 it had over seven thousand entries. Renowned as a bull market, the show emphasized carlot and pen divisions, where cattle were bought for range replacements. See W. R. Watt, "Southwestern Exposition and Fat Stock Show,"* Cattleman *43, no. 8 (January, 1957): 34–36.*]

Sat 26: Warm, partly cloudy morning after a warm breezy night. I got the day men paid then got off to Ft. Worth reaching there about 6:30. . . .

Sun 27: . . . We went down to see the bull judging. Lucile went with us. They only judged blacks and short horns before dinner. We (Joe & I) went back again after lunch & the Hereford judging was not over until between 4 & 5. CK calves won their class but were not champions (however I like them better than the champs). . . .

Wed 30: . . . went to car lot barn & to cow judging. Took some bit of time to get Jim Nail's & our bulls loaded out. . . .

[*Watt had bought the carlot of CK bulls after they won their division in the Denver show. They were shown again in Fort Worth by the CK Ranch before Watt took possession of them. Watt Matthews, interview by Janet Neugebauer, September 19, 1991.*]

FEBRUARY

Sat 2: Temp around 37° after a mild cold front. Ground hog didn't see his shadow until after eleven. . . .

Tue 12: Mild (48°) . . . It was sand stormish. . . .

MARCH

[Watt attended the Texas and Southwestern Cattle Raisers Association meeting in Fort Worth. Formed in 1877 at Graham, Texas, by area ranchers to combat rustling, this association is one of the oldest and largest in the cattle industry. It maintains brand inspectors at strategic markets and lobbies effectively for cattlemen in state and national affairs.]

Tue 18: Went to meeting in time to hear Gov Shivers speak. Later got with Tom Lasater, Walker White & Gardner Duncan & we were in Tom & Walker's rooms for some time then Tom took us to lunch. . . .

[Tom Lasater married Watt's niece, Mary Casey. He developed Beefmaster cattle, a cross between the Hereford, the Shorthorn, and the Brahman. In 1954, Beefmasters were recognized as a breed by the U.S. Department of Agriculture.]

APRIL

Wed 9: Started feeding years 3# a day . . . Had 44 of 45 cows accounted for & 39 calves. The calves are beautiful & a lot have red eyes. . . .

[Watt was feeding cottonseed cake to put a bloom on the yearlings due to be marketed the following month.]

Wed 16: Temp 48° Another clear pretty morning. Talked to John Britt [*a nephew*] to wish him happy birthday. We did some shaping of the steer years to have them ready to sell which will be shortly now with or without rain. It is too late to get much gain from grass now even if we got rain (on May 1 delivery). To have rain enough to wash them off & put out water every place would be a great thing for them. . . .

[In Shackelford and Throckmorton counties, the grass is at its best dur-

ing the fall and spring months. Therefore Watt carried his steers through these months and marketed them in late spring before summer droughts reduced grazing. They were sold as short yearlings. Watt R. Matthews, interview by Janet Neugebauer, September 19, 1991.]

Thur 24: Beautiful dewy clear morning. Temp 44° . . . Went around to feed places in Lambshead checking on years. We fed them six pounds, but they were not too hungry nor interested in the feed although they practically cleaned it up. We will probably drop back to five pounds a day. . . .

MAY

Thur 1: Temp 54°. Everything looks clean & bright after the nice shower .55 yesterday evening & in early night. Looked around about rain which has been a grand thing & changed the prospects. Good rains every where apparently except the SE 1/4 of ranch. Drove around over Phin Reynolds Ranch to see about the rain. East side got a trash mover which filled the tanks along the road & knocked gaps out. Creek ran thru W. which will help a lot. . . .

[*A water gap is a gatelike fence, usually made of old posts and old wire, that crosses a watercourse. When high water comes after a rain, the pressure of driftwood, etc., from the flood washes the water gap out, protecting the rest of the fence. After the water recedes, damaged water gaps have to be repaired to confine the cattle. See Erickson,* Modern Cowboy, *154–56.*]

Tue 6: Another clear pretty spring morning. Temp 62° . . . sold the Spanish Gourd yearlings to Jack Farmer [*a local cattle buyer*] at 40¢ [*per pound*] to be delivered next Monday.

[*Spanish Gourd is the brand used by the partnership of Matthews and Brittingham, a partnership between Watt and his sister Lucile Brittingham. Their cattle ran on the Phin Reynolds Ranch, which they leased from the J. A. Matthews Ranch Company. The latter was a partnership of Watt, his brother Joe, and his sisters.*]

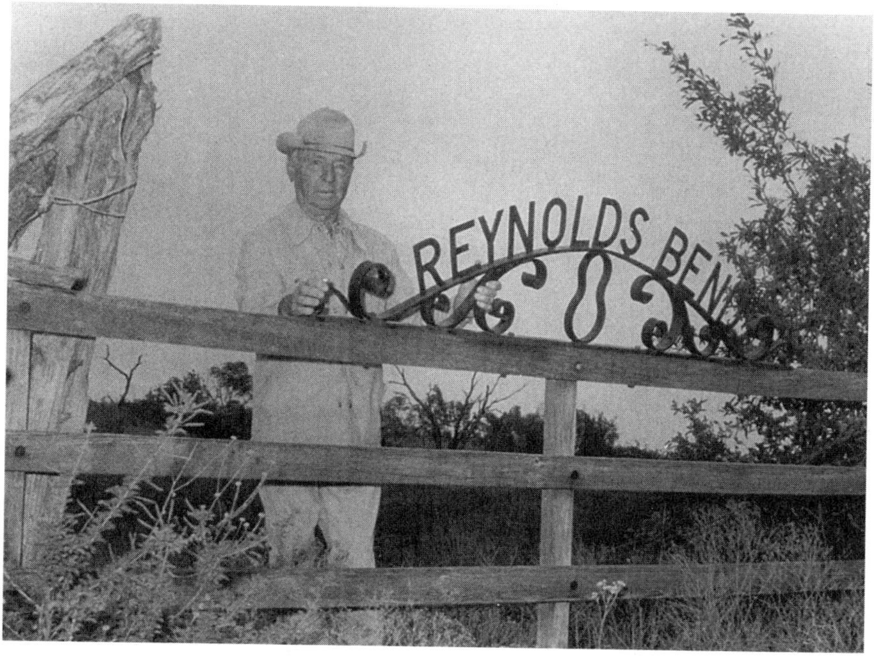

Watt Matthews at the entrance to Reynolds Bend, home of his maternal grandfather, Barber Watkins Reynolds. The sign includes the Spanish Gourd brand used initially by B. W. Reynolds and later used by the partnership of Watt and his sister, Lucile Brittingham. Courtesy Watt R. Matthews

Sat 10: Cool 53° with fairly strong north wind . . . Jack Farmer & I went out & looked at the steer yearlings. I offered to take 500# ($200) & he offered to give $195 (487-1/2#). . . .

Mon 12: Temp 53°. Clear, pretty morning. Oscar, Carrol & I went over to Phin Reynolds Ranch. Oscar, Tom & I went to W pasture to help Weaver & Farmer's men across Trout [*a creek that flows into the Clear Fork of the Brazos*], etc with the steer yearlings. We shaped them up, trucked them to scales, then back to Phin Reynolds Ranch where we branded them, then trucked them to Cook. They weighed 492. We were thru before 1 P.M. . . .

Thur 15: . . . Temp got above 100° again. . . .

Fri 30: Clear pretty morning. Temp 56° . . . then to Hayford where we doped the ugly & sore brands on the young CK bulls. We were short one & he will have to be located soon before he gets a case of worms. . . .

[*Animals with an open wound were treated with EQ 335, a solution containing lindane and pine oil; or SMEAR 62, which consisted mainly of benzol and diphenylamine, as a precaution against screwworms, a parasite of warm-blooded animals. The female fly deposits eggs, about two hundred at a time, along the edges of wounds, such as brands or castration wounds. They hatch within hours, and the worms immediately start feeding on live tissue. A grown steer with an untreated infestation has been known to die in less then ten days. See Scruggs,* Peaceful Atom and Deadly Fly, *17, 126–27.*]

JULY

Mon 14: . . . Mr. Benner phoned. He had a man to give 27¢ for the Spanish Gourd heifers. I told him he could have 300 AV at that.

[AV *was the brand used by the J. A. Matthews Ranch Company, a partnership of Watt, his brother Joe, and his sisters. Its cattle ran on Lambshead Ranch.*]

Wed 16: Temp 76° . . . Coyote howling after daylight or near sun-up & I trust there will be more showers today. . . .

Fri 18: Temp 75°. Pleasant morning. Got up at 4:45 to go over to deliver the Spanish Gourd heifers. They were in the pen by about 5 min past six. They weighed 573+ & net $149.40 per head . . . did some desk work until train came. We loaded them about 2 P.M.

AUGUST

Sat 9: . . . Temp about 79° . . . Turned out to be another hot day. The weather is taking an awful toll on the vegetation, which is all I mind about it. . . .

Tue 26: Another pleasant morning with no signs of a break in the dry, hot weather. Took a drive up thru South & West pastures around river by Burkett Bend, Mouth of Paint Creek, etc & have to admit the water has gone faster than I have ever seen it and the river is probably lower than I have ever seen it or soon will be. You can walk up the channel close to 1/2 mile at MK crossing. Doing fairly well at Bend. . . .

[*The Clear Fork of the Brazos River supplies water for most of the cattle on Lambshead Ranch. Entering the ranch in its southwest corner, the river makes a large half-circle to the north and leaves at the southeast corner nearly thirty miles downstream. Archaeological evidence indicates that prehistoric hunters lived along the banks of the clear waters, hunting the game animals that grazed nearby. Watt's maternal grandfather, Barber Watkins Reynolds, also understood the importance of the river and settled in the Bend, a section of present-day Lambshead that is located in a large bend of the river. Local ranchers attribute part of the ongoing success of Lambshead Ranch to the abundance of good water there.*]

SEPTEMBER

Tue 2: Temp 59° which is a big change & this will be the first day since July 19 (44 successive days) that the maximum will not be above 100. Got cold & had to get a blanket. . . .

Mon 29: Cool (52°) . . . Worked Road & sent 120 cows & 24 calves to Ft. Worth. (6 trucks). There were some good old cows that make you sad to see go. We have about 70 more in Road most of which will go. . . .

[*Road is a pasture where Watt gathered cattle to be shipped. He believed that he would be short of water, as the river would dry up completely in a month or so.*]

Tue 30: Temp about 53° Clear & no sign of rain. Hope river has past Buzzard Peak crossing by now & trust it will fill hole at Buzzard Peak corrals before it quits running so we can fill vat without laying more pipe. Worked Road & sent 44 more cows to Ft. Worth. Those there today topped market on cutters & fat classes & we are pleased with the way they sold considering market conditions. The calves sold mean [*low*]. Carrol Putnam came by & we checked on river, etc. It was coming across Buzzard Peak crossing.

OCTOBER

Fri 3: . . . Left about 5 to take bus for football game with Cougers. Anson 19, Albany 7 & a pretty good game.

[*Interest in high-school football is a sentiment common throughout Texas. In small towns, especially, everyone becomes involved in one way or another; often the football team is as potent a force as the Chamber of Commerce. See Winningham,* Rites of Fall, *7–10.*]

Sat 4: . . . Listened to World Series. Jack, Sam & I took a baby calf they had found in South up to its mother. This is the first calf of season that any one knows of & is early . . .

[*Bulls were put with the cows in February, to produce a calf crop that would begin hitting the ground in November, when cool weather would discourage screwworm problems.*]

Mon 13: Temp about 50° . . . Boys got off before 7 to round Paint. Those cows look well & we cut out a bunch. 36 fine old cows to ship which we hate to see go & would be money makers for anyone with a place to take good care of them. . . .

Wed 15: Temp about 48° . . . They rounded heifer yearlings & got 256 which is short quite a bunch. They have lost ground but are a fine bunch of heifers. We will have to clean out West pasture for them soon if we don't get rain. . . .

1953

[The cattle industry is cyclical in nature. When prices are high, ranchers expand their cow herds to generate more income. As additional calves hit the market, prices soften. Fearing further price breaks, cattlemen retrench, and the market becomes glutted until herd sizes are reduced. As supply diminishes, prices climb slowly until herd expansion begins again. Historically, cycles have been about ten years in length. In 1953, record-breaking numbers of cattle hit the market, reflecting high prices during the Korean War and the onset of a drought in the Southwest. Prices dropped as much as 50 percent. Cheap retail prices further fueled growing consumer demand for beef, however, which ultimately proved beneficial for cattlemen.]

JANUARY

Sat 3: Temp 30°. Worked around the cookshack with the mail. . . .

FEBRUARY

Sat 28: Low 42°. Partly cloudy & damp feeling. Carrol & I fed Valley & got all 7 bulls and all (124) cows, but 7. [*Watt used five or six bulls per hundred cows; studies indicate that bulls become sterile when overused.*] The green stuff is coming down there & with one good rain the troubles would soon be over. The Varnon outfit brought 375 sacks of feed, which I hope will see us through. . . .

MARCH

Mon 2: Low 44° . . . Went to Blanton's for the day. Bro. Lynn had a family dinner as a memorial on Papa's 100th birthday which was mighty nice & fine of him to do. . . .

[*Bro. Lynn was Thomas Lindsay Blanton, Watt's brother-in-law. After the family celebration, he published a book entitled* Pictorial Supplement to *Interwoven*: Centennial Memorial Commemorating the 100th Anniversary of the Birth of Judge John Alexander Matthews, March 2, 1853. *A testament expressing the gratitude he felt toward his in-laws, the book was distributed only to members of the Matthews and the Reynolds families. Over the years it has become rare and is an item highly prized by collectors of Texana.*]

Fri 6: Low about 31° . . . Did some more work on income reports. We worked the steer yearlings & after weighing & dipping put 402 in South. 100 in Lambshead, and 32 in Weigh Out. 533 avg 402#. They would really be a beautiful bunch if they could put on another 100 lbs. They are the most uniform with less tail than any yet for that matter. . . .

[*Feedlot owners pay premium prices for loads of cattle that are alike in fleshing, conformation, and weight for age. Animals that have developed uniformly for a year can be expected to continue this pattern and should be ready for slaughter at the same time.*]

Mon 9: Low 45° . . . Raining a beautiful slow rain which is ideal to start off with. We had .78 total by 7:30 & I hope it keeps coming for some time. One inch by six & I hope we get more tonight. . . .

Tue 10: Low 48° . . . Foggy, misty morning which will drive the moisture down & be a great thing even tho it doesn't rain much. . . .

Fri 20: High 90°. Low 60°. Clear windy morning. Barometer getting low. Fairly windy all day but no dust storm. Carrol & I tried to feed the Lambshead but didn't get half the yearlings. We had better luck in W.O. Went to Bend to see about cleaning up. Richard & J D were getting every thing in good shape. We branded 162 calves (76 heifers & 86 steers) in W. D. Reynolds in just over 2 hrs. Fencers

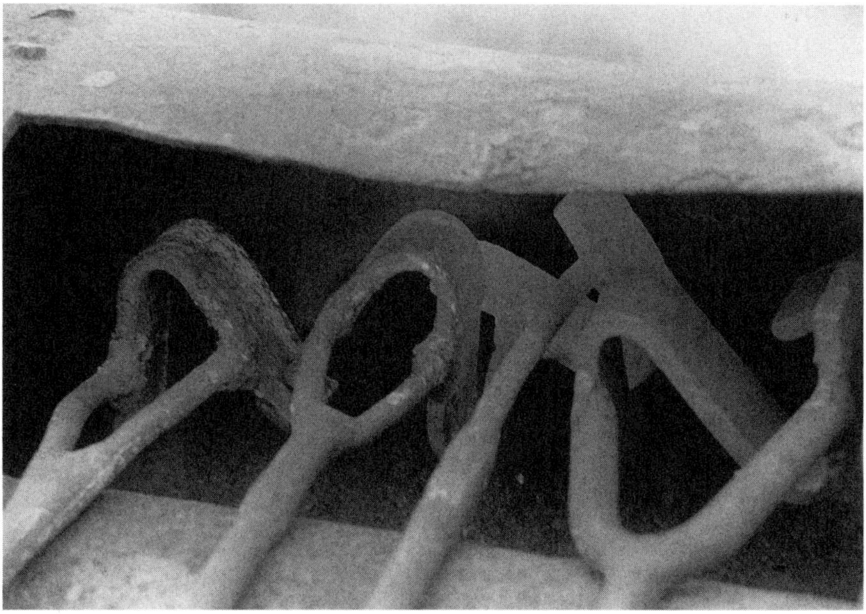

Grey-hot irons used to put the AV brand on ranch cattle.
Photo by Janet Neugebauer

moved to Phin Reynolds Ranch to put up some corrals in NW corner of Trout.

APRIL

Wed 1: Low 46°. Partly cloudy. Got up and went in to meet Chuck & May to go to Austin. We didn't get off until about 10:30 on account of clouds around Austin. Got there just before 12. Had lunch in Andrew's room, then went to hearing at Capital. It was hot & muggy. Max & I went by game commission offices. . . .

Thur 2: . . . Got to talk to Chairman Fuller of Senate Committee on Wildlife. Saw our Senator Moffet at breakfast . . . We left Austin 8:45 and got to Albany by 10. Came here (Lambshead) for lunch. Drove around some then got ready & went in to communion service.

Fri 3: Norther on. Temp 7 A.M. 46° . . . I went to court house & got

Maxine to write some letters in regard to closing season on turkey and quail.

Fri 10: Warm low 66° . . . Went over to get Carrol Putnam [*neighboring rancher*] to sign letter to try to get season on turkey & deer closed. . . .

Fri 17: Low 62° . . . Carrol & I hunted the pear cutters but didn't find them. They have a lot cut that are not piled. We then went by Mouth of Tecumseh to Hitson by the tank job etc. Back by Bend. Joe here when we got in. Did a lot of talking over phone about selling some horses. Finally sold four, I guess. . . .

[*Good range management for maximum grass production includes control of the prickly-pear cactus (*Opuntia engelmannii*). Prickly-pear drops some of its joints; these take root, and each becomes a new plant. Thus large colonies are produced in a short time.*]

Sat 18: Stiff norther blowing since about 10 last night. Temp 37°. We will be lucky to miss a freeze in the morning. . . . 28° by Jacks!

Wed 22: Low 54°. Spring like morning with soft air. Day got hot as it wore on and what little grass there is was burning up & a few more days would see the country looking wretchedly. . . .

Thur 23: Low 59° . . . Started showering a little about 12:30 this morning & has amounted to .44 by 7 A.M. . . .

MAY

Fri 1: Low about 62°. Wind got high and air full of dust, but not as bad as Wednesday [*April 29*] which was reported by a lot of people to have been the worst they ever saw. . . .

Tue 5: Low 43°. Clear & dry . . . We sold AV & Spanish Gourd yearlings to Dinklage [*a Nebraska cattle feeder*]. Steers 20¢, heifers 17¢ . . . Joe thinks country hardest he has seen it as of this date.

[*In 1952, the yearling steers had brought forty cents per pound. See May 6, 1952. In the Southwest, prices were driven still lower by the onset of a severe drought that forced additional cattle on an already glutted market.*]

Thur 21: Warm morning after a mighty warm night. Windy & partly cloudy. Day got to be a regular summer one with heat above 100° . . . We worked two year old heifers. Tipped & sprayed 255 at Buzzard Peak. They should make big, fine cows. . . .

[*The best heifers were retained as replacements in the cow herd. Removing the tips of their horns reduced harm to other cows but left enough horn to protect their future calves. Watt Matthews, interview by Janet Neugebauer, September 19, 1991.*]

Mon 25: Cool morning with temp about 72° . . . Mr. Rice, piano tuner, got here fairly early . . . Took Mr. Rice to Bend to tune those pianos. . . .

JUNE

Wed 3: . . . found turkey nest with 12 eggs in it. I came home & phoned around to try to locate a hen to put them under. . . .

Tues 30: Started raining in early morning. We have had a wonderful rain, 3.58 up to 10:15 & may get more. I believe creek got higher than any time since 1910 . . . caught lots of water . . . River all over bottom at Mouth of Paint. . . .

[*Weather conditions improved during July. Rain and cooler weather helped the grass recover, and on July 19 the river came close to overflowing—its highest level since 1932.*]

AUGUST

Sun 2: Some clouds with rainbow this morning which I hope means we are due to get a rain soon.

[*The late June rains continued through August. The grass began to spread and, where any turf was left, actually grew lush.*]

SEPTEMBER

Tue 8: Mild, pleasant, clear morning. Will soon not be daylight by six o'clock. . . .

OCTOBER

Sat 3: Warm cloudy morning temp about 70°. Carrol got off for town with 3 AV and 1 Blanton cow for CROP at 7:35. . . .

[Under the direction of the county agricultural agent and local pastors, Albany participated in the Christian Rural Overseas Program (CROP). The effort was organized to collect and ship food packages to needy countries overseas. Shackelford County citizens furnished thirty head of cattle, which were to be canned free of charge at Fort Worth and shipped free of charge to overseas destinations. It was believed that CROP could do more to create good will abroad than government money.

The fall equinox was hot and dry, but October rains caused the grass to grow well, so the cattle started winter in fine shape. End-of-year cow work included shaping calves up for shipment and culling cows which had not bred during the season. The cow herd then was dipped to remove vermin and checked over before being moved to winter pastures. Finally, the bulls were dipped and shaped up. After everything was in order for the coming breeding season, Watt, his brother Joe, and several cousins joined their Reynolds kin for a hunting trip to the Reynolds' Long X Ranch near Dalhart, Texas.]

1954

[High prices following World War II lured speculators into the cattle business. After the heavy losses of 1953, these "hobby ranchers" led a march in Washington, D.C., seeking federal price supports. Ranchers who had grown up in the industry, fearing they would lose control of their own businesses, continued their opposition to government intervention. Instead they worked within their cattle associations to launch a nationwide "Eat More Beef" campaign. They believed that increased consumption would eliminate the current surplus and make room for future growth.]

JANUARY

Fri 8: Temp 50° . . . Mild & windy. 8th straight day with temp getting above 60°, which it is by 12:30. . . .

Sun 10: Temp about 23°. Cold north wind. Got organized & packed up to leave for Colorado Springs [*to attend the American National Cattlemen's Association annual meeting*].

Mon 11: Temp Lambshead 20° . . . went to Executive Committee meeting. To bed early.

Tue 12: Temp Lambshead 30°. We got up and went to opening session . . . Joe [*Matthews*] was busy on Resolutions Committee all afternoon. . . . [*Members supported the new farm program submitted to Congress because they hoped it would lead to decontrol of agriculture. They also approved the government program of beef buying for public schools to support sagging prices, but emphasized that the program was funded through import duties on foreign beef, not U.S. tax dollars. Advertising to promote beef consumption received solid support, as did voluntary calf vaccination for brucellosis control. Finally, USDA was urged to establish research centers to combat livestock diseases. Ranchers were not opposed to all forms of federal support. They simply wanted indirect support with no threat of controls over production or prices. See "American National Meets in Colorado Springs,"* Cattleman *40, no. 9 (February, 1954): 26, 53, 54–56; and "Cattlemen Display Optimism in Industry,"* American Hereford Journal *44, no. 19 (February 1, 1954): 100–102, 108–11, 115, 118–20, 124–27.*]

Wed 13: Temp Lambshead 29° . . . We went to convention & spent morning. Magic barrel meat cutting, etc. Tom, Joe Reynolds, & I had lunch at the Antlers. Back to convention hall early for Secretary Benson's speech at 1:30. Tom & I stayed for tax conference. . . .

[*Secretary of Agriculture Ezra Taft Benson won the approval of cattlemen when he told them that the new farm program of flexible price support would provide relief from the squeeze in which they were caught—between high support prices for feed grains and declining live cattle prices. See "American National Meets in Colorado Springs,"* Cattleman *40, no. 9 (February, 1954): 26, 53, 52–56; and "Cattlemen Display Optimism in Industry,"* American Hereford Journal *44, no. 19 (February 1, 1954): 100–102, 108–11, 115, 118–20, 124–27.*]

Thur 14: Temp Lambshead 40°. Mountains beautiful with the sun rising on them . . . went to meeting. Didn't leave there until all was over about 2 P.M. Reno got next meeting which pleased me. We went back to hotel & got set to leave.

Thur 28: Temp 40° . . . Worked with pecan losses trying to decide whether to charge off something. . . .

[*Drought killed many of the pecan trees on Lambshead Ranch, and Watt charged off the loss on the J. A. Matthews Ranch Company partnership tax return.*]

FEBRUARY

Thur 4: Temp 42° Clear beautiful day. Sun rise Ft. Worth 7:22, sets 6:04. We worked with the bulls all day checking numbers, etc. Put C on hip of those checking clean. Sent 10 clean CKs to Paint . . . Bet Jake $5 will be 10-1/2 hrs from sun rise to sunset in Ft. Worth on this day. Dec 29, '53. Rise 7:31—set 5:31.

[*February was hot and dusty, with temperatures reaching into the high eighties. With less than an inch of moisture, grass growth was slow.*]

Sun 7: Temp about 26° . . . Lucile & I oiled my luggage. . . .

Wed 17: Temp 28° Beautiful morning. We got 166 steer yearlings in from Lambshead before 8 A.M. & weighed them. Average 561 which pleases us. . . .

Fri 19: Temp 50° after a blustery night with a .05 sprinkle about 2:30 this morning. Bad dust storm got going before noon & by 2 to 3 o'clock it was about as dark & thick as it ever gets. Houses were very dark and lights had to be burned on cars. . . .

APRIL

Sat 3: Temp 55°. Boys got off early to work Phin Reynolds Ranch. They made a good round on North Pasture & we branded 204 calves (106 steers & 98 heifers) and marked 1 dwarf. Richard cooked steaks & fixed a big salad to go with the beans, bread & bread pudding that Jake fixed & we had a good dinner for twenty odd. Cattle looked well. We sprayed them & got done just before five . . . Weighed 5 lbs less after finishing, than about 10 A.M.

Mon 12: Temp 51°. Having wonderful rain. 1.35 [*inches*] by 8 A.M. . . . Has fallen fine so far. Stayed around cookshack all morning enjoying the rain . . . Went to town after lunch. Got mail. Had station wagon inspected. . . . to bed early. Lambshead 1.81, Farm 2.90, Hayford 2.30, Tecumseh 2.25, Bend 1.69.

Wed 14: Temp 59° . . . Joe & I left Albany for Ft. Worth about 7 P.M. Had visit with Lucile.

Thur 15: We got up & went down to Texas Hotel where we met in Room 310 with Henry Biederman, Mary Clark & Lewis Nordyke who read his manuscript. Joe Reynolds got there later. We had lunch in that room & stayed with it until 5 o'clock. . . .

[*They were reading Nordyke's manuscript for* Great Roundup: The Story of Texas and Southwestern Cowmen. *Henry W. Biederman was editor of the* Cattleman *and director of information for the Texas and Southwestern Cattle Raisers Association. Mary Whatley Clarke, a freelance writer, contributed many articles to the* Cattleman.]

Wed 21: Cloudy & Mild. Soft air. . . .

MAY

Tue 4: Temp (low) 36°. Considerable frost. . . .

Sat 29: Temp 59° . . . checked & doped fresh branded calves in W. T. They have done extra well & there were not even any blowflies . . . I have never seen grass making such a recovery as the past six weeks.

[*Blowflies breed in animal flesh. The maggots spread over the animal's body, feeding on the skin surface and destroying its ability to function. Infected animals become weak and fevered; thus production is lowered. Infected animals were treated twice weekly with Smear 62, the same treatment used for screwworm maggots. See Ensminger,* Stockman's Handbook, 920.]

JUNE

Thur 3: Temp 58° . . . Went to Bend & checked on things. Shorty was cutting weeds & the mesquite grass is spreading over the big yard well. . . .

[*Curly mesquite grass (*Hilaria belangri*) forms the bulk of forage on ranges in Throckmorton and Shackelford counties. Young curly mesquite grass averages 8.86 percent protein, .36 percent phosphoric acid, and .56 percent lime. It is grazed from May through September. See Fudge and Fraps,* Chemical Composition of Grasses of Northwest Texas, 6–55.]

JULY

Sat 3: . . . Met Carl [*Rister*] & Mattie Rister in my office at 11 A.M. Let them have my copies of *Quirt & Spur* and John Brown's book, & map J. R. Webb gave me. Took Risters & Webbs to lunch at Steak House. Showed Risters some letters & stayed in office until nearly five. . . .

[*Carl Coke Rister, a professor at Texas Technological College in Lubbock, was the first nationally known historian to focus on the American Southwest. He was writing a history of Fort Griffin and wanted to use some material belonging to Watt.*]

Sun 18: Another hot day in prospect. Droughty conditions with us again. We are behind average rain fall for first six months & this will make 5 years in row if it carrys on thru year. . . .

Thur 22: Another clear day with no prospect for rain. Went over to Tecumseh & looked at bulls one of which has a bad case of pinkeye. . . .

[*Pinkeye, a highly infectious eye ailment, can spread rapidly through a herd, causing blindness or a drop in production. Caused by a Vitamin A deficiency, dust, or injuries, or spread by face flies, the disease is widespread throughout the United States, especially among range and feed lot cattle. Treatment consisted of applying antibiotics or sulfa drugs. See Ensminger,* Stockman's Handbook, 904–905.]

Sun 25: Temp 114° Clear breezy morning with more heat in store. The heat came with a bang & reached 114° by Jack's which is as high as ever recorded at Albany. Has been that high a few times. . . .

Mon 26: 114° Still, hot morning. Day got mighty hot & we had second day in row of 114°. Things are burning up & I am afraid we are going to lose a bunch of trees. . . .

Wed 28: 104° Few clouds in N.W. Sun rising red. May be we are in for a change soon. Went in & met May Bentley about 8:45 for our annual drive for Southwestern Diabetic Foundation. We got along fairly well. . . .

AUGUST

Thur 19: . . . Have done some phoning getting organized to go to Camp Sweeny in the morning. . . .

[*Camp Sweeney, at Gainesville, Texas, was the only camp in the South exclusively for diabetic children. It was operated by the Southwestern Diabetic Association. In addition to enjoying sports and recreational activities, campers learned about the role of diet in their health. They also learned to administer insulin to themselves. Watt helped the Southwestern Diabetic Association raise funds in Albany and spent time working at the camp. See* Texas in Review, *August 8, 1955, Film Files, Southwest Collection, Texas Tech University, Lubbock, Texas.*]

Fri 20: Nice morning. Boys off about 5:10 to help Sam Jones. Will be off for airport about 6. Bob Green, Bob Nail, & I off for Gainsville (about 7) in Bob G. ship. We got there about 8:20. Jim Campbell & Bob Brown met us. Bob went right to work when we got to camp. Worked hard until nearly 3 P.M. when we left for airport in a down pour. Was not raining at airport. We took off toward a broken to clear spot & while it was a bit rough we got along well. . . .

Thur 26: Clear, pretty morning. A little red in the east. . . .

SEPTEMBER

Sun 5: 100° . . . Cattle are shrinking but still look well. It is a shame we cannot get some rain before it is too late for the summer grasses. . . .

Mon 13: 52°–101° . . . Abilene to get eyes checked. Was delighted to be told by Dr. Nystrom that I only need glasses for reading. . . .

NOVEMBER

Wed 3: Temp 43° . . . Went to town. Worked on beef council business. . . . [*In the fall of 1954, the Texas Beef Council was organized to increase beef consumption by convincing Texas housewives that beef was affordable if they used economy cuts. Recipes also were provided. Grocery and restaurant chains reported as much as a 30 percent increase in sales. See "What the Texas Beef Council Is Doing for the Cowman,"* Texas Hereford *4, no. 9 (April, 1955): 7–9*].

Thur 11: . . . Saw Roy Parks [*president of the Texas Beef Council*] & James Snyder [*Watt's friend who ranches at Baird, Texas*] on TV Beef program.

Sun 21: Temp 42° . . . Spent morning reading & trying to clean up table. Have four chapters of Carl Rister's history of the Ft. Griffin area which I enjoyed. . . .

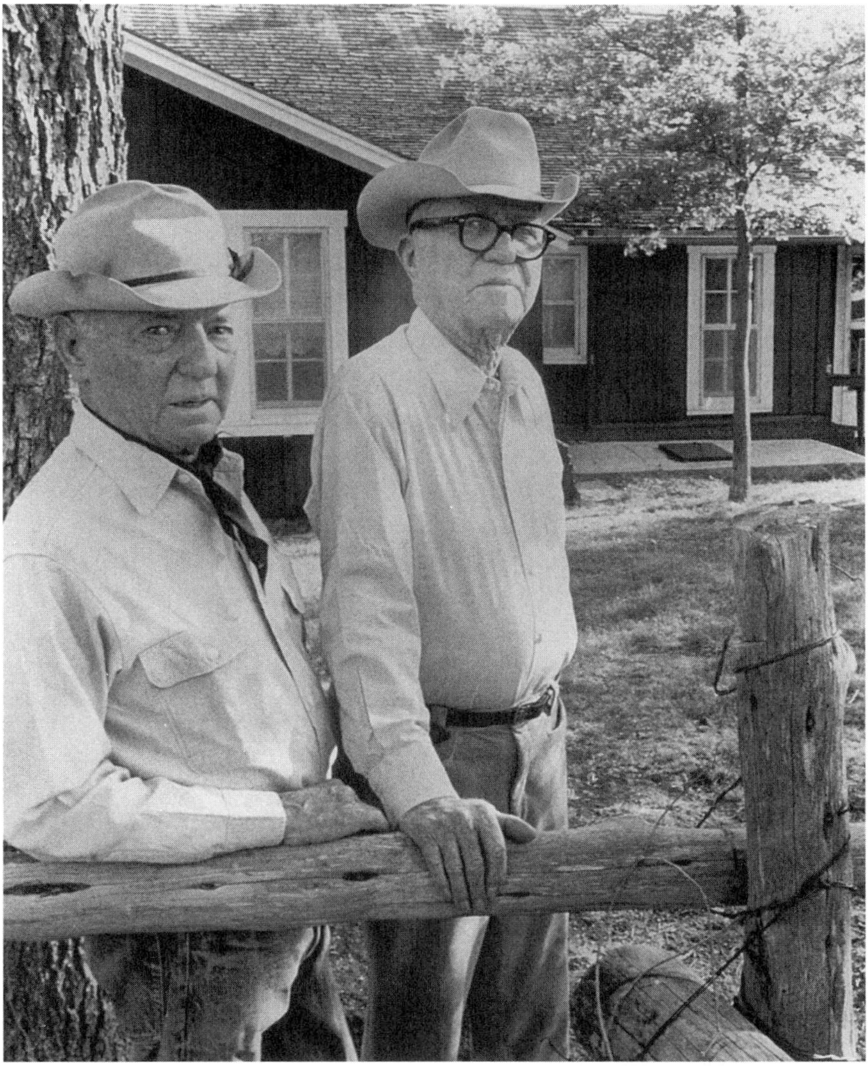

Watt and Joe Matthews after a routine tour and discussion about the management of Lambshead Ranch. Courtesy Watt R. Matthews

DECEMBER

Wed 1: Temp 47° . . . Went to Valley pen & helped spray the Valley cows. 63 accounted for & 32 calves. Joe got there soon after we got thru but I kept them in the pen for him to see. They line up on the fence like a bunch of show cattle. . . .

[*Spraying cattle twice a year with a solution of 5-percent Rotenone effectively reduced heel flies and grub infestations. When a solid stream of spray about one inch wide was applied against the lay of the hair coat on the backs of cattle, the force of the spray drove it into the grub openings, allowing the insecticide to contact grubs under the skin. See "Research Frontier,"* American Hereford Journal *44, no. 18 (January 15, 1954): 136–37.*]

Sat 11: Temp 54° . . . Raining a little. Had shower about 9 A.M. which brought total up to .17. Will wash dust off grass & do a lot of good in that respect . . . Call John Burns [*a nephew; birthdays of family and friends were noted in Watt's diary*].

Sun 19: Temp 45° . . . Hot water & salts & finger in lemon has finally got my finger to draining after being terribly sore for the past four days & throbing & keeping me from sleeping much at night.

Mon 20: Temp 33° . . . Got off for Ft. Worth just after nine. . . . Tried on my jacket & top coat at John Graves [*Watt's tailor*]. Got diary for 1955 . . . Kept lemon on my finger going and coming on trip.

Fri 24: Temp 43° . . . Fixed up Christmas checks for men, etc. . . .

Sat 25: Temp 45° after a low of 39°. Max 75° When I went to bed a drippy morning with the rocks all wet. Lucile & boys got over fairly early & after breakfast we had our stockings then the tree with many presents. 15 Blantons, 6 Joe B. Matthews, 6 Caseys, 3 Brittinghams, Nozel, Viejo, Richard, Ann & Jenny, Jake, Sedalia, Sue & I here for dinner. A fine 31 lb turkey. Very warm sunny day. . . .

1955

JANUARY

Tue 4: Temp 55° . . . Went to Dead Man Creek Water meeting in back of bank at 2 P.M. which lasted until late and took up my whole afternoon. . . .

[*Many creeks in West Texas are named because of a connection between the creek and some circumstance. Dead Man Creek was so named because a man was found dead in it in the early days of settlement. See Sallie R. Matthews,* Interwoven, *126.*]

FEBRUARY

Thur 17: Temp 28°. Clear . . . Oscar rigged up for shearing the 222 sheep here which they finished about 10:30. Tone [*Watt's nickname for his nephew, John Brittingham*] & James got those in Bend (34 of them together). Short 2. . . .

[*Watt kept a small flock of Suffolk sheep to graze the grass around the houses located on Lambshead Ranch.*]

Tue 22: Temp 15° . . . Joe phoned out about Mr. James B. Masher of Prophetstown, Ill who wanted to see the cattle. I met him at the other side of Sam Jones. We looked at years in Lambshead, then in W. D. Reynolds & took him by & saw the houses . . . He was impressed with the cattle & enjoyed the trip. . . .

MARCH

Sat 5: Temp 63° . . . Worked most of morning cleaning up table [*a table in the cookshack upon which the mail was left until Watt read it and took any necessary action*] & bringing tally books up to date. . . . [*By the end of March, the tally books showed the addition of six new CK bulls that "looked like might be worth the money." The average cost was $732 per head. The herd at Lambshead included 100 registered bulls, and approximately 1,300 cows.*]

APRIL

Fri 1: Temp 45° . . . Went to Bend after helping Roy Matthews load branding table. . . .

[*A branding table is a device that mechanically holds calves so they cannot kick or twist. It tips over on its side like a table and hinged panels open, allowing a team of cowboys to brand, dehorn, castrate, and vaccinate the animal. Calves are driven through a chute into the clamp, eliminating the need to rope the animals and knock them down.*]

Fri 15: 48°. Clear & not too much wind. Nice spring morning. Checked on white buffalo story. Gathered some pictures to take to Carl Rister. Tone & I went in for lunch (C.C.) at hotel where Carl spoke & which we enjoyed. They had a full house (eighty odd). . . .

[*Watt's mother, Sallie Reynolds Matthews, recorded a story in* Interwoven *about a rare white buffalo killed near Fort Phantom Hill, approximately thirty miles southwest of Lambshead Ranch.*]

Sat 16: Temp 58° . . . A little hazy. Drove Will & Watt [*Reynolds*] out to see the steer years in Lambshead which Carrol & John fed. Got word of Carl Rister's death when we got back [*Rister died unexpectedly of a heart attack*]. . . .

Sun 17: Temp 66°. Pretty morning. Tone & I are about ready (6:45) to go pickup Carrol & Ethel & head for Carl Rister's funeral at Lubbock. . . .

Fri 22: Temp 67° . . . Was mighty hot. Snakes were on move (killed one rattler) this morning. Bet Tone would rain by Sat. mid-night . . . Showered .52 here at Lambshead. . . .

Aerial view of Lambshead Ranch, circa 1955. Courtesy Watt R. Matthews

MAY

Mon 9: Temp 67°. We got off about 4:35 to get heifer years [245]. Had them in pen soon after six & the three trucks were loaded & gone by a little past 6:30. A pretty bunch of heifers. Average weight 547.8. More than held their weight since we put them in Weigh Out. They weighed them again at stock yards 5 hrs after weighing here & trucking in & they had gone off 3-1/2% which is about right. . . .

[*The weight loss was excretory shrinkage due to loss of digestive tract contents when cattle are without food or water during shipment. Cattle that have been on grass can shrink up to 4 percent. The weight is quickly regained when the animals receive food and water again. See Minish and Fox,* Beef Production and Management, *2d ed., 205–206.*]

Fri 20: Temp 57° Cloudy. .15 more rain last night & late afternoon. Ideal for getting the grass started & growing well . . . Jay Pumphry [*6666 Ranch*] came just before 12 & he, Matt & I had lunch together and went over plans for Hereford Tour on June 23. . . .

[*The West Texas Hereford Association sponsored an annual two-day tour of ranches having some of the top Herefords in Texas. The first day was spent visiting commercial herds in the Albany-Throckmorton area, and purebred herds were inspected the second day. Lambshead Ranch, a commercial cow-calf operation, was selected because, year after year, its cattle were in demand by Corn Belt feeders. See Reeves, "West Texas Hereford Tour,"* Cattleman *42, no. 3 (August, 1955): 34–37.*]

Tue 24: Temp 59° . . . We shipped 13 cows (nearly all sore-eyed), 2 heifer years, 1 steer calf, 1 heifer calf, & 5 dwarf calves. Sent 5 dwarfs to be butchered. . . .

[*Beginning in the late 1940s, dwarfism became a serious problem for all breeds of purebred cattle. The snorter dwarf, so named because of its breathing difficulties, was most frequently produced. Research proved that a recessive gene caused this condition. Thus, in matings of two carrier animals, 25 percent would be dwarfs, 50 percent would be normal size but carry the dwarf gene, and 25 percent would be normal size and free of the gene. Dwarf calves were an economic loss because they did not live to maturity. In 1955, the American Hereford Association took the lead in eliminating dwarfism through pedigree checking and progeny testing. Both procedures, though costly and slow, were necessary to restore the quality of purebred cattle. By the mid-1960s, dwarfism had been virtually eliminated. See McCann,* The Battle of Bull Runts, *and McCann, "Mission Accomplished,"* American Hereford Journal *52, no. 5 (July 1, 1961): 135, 138, 140, 142.*]

Wed 25: Temp 67° . . . Lucile & I went up & showed Clyde where to work on air strip for John [*Brittingham*]. . . .

Thur 26: Temp 65° . . . Martin bought 30 of our heifers at 17¢ and 40 steers at 20 to go June 25 to July 1 . . . Joe & I went out & saw Tone's new plane (Tripacer). . . .

JUNE

Wed 29: Pleasant morning. Took Jesus down to Overton and showed him pears which they will get on soon. . . .

JULY

Fri 8: Stays dry & getting more serious every day . . . Carrol putting out salt. . . .

[*Because salt stimulates the appetite of grass-eating animals, cattlemen consider it their cheapest feed. Generally, three-fourths of an ounce daily is provided for each one thousand pounds of body weight. See Bailey,* Veterinary Handbook for Cattlemen, *5th ed., revised by Irving S. Rossoff, 404–405.*]

Mon 15: . . . Tone, Carrol, & I are going to work with creep jobs. We had thirty odd at Pot Hole tank but didn't have much luck getting them to go in creeps. Later on a few went in & I hope will get started in numbers. . . .

[*A creep, an enclosure with an opening large enough for calves to enter but too small for older cattle, contains feed which fattens calves faster than the usual grass. Cottonseed cake or ground sorghum grain is generally used for creep feed in West Texas.*]

AUGUST

Thur 4: Carey & James gone to Bend to get sheep together & ride out Gentry, etc. Tom Gordon [*a veterinarian*] coming over to see what's wrong with the sheep here & at Bend (Blue tongue). . . .

[*Bluetongue, a viral disease that is infectious but noncontagious, affects sheep and sometimes cattle. Transmitted by insects, it produces symptoms including high temperature, loss of appetite, extreme weight loss, and reddened mucous membrane of the mouth. The mouth itself turns purplish or blue in color. Vaccination is an effective preventative, but treatment is geared only to control secondary infections. The mortality rate is low. After being diagnosed by a veterinarian, the disease must be reported to state and federal officials. See Ensminger,* Stockman's Handbook, *880–81.*]

Mon 15: Temp 58° . . . We worked NW side of Culver and put 69 cows in Road & sent 44 to Ft. Worth. They are fine old cows & we took some fine big calves off of them. It was nearly three when we got in for lunch. One truck left soon after four. . . .

Wed 17: Temp 64°. We got another shipment ready out of Road & sent 43 more old cows to Ft. Worth. Jack Evans trucks got off about 10:30. We went down and checked on long horns & grass in Ft. Griffin State Park. . . .

[*As range conditions deteriorated during June and July, cow herds were culled closely. In an entry two weeks earlier, Watt had written that a neighboring rancher sold four hundred cows and calves to reduce his herd.*]

SEPTEMBER

Wed 14: . . . Carey got kicked by Barney when they were unloading horses. John White's cousin was bitten by rattle snake when leaving Hayford with Herman. . . .

Sun 25: From 5:30 yesterday evening until breakfast time this morning we have had 5.57 in of rain. Lambshead [*Creek*] got almost to corner of yard & may have which is highest it has been since June, 1910. . . .

[*During "droughty" years, rainfall is unevenly distributed. A cloudburst can produce several inches that come too fast to be absorbed, and the runoff produces a flash flood. This condition often is followed by lack of an adequate amount of moisture.*]

Mon 26: Cool (60°). Cloudy morning. Tone & I went up & checked on river which is about 18" or 2' lower than crest July 2 yrs ago, if this crest is final. We drove around checking on tanks, etc. Everything we have seen except old Swag Valley & Dipping Vat running around & they only lack about 2' each. Roads washed pretty badly in places & a good deal of fencing to do but we are helped an awful lot by the rains. The biggest 12 hr rain I believe I have ever seen to cover the whole ranch from 5" to over 8".

Thur 29: Another warm grass growing night & things continue to improve. Tone & I went to Bend then to Buzzard Peak & checked river there & it was still pretty deep (4 or 5 ft). . . .

OCTOBER

Sun 2: Gentle rain falling. Just the thing for the grass which is jumping. . . .

Fri 7: Temp about 48°. I am glad it is no colder & I hope we can have more rain & another six weeks before frost. Range conditions were mighty bad when rains started & the prospects for winter are now about to get good. The bare spots are covering as fast as I have ever seen. . . .

Mon 31: Temp about 48°. Carrol & I took men & horses to Tecumseh to round 3 year old cows back this way. They got to Buzzard Peak before 12. We dipped them which was slow without electric prods. . . .

NOVEMBER

Wed 30: Temp 31° . . . Took some leather to Mr. Holder to make me some boots. Brought my church books up to date. . . .

DECEMBER

Fri 2: Temp 44° . . . Talked to Willard Simms, Gen Manager Denver Stock Show. Tom & Jack Vines got out with clippers, etc., & we got started clipping tails & poles by 10. . . .

Sat 10: Temp 31°. Clear & calm. Weighed calves & they only lacked .2 lbs per head averaging 14 lbs gain per head for past 2 weeks which is good considering all the chasing they have had . . . Tone killed an old boar & late coming back. I killed a small buck near tank. . . .

Thur 22: Temp 24°. Biggest frost of season. Holed up most of morning working with bull certificates. . . . [*Bull certificates are filed in the headquarters of the appropriate breed association to register the ownership of purebred animals.*]

Sat 24: Temp 64°. Warm blustry morning. Day finally got hot with temp in nineties. I believe it is probably a record high for Christmas Eve . . .

Maximum temperature 91° Albany. All time high, Ft. Worth for Dec 24 (eighty odd).

Sun 25: Temp 49° by about 7 A.M. after a warm night. Light norther on since early morning. Opened my many packages (a lot more than I deserve). . . .

1956

[Exhibiting animals is one of the oldest traditions of cattlemen. Stock shows bring all segments of the industry together to compare and select the cattle that will produce beef most economically. These competitions are hailed both as inspirations to breed improvement and as marketing opportunities, since prospective buyers remember the herds with good stock. The lure of the show ring is strong.]

JANUARY

Tue 3: Temp 38°. Clear, mild morning. We got organized for washing & trimming calves & got started before too late. Bill Couger was here early & Jack Vines before very late. He had a good system & got along well. . . .

[The training and grooming of animals begins four to six weeks before the show, with frequent washing and brushing to encourage heavy growth of hair. The tail is clipped to show the fullness of the twist and the thickness of the hindquarters. The evening before showing, the switch on the tail is washed, with a small amount of blueing in the water to whiten it, then braided. On show day, it is brushed and fluffed. Proper grooming can give animals a slight edge in the fierce competition of the show ring. See Ensminger, Stockman's Handbook, *1044–48.]*

Tue 10: We got to stirring around & got the calves loaded & started by 7:45. Should have got them going earlier. I tended to a lot of last minute items, packing, etc., & didn't get away from Albany until after eleven. The trucks had left at 8:45. I caught them at Plainview. Tone got in with me there. We plugged on & the trucks reached Dalhart at 7. I phoned T. A. Baridgman & he came & let us in pens. Joe Scott got to XIT Motel & after the calves were unloaded took us to his house for drinks before we went to supper.

Wed 11: We got up at 5:30. Had calves loaded a little after six . . . trucks got off about 7:15 . . . We got to Denver stock yards at 4:30 . . . Got them unloaded & in pens by six. They stood trip well. We ate supper at Nuestro & to bed early.

[*Watt was one of the judges of the National Western carlot bull show. He wrote: "Rough competition. The 10 pens of junior calves CKs champion & Bridwells reserve." Judging livestock shows helps a rancher develop the sharp eye needed to select herd bulls and replacement heifers wisely.*]

Fri 13: . . . We put in long hard day washing & combing 22 calves, moving them to show pen, getting feed, etc. Several visitors. Tone & I didn't take time out for lunch. Got in after dark. . . .

Mon 16: Got out fairly early & cleaned up calves which were judged in early afternoon & won 1st & 2nd. Got in in time to clean up and go to party at Joe B's [*Watt's brother hosted a party in his hotel room for friends and prospective buyers*]. Weather cold & did a little snowing. Up to this weather has been might pleasant. . . .

[*The J. A. Matthews Ranch Company won both first and second places for their two loads of yearling feeder steers, all of which were sired by CK bulls. See "CK Ranch" (advertisement),* American Hereford Journal *46, no. 19 (February 1, 1956): 38–39.*]

Thur 19: We went out & got calves ready for sale . . . Yearlings brought 22.25 [*cents per pound*] average 737 [*pounds*] & 20.50 [*cents per pound*] average 706 [*pounds*]. . . .

FEBRUARY

Thur 2: Sleety cold bad day. Below freezing all day. Ground hog never did see his shadow here or at the ranch. A hard spell on the cattle. . . .

Sat 11: Temp 25° . . . Cattle look remarkably well after all the bad weather

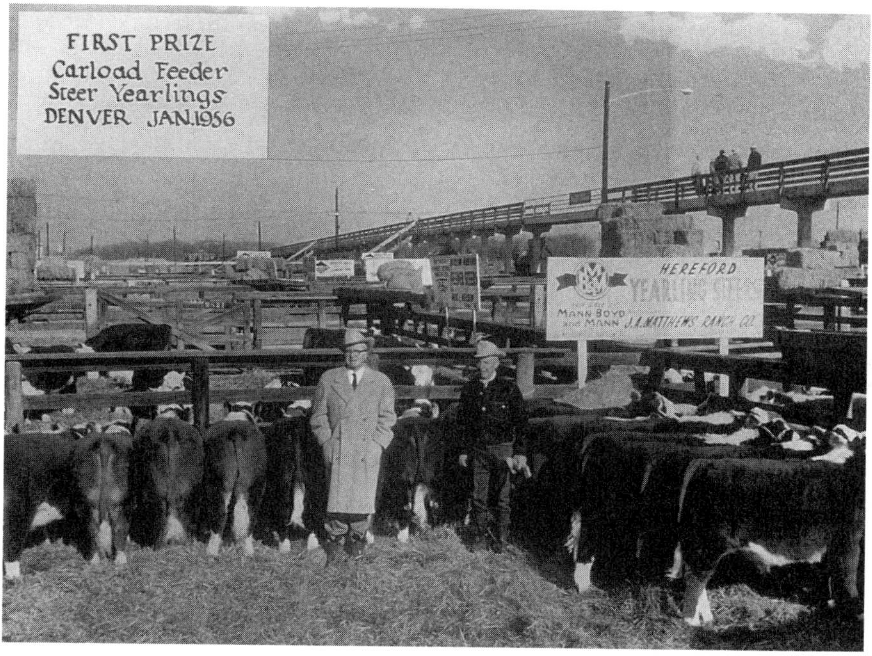

Joe and Watt Matthews with their prize-winning Herefords.
Courtesy Watt R. Matthews

. . . We got in fairly late & had to rush to make calf show [*in Albany*] at 1:30. AV calf won cup for best type. . . .

[*"Type" is that ideal combination of traits that best fits an animal for a specific purpose. Through selective breeding, high-grade beef animals come to possess certain well-defined characteristics which indicate efficient conversion of feed into beef rather than milk. See Fowler,* Beef Production in the South, 49.]

Mon 20: Temp 28° here in this low spot with a lot of frost, butno ice on pot or anything . . . We got the bulls in [*into a corral*], checked tallies etc & scattered them. 10 to West, 8 Paint, 17 to South, 4 Valley, 1 Overton, 1 Road, 10 Long, 6 to WN, & 2 left in W. D. Reynolds. Trimmed some feet & doctored some eyes.

[*Range bulls with feet sore from untrimmed hooves cannot breed the cows assigned to them.*]

MARCH

Wed 14: Got ready & went down to Texas [*Hotel*] for 7:30 breakfast with Resolutions Committee [*at the Texas and Southwestern Cattle Raisers Association annual meeting in Fort Worth*]. Then to meeting . . . Went to lunch for directors. They put me on in Joe's place which made me feel sad. [*Joe became an honorary vice-president.*] Joe & I went out to Merle's [*a cousin*] for cocktails (took Evetts Haley [*a rancher and well-known Texas historian*] with us). . . .

Mon 19: Temp 21°. Clear, pretty morning. By Overton, up thru Culver & over to Tecumseh (May Camp) . . . Country looking wretched & is soon going to be worst known for this time of year. If we don't get good rains before May it is going to be panicky. . . .

Wed 28: Temp 27°. We started after yearlings at 5 A.M. Dust & norther (temp 50°). Had to wait a half hour or more for light enough to round. Daylight about that much longer coming on account of dust. Penned both bunches at 7 A.M. Beautiful yearlings probably the most uniform we have raised yet. 512 average. . . .

Sat 31: Temp 56° . . . Clear, but air feels a little softer. . . .

APRIL

Sun 15: Temp 58° . . . Ethel phoned about more dead heifers being reported. Did a bunch of phoning. . . .

Mon 16: Temp 54° Blustry. Went to see about Spanish Gourd heifer years which boys were rounding. Tom Gordon did a post [*mortem*] on one & thought lead poison was the trouble. Mule [*a friend*] & I took a piece of liver & kidney to Abilene. Prof. Arrant of H.S. [*Hardin-Simmons*] Univ checked them. Guy Caldwell went with us & introduced us. Came back to ranch . . . Got report from Prof. Arrant that definitely lead poisoning.

MAY

Sat 5: Fine morning. Worked around table & on phone a good part of morning. Carrol Putnam, his father-in-law & I went to our precinct convention at Throckmorton at 2 P.M. The Shivers' forces lost by a fairly close margin, but all others in Throckmorton County went strong for Johnson. . . .

Mon 28: Temp 67°. Clear after a stormy night with .37 rain. Wind blew pretty hard from So. Stayed by cows until eleven and they were calm. . . .

JULY

Wed 4: . . . A very quiet fourth.

Fri 6: Close morning after the closest night of the season it seemed to me . . . A mighty hot day. . . .

[*The drought intensified in 1956. Many weather stations reported higher temperatures and less rain than any year on record, which laid the ranges bare over most of West Texas.*]

Sat 14: . . . Did some reading & resting in afternoon. . . .

Tue 17: . . . Webbs & I went to Anson to their 75 year celebration. They had a pretty fair show. Got home about 11:30. Had cool front & little sprinkle between 5 & 6 P.M. Was really cool at Anson.

[*Anson is the county seat of Jones County, which was created in 1858. It borders Shackelford County on the west.*]

AUGUST

Sat 4: August is going by and no relief in sight. In fact I think it will take a gulf disturbance to ever move the weather off dead center. . . .

[*The weather was on dead center because of a high-pressure ridge in the upper atmosphere that perennially drifts northward during the spring, causing warm, muggy nights and oppressively hot summer days in Texas. If this high-pressure cell, known as the "Bermuda High," becomes entrenched, its descending air currents squelch any vertical development of clouds, turning the blessing of fair weather into the dreaded curse of drought. Once it settles into position, the cell moves very little for weeks at a time and forces weak low-pressure systems from the Pacific Ocean, which could bring relief, northward to Canada. The Gulf disturbance that Watt hoped for was a hurricane that would make landfall in Texas. Only a rainmaking system as massive as a disintegrating hurricane could break the drought that gripped Texas. See Bomar,* Texas Weather, *86–87, 145*]

Wed 8: . . . Went to meeting at bank on rain increasing. There was a poor turnout & nothing done. . . .

[*Interest in rainmaking often grows during a drought. Unfortunately, this is when most techniques for artificially stimulating precipitation are least effective. Clouds of the proper depth or temperature must exist for successful seeding with dry ice or silver iodide, the most popular rainmaking methods. Cloudless skies typically characterize droughts. See Bomar,* Texas Weather, *155.*]

Thur 9: . . . Went in for DAR party to sell Ft. Griffin books. Mattie Rister [*Carl Rister's widow*] inscribed a lot & I did quite a number. . . .

[*Carl Rister's book,* Fort Griffin on the Texas Frontier, *was dedicated to Watt.*]

Wed 15: . . . watched convention on T.V.

Fri 17: 107° (high). This summer is going to set a record for days with temperature 100° or above as it is far ahead of 1954 as of this date. Got packed up & went in & Alice [*Reynolds*] & I got off for Kent at 8:15 . . . to ranch at 6:30. They had eaten supper.

Sat 18: 107° Watt [*Reynolds*], Alice [*Reynolds*] & I went to Camp Meeting. To church & had a nice visit with a lot of folks. Ate lunch at Evans & Means camp. Had fine beef & Mutton & were well looked after. . . .

[*They attended the Bloys Cowboy Camp Meeting in Skillman Grove, between Fort Davis and Valentine, Texas. Named after the first minister to conduct the services, this meeting is one of the nation's oldest and most colorful religious institutions. The three cousins were following a family tradition dating back to August 1903, when the J. A. Matthews family traveled three hundred miles by covered wagon from Lambshead Ranch to the Reynolds' Long X Ranch, near Kent in Jeff Davis County. Joining their Reynolds kin and cowboys, the group traveled another ninety miles to attend the annual meeting conducted by Rev. W. B. Bloys, a Presbyterian minister. In 1890, a few ranch families gathered for three days in a grove of live-oak trees to hear Bloys preach the gospel. Because great distances made opportunities for worship scarce on the frontier, these annual interdenominational meetings were popular. Watt's uncle, George T. Reynolds, who moved to the area in 1895, was a strong supporter of the meeting. Attendance grew until it numbered nearly three thousand in 1956. Cars and airplanes replaced the covered wagons, and a modern tabernacle replaced the first brush arbor. Each family has a regular campsite that is used year after year. Visiting with the Evans and Means families also was a family tradition. For years, the Reynolds and Matthews families spent a night at these ranches on their way to the camp meeting. Watt's group returned to Albany on August 21. See Joe M. Evans,* Bloys Cowboy Camp Meeting, *20–26.*]

SEPTEMBER

Sun 9: 44° (low). A chilly morning and a real reminder of fall. Buster got the milking & tending to doggies, creeps filled, horses wrangled & one saddled & loaded in Power Wagon & off for West Pasture by 6:45. He is really industrious & a drifter & it is a shame he is not stable. . . .

Tue 11: 53° (low) . . . Ate lunch at Bend. BCM [*a friend*] brought out doves which were mighty good. I ate 7 & practically nothing else. . . .

Wed 12: 68°. Boys off soon after six to work Hoover. Got along well & were thru about 11. That was a depressing job & they look sad. Cattle are going down & a person doesn't know which way to jump or what to do about it. . . .

Wed 19: 106°. The dry hot weather continues with no let up. A new all time record for number of days 100° or above & lack of rain. .90 of rain since May 28 & 92 days of 100° or above up to today which will probably hit 100°. Hit 106° which is pretty high for this late in year.

Mon 24: Trying to decide how to go at cow work which is a problem the way conditions are. Went over & checked on river at Buzzard Peak & we will have to lay more line to be able to pump water unless river runs. . . .

Tue 25: A pleasant surprise of rain came about 2 or 3 A.M. .80 here before six . . . Great to get the dust settled which was worse around trap [*the yard area around the headquarters buildings*] than I have ever seen it, I believe. Tone & I took a round checking on tanks. Lambshead & Culver pasture tanks caught a lot of water. Boys fixed some water gaps. . . .

OCTOBER

Mon 8: Low 49°–High 101° . . . We heard a little of Don Larsen's perfect game pitched in World Series. Yank–2, Dodgers–0. Not a Dodger got on base. It is getting mighty dusty again. . . .

Fri 12: Boys rounded bal of Culver going over whole thing & then Tone checked it with his plane & they picked those up . . . We are only short about 18 calves now which is good for the first complete round. Had such a busy day didn't get a chance to feed steer calves. . . .

[*Using his airplane, John Brittingham could spot cattle which were hiding to avoid being rounded up. He would write their location on a piece of paper that was dropped to the cowboys, and the cattle were moved.*]

Thur 18: Got to work combing Ft Worth calves (Tone, Carrol & John) . . . About time we were weighing all calves & loading these for Ft Worth got to raining. Light 10 calves averaged 545, heavy 10 averaged 632. Several here to see them . . . Denver calves 632.8. Lambshead got .39 rain before Tone, Penny & I left for Ft Worth after lunch. Delayed a while in Albany. Tone, J. D. & I went to yards & combed calves which had dandy pens. Strawed down in good shape. Britts & I ate supper at Garcia's, then by Aunt Susie's.

Fri 19: J. D. [*Lucile Brittingham's butler*] had breakfast ready for Tone & me soon after five & we were at yards well before six. Calves had filled some & were looking better. By the time they were weighed they had most of their weight back. Lights averaged 534.5 at 24¢ & heavies 624.5 at 21.50¢. The lights were grand champions & both pens got a lot of attention & favorable comments. Rained .25 more at Lambshead during early morning, but no rain except few drops in Ft Worth. Didn't get back to house until 12:15 then ate a fine big lunch Martha had fixed us. Got to Albany between 4 & 5. . . .

[*Watt entered cattle, and was a judge, for the final stocker-feeder show of the year, held in Fort Worth on October 19, 1956. His steers were grand champions and second place in the competition of ten head. Watt judged the pens of heifers. His steers, which were sold for $24.00 and $21.50 per hundredweight, brought the highest prices paid at the show.*]

Sat 20: Thundered around in early morning, but no rain any place on ranch that I know of . . . All look well except those to Valley. There is absolutely nothing to eat in there except leaves & beans [*mesquite beans*] & we have to watch & see how they do. The range is in a sad shape. . . .

Wed 24: Fairly strong south wind. Boys rounded Long & went back in there & Stone Ranch after lunch & got all the heifer years we know of. I ate lunch at Mexican camp & drank some pecan leaf tea which was better than one might think. . . .

NOVEMBER

Fri 9: Cold, clear, frosty morning. Had to bring pump in by fire to thaw it out. They wet the calves & combed them [*grooming for stock shows*]. The cold water should make their hair grow. . . .

Sat 10: Temp about 48° South breeze. Busy day. Organ dedication went off in good shape. About 130 in church & I think the music was well received. We fed around 80 at Bend. Cleaned up 12 lbs of beans & made a mighty hole in about 160 lbs of beef. A lot of the people were strangers from out of town. George Leslie, Lucile, Sallie & I went in for the evening program. 108 there.

[*The organ was dedicated to Watt's paternal grandmother, Caroline Spears Matthews (1824–95), a pioneer who helped to establish Christianity in the area. The church, Matthews Memorial Presbyterian in Albany, Texas, was built in her memory in 1898. When the interior was remodeled in 1954, the organ, which initially had been dedicated to Mrs. Matthews in*

1928, was sold and the proceeds applied to the price of a larger one. Thus the original donors were permitted to share in funding the new instrument. The organ, built by Otto Hofmann of Austin, Texas, was housed in a case designed by Joseph E. Blanton, Mrs. Matthews's great-grandson. See Susan Matthews Reynolds, Reference File, Southwest Collection, Texas Tech University, Lubbock, Texas.]

Thur 15: . . . There is quite a jag of green stuff & it is too bad it cannot rain some more & keep it coming. We could have a green winter yet & we really need one in the worst way. . . .

Sun 18: . . . About set to go in & help examine bank. We got along pretty well & were done by noon. . . .

DECEMBER

Tue 11: Temp 45°. Strong south wind. Joe came out with Frank Reeves about 9 o'clock & Frank took two or three dozen snap shots of the calves. We had them combed up in pretty fair shape. . . .

[*Frank Reeves, known as the dean of Texas livestock reporters, documented the cattle industry in word and picture during his thirty-two years with the* Fort Worth Star-Telegram. *Many of his articles also appeared in the* Cattleman, *the official publication of the Texas and Southwestern Cattle Raisers Association. Reeves used the photographs mentioned here in an article he wrote about Lambshead Ranch for the* Star-Telegram.]

Fri 21: . . . Spent day around cookshack, etc trying to get ready for ranch Christmas tree & supper, which went off well & and is always a satisfaction to me. About 32 all totaled, inc Jake's folks, Jean Clearance & Issac.

Sun 23: . . . After late lunch I rushed up to get in to meet Joe & Louise & over to christening of little Matt [*Matthews*] at 4:00. Their new church is fine. . . .

1957

[For most Americans, the top news story of 1957 was the launching of Russia's Sputnik. For Texas ranchers, however, the biggest news was the end of the drought. Early spring rains sent stocker prices zooming upward as the pastures grew lush.]

JANUARY

[Watt again entered cattle in the feeder division of the National Western Livestock Show in Denver. His yearling steers got a blue ribbon, and even though the calves didn't make it beyond the first round of judging, they sold for high prices. Watt was pleased with the results. He flew home with John Brittingham and described the flight as "a quick easy trip that saved several days time."]

FEBRUARY

Fri 1: Rained .32 during night. A nice birthday present. Temp 40° and clear early. Dark & cold front came from north about 9 or 9:30 . . .

Thur 7: Started another gentle wonderful rain after midnight and has rained most of time since (10:45) & raining a little now. Total got to be 2.64 for the day. A winter rain to date from. In fact one of the finest rains in my memory regardless of time of year. Went in to town after three & creeks still running mighty bold. . . .

MARCH

Tue 12: Warm clear breezy morning. Temp 35° . . . Talked to Baker M about making some T branding irons. . . .

Sun 24: Temp 35°. High wind, cloudy & lower barometer than yesterday

. . . Got to raining & snowing a little & was disagreeable. A bad storm is on in Panhandle & northern Plain states.

[*Nearly thirty thousand cattle were lost when winds up to ninety miles an hour piled snowdrifts thirty feet high. Even though the temperature did not drop much below freezing, the lungs of animals were filled with water from the force of drifting snow, and they suffocated.*]

Tue 26: Temp 26° Heavy frost & ice about 1/8 in thick. Worked Long & Tecumseh . . . Tone flew out about 6:20 (?), but had to turn right back. Baby boy [*John Clark Brittingham, son of John Brittingham*] arrived about 5 P.M. . . .

APRIL

Tue 2: Temp 58°. Partly cloudy. Low barometer & storm warnings . . . heard election returns. Yarborough won. Dallas had a bad storm that killed about 9 people.

[*U.S. Sen. Price Daniel defeated Ralph W. Yarborough in the 1956 Democratic gubernatorial runoff, which assured his victory in the November general election. When Daniel resigned his Senate seat, Yarborough won the special election to fill the unexpired term. See* Texas Almanac, 1958–59, *455–58.*]

Sat 13: Temp 28° . . . Took Alice [*Reynolds*] out on Throckmorton Road to see wild sweet peas which are more profuse along road than I have ever seen I believe. . . .

[*Wildflowers bloom most profusely just after a drought. Domesticated vegetation usually dies during a prolonged drought, leaving all of the nutrition and moisture for wildflowers, once the rains return. Watt R. Matthews, interview by Janet Neugebauer, April 13, 1989.*]

MAY

Wed 29: Clear morning with big dew. A fine thing on river which has stayed high longer than I can remember, I believe. It has not been fordable for a horse any time to speak of since late April & then the banks were too muddy. . . .

JUNE

Fri 21: . . . First time to cross river since before April 19. . . .

Fri 28: . . . Spent a long time on the phone getting things lined up for [*Fandangle*] parade. We hitched a four up to Caliope about 3 P.M. & moved it up on hill. The horses behaved well & parade was probably the best yet . . . Dished out tickets & all used of about 44, except 2 or 3. Matt fed about 220 & had everything mighty nice. Show went better & faster, but still too long. 8:42 to 11:13. Packed house.

[*In 1938, Robert E. Nail, Jr., an Albany native and a graduate of Princeton University, wrote* Dr. Shackelford's Paradise, *an outdoor drama depicting life at Fort Griffin, Texas. During the late 1930s, a surge in the growth of outdoor historical dramas occurred in the United States. Nail's play was presented by the senior class of Albany High School, where he taught English and speech. It was so popular that it became a community pageant entitled* The Fort Griffin Fandangle. *The Fort Griffin Fandangle Association was formed in 1947, in an effort to make the pageant an annual event, but the play was produced only sporadically until 1965, when the J. A. Matthews family leased the association thirty acres of their Phin Reynolds Ranch. Citizens of Albany pitched in with time, money, and equipment to make a prairie theater. Each summer, during the last two weekends of June, they gather there to tell the story of their heritage in song and dance. The pageant has become the single most unifying force in the community—most people boast that they "grew up with the Fandangle." See Nail,* Fandangle.]

JULY

Tue 2: . . . All Blantons, except Bro. Lynn, Joe B., Ethel, Craig all out for birthday dinner with Lucile & her bunch.

Wed 3: . . . Got girls (6) off on ride with R. B. after considerable rigging. They rounded H P & we shaped it up some then we shaped up the Weigh Out . . . we all went to supper at cabin & to rodeo. John Bennett had 13 extra seats put in my box for the young folks.

[*They went to the Texas Cowboy Reunion and Rodeo at Stamford. Organized in 1930 as a community project to provide entertainment on July 4, this four-day event has grown to be the largest amateur rodeo in the world.*

The grand entry march, cutting horse events, barrel racing, and quarter-horse shows originated here. Chuck wagons came from neighboring ranches to feed the crowd. Several times during the early years, the Lambshead wagon came. See Frank Reeves, "Texas Cowboy Reunion," Cattleman *46, no. 4 (September, 1959): 42–43, 70, 72, 74.*]

Fri 5: Temp 101° [*high*]. Up at 3:45 to get organized to get after the years in Weigh Out & Road. We had those from Weigh Out in pen by 6:30 & they could not have handled better . . . We loaded 9 Nebraska trucks with 316 head which is a big convenience & worth about $1 per head to us. Several people out from Throckmorton & Albany. Fine bunch of years.

[*It is a courtesy of the ranching world to watch a neighbor's or friend's cattle being loaded for sale, hence the visitors. By 1957, two-thirds of all western range cattle were sold through direct marketing. Producers who sold at home took on the responsibilities formerly assumed by agents or commission firms and saved the cost of such services. See J. G. McNeely, "A New Market News Report,"* Cattleman *44, no. 5 (October, 1957): 22.*]

Sun 7: Temp 103° . . . to bed early which made the most restful day I have had since probably early June.

Tue 9: Temp 98° . . . Britts & I had supper at Cougers & saw Fandangle Parade, etc on TV—Texas on Parade.

[*Actually Watt was watching* Texas in Review, *which was telecast from 1952 until 1958. The program documented a wide variety of community activities, technological advances, sports highlights, and special events. When the series ended, its sponsor, the Humble Oil and Refining Company, donated the film to the Southwest Collection, Texas Tech University, where it has been preserved for researchers. Watt was driving the chuck wagon in the Fandangle Parade, which is as much a pageant as the play. See* Texas in Review, *Film Files, Southwest Collection, Texas Tech University, Lubbock, Texas.*]

Fri 26: 99° . . . Went to Bend fairly early. They had caught a 16-1/2 lb yellow cat & a few smaller ones . . . to Abilene airport where I met Buck Schiwetz on 6:13 plane. We came back by Craig's & ate supper at Steak House.

[*The first edition of* Interwoven *had been out of print for some time, and preparations were under way for a second edition to be printed by a nationally known typographer and book designer, Carl Hertzog of El Paso. Edward Muegge (Buck) Schiwetz, one of the outstanding Texas artists of the twentieth century, was at Lambshead to begin creating illustrations for the 1958 edition.*]

Sat 27: 100°. Clear pretty morning. Buck & I will try to get going on drawing of Stoneranch, etc. We had good luck & before it got very hot we were back & Buck got going. He practically finished the drawing of the Bartholomew. Did some work on the one & the Stoneranch & made a few corrections on others. A bunch (about 25) had supper at Bend. The Hertzogs, also A S Jackson [*a botanist*] got there in time to eat.

Mon 29: 105°. Carl [*Hertzog*] & I took Buck to Bend where he did interior sketches in Reynolds house . . . Spent afternoon on *Interwoven* problems. . . .

Tue 30: 100° . . . got the pictures of Mama & the copy of pictorial supplement to *Interwoven.* Carl, Mule & I took Buck to Abilene for 11:46 plane. Went by to see a book binder . . . Carl & I on back after checking map in ASCS [*Agriculture Stabilization and Conservation Service*] office. Hertzogs left just after 5. . . .

AUGUST

Sun 11: Cool morning. Temp 62°. The summer is slipping away & fall will soon be here. This is one year we will probably welcome an early freeze to stop the worms [*screwworms*]. Patty [*Blanton*] called me about eight that Bro. Lynn was dead. I just happened not to be gone. He had apparently died between 4 & 5 A.M. After phoning Joe & the girls [*Watt's sisters*] I went in and helped with everything I could. . . .

Mon 12: 103° . . . funeral at 5 P.M. . . . Big crowd at funeral, which was dignified & nice. Presbyterian ladies brought in lots of good food for supper. Susette, Lucile, Sallie & I came out fairly early.

Wed 14: 103° . . . Visited with sister May & girls. . . .

SEPTEMBER

Sun 15: 103° . . . Killed biggest rattlesnake I have killed this year. Have killed & let get away more this year than for many years. . . .

Thur 19: 63°–92°. Pretty morning. Not so cool. Went to airport by 7 and Joe, John & I got off around 7:20 for A&M & got there in 1 hr & 30 min. We started to demonstrations, etc. soon after 10 & had a full one interesting day ending with a barbeque at Hilmar Moore's place. . . .

Fri 20: 53°–98°. John & I got up early and went on tour of animal husbandry facilities which was impressive. Back for meeting of directors soon after nine which was a good one. Then lunch & beef demonstration. Off for home at 3:17. . . .

[*Reports on new developments and problems affecting the beef cattle industry were presented to the directors of the Texas and Southwestern Cattle Raisers Association at their quarterly meeting at Texas A&M College, September 19–20. Directors received up-to-date information about cattle production, disease control, and market conditions. See "A Quick Look at Texas A&M Research,"* Cattleman *44, no. 5 (October, 1957): 18, 20, 22–24, 27, 74–76, 78.*]

Sun 22: 50°–77° . . . Brilliant display of northern lights when I got home about 11:30.

NOVEMBER

Thur 7: 43°–67° . . . Got off after eleven. Went in and had lunch with Blantons. All but Matt on my list for every member canvass [*for annual monetary pledges*] for church. . . .

Tue 12: 43°–55° . . . I went to hospital board meeting at 1 P.M. & from there to bank meeting. . . .

Sat 23: 23°–48° . . . I killed a smooth 10 pt buck near round hill on Right Hand in West pasture. . . .

DECEMBER

Sat 7: 32°–67° . . . Susette & Lucile took our turkey in. The Bazaar was a success & took in $1280.00. . . .

[*The bazaar was an annual fund-raising event for the Matthews Memorial Presbyterian Church in Albany. In addition to serving a turkey dinner, the women also sold handmade items and baked goods.*]

Sat 14: 28°–79° . . . We got 3 fine hogs (old) for Christmas. . . .

[*Hogs were allowed to run wild at Lambshead, where native pecans provided feed.*]

Thur 26: 31°–65° . . . Boys combing calves. They have hardly missed being combed a day since Nov 21. . . .

Sat 28: 27°–60° . . . Wattie Reynolds [*Watt Reynolds's oldest son*] died about 10:30.

Sun 29: 21°–75°. Another cold frosty beautiful morning. Got off late & went in & ate dinner with Blantons. Left for Ft Worth about 2 P.M. & got there about 4:30. Britts were at Watt Reynolds'. I cleaned up & went over & had a nice visit with them even though there were a lot of people in & out. Wattie's death a bitter pill, even tho expected. Home & visited with Bob [*Brittingham*] & Tom [*Brittingham*] & to bed early.

1958

[There is an old saying that if you stay in the cattle business long enough, the good takes care of the bad. 1958 was a good year for ranchers. Ranges were in better condition than they had been for nearly a decade, and so were cattle prices.]

JANUARY

Wed 1: 24°–57°. Year came in with clear, still, frosty cold morning . . . Got fires started in all three places in Reynolds' house. Got organized & had little John christened about 5:30. A nice service. All then had turkey dinner . . . about 31 of us. . . . Home early.

[John was Watt's grand-nephew; see March 26, 1957. Watt, his crew of helpers, and his best calves again were on their way to the National Western Stock Show in Denver, Colorado.]

Mon 13: 38°–56° (Albany). Out at yards all day again. Our calves were judged around 2 P.M. & got first & the announcer gave us a big laugh. In & got ready for Monahan's party after going by Biederman's room (Sallie & I). Tom, Edna [*Blanton*] & I stayed & went to their dinner party for about 22 in Emerald, which was nice. Bunch of us in Tavern later where June Wood joined us. To bed late.

Tues 14: 31°–56° (Albany). Fine day. They got calves looking nice. Durwood Lewter by pens for quite a visit. He had lunch with Tom, Henry Steele, Ray Thompson, & me. . . .

[*Durward Lewter operated one of the largest feed lots in the Southwest, at Lubbock, Texas. The site was selected to take advantage of the abundant grain sorghum and cottonseed in the area. Lewter was recognized for proving that cattle finished on a ration of milo maize and cottonseed meal would grade as high when slaughtered as those finished on corn. After seeing the potential in Watt's herd, Lewter would have been interested in buying Lambshead cattle for his feed lot. See Frank Reeves, "Factory on the Hoof,"* American Hereford Journal *48, no. 17 (January 1, 1958): 28–30, 154; and Durward Lewter, interview by David Murrah, June 13, 1973.*]

Thur 16: 26°–69° (Albany). . . . Tom & Goop went out to yards & I packed up & went out later. Our calves sold 68th & brought 41.50 & weighed 716#, which was good . . . left for airport. Off about 4:05 CST & arrived Abilene 7:20. Louise [*Matthews*] out there. . . .

[*This year's Fort Worth show was characterized by a strong demand for feeder cattle. The first-place load of twenty-five senior steer calves shown by J. A. Matthews Cattle Company went to Wertheimer Cattle Company, Montgomery, Illinois. See "Denver's 15,859 Feeders,"* American Hereford Journal *48, no. 19 (February 1, 1958): 202.*

FEBRUARY

Fri 7: 28°–51°. Raymond Fisher, Donald Hunter, & Ray Winter of Iowa [*feedlot owners from the Corn Belt*] came out fairly early & I took them on tour of cattle. . . .

Sat 15: 21°–40° . . . Mac Tidmore came out before noon with a lot of maps, etc. RE: McKenzie Trail. Clyde & I took him to near southwest corner & showed him where Trail touches us. Then took him to Camp Cooper. . . .

[*Max Tidmore, a Lubbock businessman and local historian, was mapping the trail blazed by U.S. Army Col. Ranald S. MacKenzie in 1871, from Fort Griffin, in Shackelford County, to the Llano Estacado. MacKenzie's trail became the primary route for buffalo-hide hunters and settlers who later made their way to the Staked Plains.*]

Watt Matthews with hot branding iron, April, 1958. Photo by Frank Reeves. Courtesy Southwest Collection, Texas Tech University, Lubbock, Texas

MARCH

Sun 16: 30°–70° . . . Joe & I left for Abilene at 1:30. John flew us out of there at 3:15. We were at our hotel by 5:30. Watt Reynolds was in room when I got there (Gunter [*Hotel*]). We got ready & went to party at National Bank of Commerce, which was mighty nice. J. M. Bennett, Jr., Chairman.

[*Watt was in San Antonio for the annual meeting of the Texas and Southwestern Cattle Raisers Association.*]

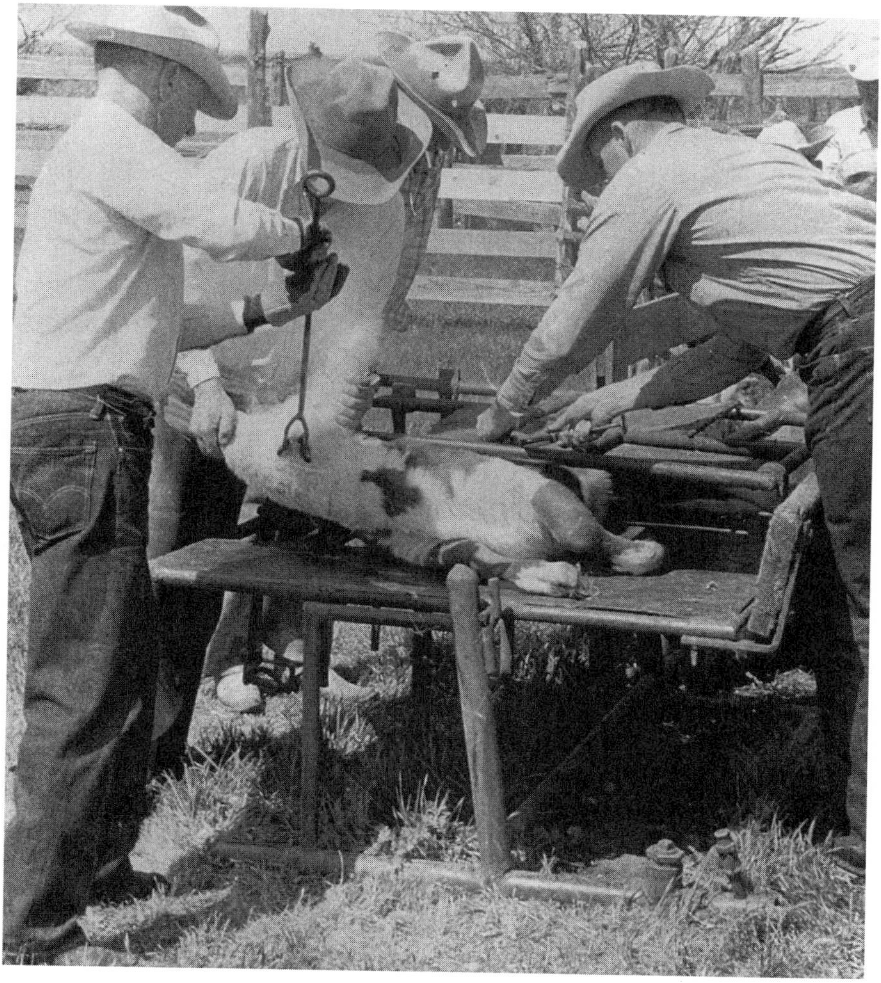

Watt Matthews branding and John Brittingham vaccinating a calf, April, 1958. Photo by Frank Reeves. Courtesy Southwest Collection, Texas Tech University, Lubbock, Texas

Mon 17: 35°–42° . . . To Director's meeting at 2 P.M. which was a good one. John Matthews made a good talk. Bob & Dick Kleberg inscribed my King Ranch book . . . Got ready & went to big party at St. Anthony [*Hotel*] (Ewing Halsell & Lorance). Got to bed at reasonable hr.

Tue 18: 29°–53° . . . Had a good visit with Watt & glad I was rooming with him as it was a sad time for him. Went to meeting of nominating Committee, then to last part of Resolutions Committee meeting. . . .

Wed 19: 31°–60°. Heard Dr. DeGraff's talk. Bunch of us went to Buck Pyle's room, then to Director's luncheon. Got ready to get off & we flew just before 3. Took Jack Mansfield by San Angelo, then Joe, John & I got Abilene about 4:30. Joe & I to Albany before 6. . . .

[*In 1957, the American National Cattleman's Association appointed Herrell DeGraff, a professor of food economics at Cornell University, to be research director of a fact-finding committee to study the factors involved in the production, marketing, and merchandising of beef. The industry was suffering from the combined effects of drought and low prices. It was hoped that, if the producer understood what was happening, adjustments could be made faster and so moderate the roller-coaster effect of the cattle cycle. In his report, DeGraff recommended more competitive marketing, improving the beef-making and eating quality of cattle, and controlling the flow of animals to market, so as to eliminate gluts and shortages. Cattlemen were encouraged to work cooperatively to control the destiny of their industry. See "Analyzing the Cattle and Beef Industry," part 1,* Cattleman *44, no. 11 (April, 1958): 28–31; and part 2,* Cattleman *44, no. 12 (May, 1958): 44–47.*]

Mon 24: 40°–58°. Lucile, Frannie & I went to farm & checked on little bulls & fencing after lunch. Carrol & I cleaned up most of the bulls & put a horn weight back on one. . . .

[*A well-curved set of horns gives the animal's head a smooth, attractive appearance. The desired shape can be obtained by applying half-pound weights when the horns are three or four inches long. See Ensminger,* Stockman's Handbook, *1044.*]

APRIL

Tue 1: 39°–83° . . . Boys off to work Long at 6:35. Took Frank [*Reeves*] & Don [*McCarthy, from the American Hereford Association*] over later

& they took an awful lot of pictures. Don took 500' of movies, Frank took 90 pictures. The heifers & calves looked mighty nice . . . Oscar back to live here.

Wed 2: 55°–83°. Mild, partly cloudy morning with big dew. Boys off to round Stone Ranch 6:50. Frank, Don & I met them at Buzzard Peak crossing & they took pictures of cattle crossing river. Got out top bull calves while some looked out pasture again. Durwood Lewter bought a club calf. There was quite a crowd out for lunch. About 30 of us ate. . . . Got stormy looking. Got thru early. Frank Reeves left for Ft Worth about 4 P.M. . . .

Thur 10: 37°–64° . . . We went by Farm & looked at young bulls & took off some of the weights. . . .

Mon 21: . . . made sketch of layout of Horse Creek Ranch & the house to take in to show sister May. Tom & I sent check to Dalhart bank for J. C. Parker & wrote him a letter (Tom did). Got involved in getting up money for scale & corral repairs. . . .

[*Horse Creek Ranch, near Simla, Colorado, was purchased for the J. A. Matthews Ranch Company because steers that were fattened on grass there through the summer were in excellent condition for fall marketing. The place also provided alternative pastures during droughty spells at Lambshead. Joe B. Matthews, who had a summer home in Boulder, managed the ranch. Five of Watt's nephews also owned ranches nearby.*]

Thur 24: 65° [*high*] . . . River fairly deep fording for cars with beautiful clear water. The range is lush & getting rank and the cattle couldn't be doing better than they appear to be doing. . . .

MAY

Tue 20: 55°–85°. Off to get steer years before daylight. Had them by 6:15 & had 4 trucks loaded & off by 6:50. A beautiful morning with patches of fog & as big a dew as I ever saw I believe. They missed 6 head in Weigh Out but got them later. The AV years averaged about 665 and they just did miss averaging $200 per head. Gourds averaged 656 & we got them loaded by 1:30. . . .

JUNE

Sat 7: 71°–97° . . . They got 900 bushels of oats out of field here which is pretty good & they are nice oats.

JULY

Fri 4: 73°–97° . . . Dr. & Mrs. Carrol came & Cougers & I stayed here with them to go over some early history of this area. We took tour after late lunch. . . .

Sat 5: 75°–89° . . . Drove Bailey Carrol up thru So., down Right Hand by Stone Ranch. . . .

[*Dr. H. Bailey Carroll was professor of history at the University of Texas at Austin and director of the Texas State Historical Association.*]

Sat 12: 69°–100° . . . Used coral spray for first time. . . .

[*A new spray treatment known as Co-Ral (Bayer 21/199) killed grubs before the hide or meat could be damaged. Part of the spray remained on the hair and some was absorbed into the animal's skin, killing young grubs. Only one treatment per year was required, if applied soon after heel fly activity ended (July through September in Texas). It offered the added advantage of controlling screwworms, hornflies, lice, and ticks. See "New Systemic Insecticides Kill Cattle Grubs,"* Cattleman *45, no. 3 (August, 1958): 94, 96.*]

Tue 29: 73°–102° . . . Mike gone with Louis hunting bulls. We only lack 4 or 5 having them in now. . . .

AUGUST

Sat 23: 70°–95°. Heifer years showing very few flies six weeks after spraying with coral. . . .

Sat 30: 65°–98° . . . These nights & cool mornings are bound to stimulate the calves & make them put on bloom. I looked at calves in Overton & I can see a change since I saw them Sunday. . . .

SEPTEMBER

Wed 24: 74°–90° . . . I went up to the unveiling of the Butterfield marker at Bud Matthews, which is a nice thing . . .

[Smith Station on the Butterfield Overland Mail and passenger stage line was located at present-day Bud Matthews, Texas. The site, a cattle-shipping point on the Texas Central Railway, was named for Watt's father. Cattle can still be shipped, by truck, from the restored corrals. See Clayton, Chimney Creek Ranch, *30.]*

Fri 26: 66°–86°. Calves nursed last time. . . .

OCTOBER

Tue 7: 65°–90°. Another beautiful morning after a mild grass growing night. . . .

Sat 11: 62°–67° . . . Vaniers planning to fly down. Weighed calves early. 11 Ft Worth calves averaged 539, 22 averaged 529, 21 averaged 442. Went in & picked them (John & Jack Vanier & Jim Johnson) up after 11 as they didn't get off until late on account of clouds. Showed them cattle at YL. Then here for late lunch. Matt joined us. We gave calves a thorough looking over . . . went up in So & looked at 2 year heifers, then to Farm to see little bulls. . . .

Wed 15: 39°–78°. Dark wet morning. Drizzling off and on since before six. Poor prospect for a good day to get calves cleaned up & ready to go to Ft Worth with ten. Jack Vines got out before noon & we decided on what 10 to send to Ft Worth. Finished washing & combing whole bunch before one & they got dried off in pretty fair shape. . . .

Thur 16: 51°–82° . . . we had a beautiful day for final preparations for getting calves off . . . Went after lunch. Got money for trip, etc. Wrote the two Kansas City hotels who will occupy rooms. Got back to ranch (Bill Couger & I) about 3:30. Dr. Smith here . . . calves off 5:20. . . .

[Watt was shipping steer calves, sired by CK bulls, for entry in the carload division of the American Royal Livestock Show in Kansas City. The Vaniers were at Lambshead to help select the animals because a winning ribbon would draw attention to their bulls during a time of very high prices for breeding stock. See Paul Swaffar, "What's Ahead for Purebred Herefords," Cattleman *45, no. 3 (August, 1958): 38, 62]*

Fri 17: 52°–85°. Beautiful clear dewy fall morning. The country is so green & beautiful I hate to be gone. Worked around table, got cleaned up & left for town after lunch . . . Off to Ft Worth about 4:15. . . . I had dinner with all the Joe, John Reynolds families except Susan . . . Pete, Mary Fru & Mary Joe took me by their house & to 10:20 train. Helen Farmer got on same train.

Sat 18: 52°–87°. Helen & I had breakfast together. Got to KC on time, 9 A.M. Brad met Helen. I couldn't get a taxi to hotel until about noon on account of parade. Walked down to see it. Had to stand about an hour before it started, then it took 1 hr, 20 min to pass. I was glad for having seen it if I did get mighty tired. Colorful entries mighty amusing. . . .

Sun 19: 52°–87°. Boys off early to get calves fed & everything organized to wash them. I got out later and we got going on them about 9:15. Penny helped me comb them . . . TL & RA took over combing & I got with John on washing. With 2 pairs of us washing we turned them out pretty fast. We finished heavy load before lunch at the Golden Ox. We did light load before 5 & were all plenty tired. Went in after they ate. Got cleaned up & went by Vanier's room & then to big Hereford party in same Hotel Muehleback. Took Helen.

Mon 20: 52°–88°. Worked on calves. Lunch at Golden Ox. Moved calves to show pens fairly late in afternoon. Went by shady alleys as it was pretty hot. Had to wait until late for feed. Got to hotel late & didn't even clean up. By Cabana & the late supper in Muehlebach Coffee Shop. Just our crew from Phillips.

Tue 21: 64°–73°. Put in day with calves. . . .

Wed 22: Up early to get calves ready for judging. Washed their faces & mane with soap. Wet & combed them & had them looking nice when they started looking at them about 11. It looked awhile like we might be going to win, but we got Reserve Champion. . . .

Thur 23: 42°–81°. Up early . . . getting ready to get out to sale . . . our Reserve Champion calves brought 50¢ & other load 46¢. Champions 63¢ & Champion Angus 63.50¢. . . .

NOVEMBER

Sat 1: 41°–70° . . . Helped boys shoeing horses, etc. . . .

Wed 5: 50°–66° . . . Dr. Smith didn't get here until nearly noon. We got blood from 15 of the dry cows they had rounded out of Valley. The lab tests showed about 1/2 had lepto so we will vaccinate the whole herd. Took 8 cows (carriers) & 1 cow & unbranded calf to Hyfd. . . .

[*Leptospirosis, a disease which cattle spread through infected urine, causes high fever, poor appetite, and abortion. Loss to the beef cattle industry was estimated at over $100 million per year. There was no effective treatment, and all susceptible animals had to be vaccinated because carrier animals—those that have survived leptospirosis—could infect others. Streams, slow-moving ponds, and stock shows were likely places for contamination. See Ensminger,* Stockman's Handbook, *900; and "Leptospirosis Presents a Double Barrel Threat,"* Cattleman *47, no. 11 (April, 1961): 92.*]

DECEMBER

Fri 5: 31°–55° . . . About ready (6:30) to go with Joe & Britts to leave for Ft Worth by 8:30. We got down there before 11 . . . The bull sale went off OK . . . I went to Beef Council supper. Had nice time. Bob Poage [*congressman from Waco, Texas*] talked too long.

Tue 9: 20°–41°. Clear, cold morning. Jack & I took a tour thru So & down river by MO & Paint, Hayford, Bend, & William D. Reynolds. We saw a lot of turkeys (mostly gobblers) & it doesn't look like 10% have been killed . . . Jack thinks there are probably 1000 gobblers on range. . . .

Tue 30: 22°–25°. Ground covered with snow and is still coming down at 8:20. Snowed until around noon and got to be 3-1/2 in or better and added .20 moisture [to what] we had yesterday. Stayed around the fires all day. Worked with bull pedigrees, etc. Will be hard on the cattle, but the moisture will help down the line. To bed about 8:30.

1959

JANUARY

Mon 12: 34°–75° . . . Clarence & Vic got a 3 year heifer in out of South that was in bad shape from failure of being able to deliver calf. . . .

Tue 13: 51°–76° . . . Heifer died. . . .

[*First-calf heifers often had trouble delivering their calves, especially if they were bred to Hereford bulls, who sire large calves. Since the 1970s, Longhorn bulls have been used on first-calf heifers at Lambshead in order to produce a smaller calf and so protect the heifer. Watt R. Matthews, interview by Janet Neugebauer, November 11, 1988.*]

MARCH

Wed 18: 30°–77° A beautiful star lit morning. Hope wind doesn't come up with the sun. We got the cows in, separated, vaccinated & dipped in time to get started with the branding about 10 & had the 183 calves (90 heifers & 93 steers) branded by 12:30. Turned them (189 cows, 183 calves & 7 bulls) back in Culver. . . .

Sun 29: 38°–82° . . . Had late wild turkey dinner. Britts, Chris & Lennie out. We went up river & let young folks dig for arrow heads, etc. . . .

APRIL

Sun 12: 39°–58° . . . I went in & worked with colts a little & saw the new colt born. Streak face, big bellied mare had sort of roan horse colt. . . .

Mon 13: 27°–64° Freeze scorched things and killed mesquite leaves in spots. . . .

Mon 20: 48°–65° . . . A little fire near Putnam line. Was started by lightning. Guy Patters & well pulling boys put it out. Our boys wet it down. . . .

Thur 23: 39°–85° . . . John C. Britt [*the grand-nephew who had been christened in January 1958*] & I got a hair cut & I took him out to see horses. Tone, Penny, J. C., & I ate supper at Hotel.

Mon 27: 76°–97° . . . Drove Lang [*John Langley Howard, an artist sent by* Fortune *magazine to draw illustrations for a story about Lambshead*] to farm, Bend, etc and he took a good many pictures. . . .

Wed 29: 53°–94° . . . Lang did some sketching. . . .

MAY

Sat 16: 52°–82° . . . To town. Had visit with Andrew. Listened to Preakness with Craig. . . .

JULY

Wed 8: 68°–98° Clear pretty morning. Should be good day on hay. Clyde & I took trip to Tecumseh hay field where the Grothe boy is doing a good job cutting & raking. He thinks it will turn out 3500 bales . . . We crossed back at W. D. Reynolds & just barely made it as water got up to fan on jeep. . . .

Sun 19: 66°–84° . . . An unusually green, cool summer with hardly a case of worms [*screwworms*] to date & very few horn flies. . . .

Mon 20: 63°–88° . . . The girls [*Watt's sisters*] got organized clearing up a lot of stuff & moving desk down to cookshack which makes me a little office. We left fairly late (they ahead of me) for lunch at Blanton's . . . R. B. & I took little John to see colts, etc. . . . I bought a kid saddle.

AUGUST

Mon 3: 71°–102° Clear, cool morning. Boys getting off early 5:30, to round Long . . . They got more cattle than we had turned loose in there the last working which was good luck. They didn't bring but 66 dry cows to Road however . . . did some fencing to hold bulls away from heifer years in Left Hand. . . .

[*Even though heifers are capable of breeding as yearlings, they have not yet reached maturity. The small size of the pelvic area at this age can cause difficulty at calving time (see January 13, 1959). In addition, heifers calving as two-year-olds frequently failed to conceive while nursing calves and did not produce a calf the next year. The use of heifer bulls (Longhorns are one breed) eliminated calving problems. This, coupled with better nutrition, has alleviated rebreeding problems, and now calving heifers at two years is an acceptable practice. See Diggins, Bundy, and Christensen,* Beef Production, *4th ed., 114–15.*]

Thur 6: 70°–105° Another clear pretty morning. Boys off early to bring in dry cows out of Road. Okla men (Luper, Beardon & Camp) here by seven and they were in with the cows soon afterwards. We didn't get anything done on a trade. T. B. Mayhall family got here around 11. Capt. Newton Givens was a great-great uncle of Mr [*Mayhall*] who is working on an article about him. I toured them to Stone Ranch, Bend, Camp Cooper, etc. They left for Austin after lunch . . . [*See July 27, 1951.*]

Fri 7: 69°–104° . . . Men after cows again which we plan to test for pregnancy. The test didn't turn out well & I am sorry we didn't ship all drys with the first shipment while they were so high . . .

Thur 13: 64°–98° Pleasant morning. Merle Thompson out early and spent practically all morning going over the Great Plains Conservation plan . . . I got my diary up to date and cleaned up most of the mail. . . .

Fri 14: 69°–100° . . . Mr. Clarke of the Throckmorton Soil Conservation Office was down & I drove him around some. Checked on hay hauling & bulls at farm . . . Rodgers for supper & the fast ball game over TV.

[*Implemented by USDA and the Great Plains Agricultural Council, the program was designed to help farmers and ranchers develop a land-use program that would prevent many of the problems caused by the recurring droughts common to the area. It was recognized that some of the worst problems were outgrowths of farmers' and ranchers' patriotic response to the government's pleas for greater production to meet wartime demands. See U.S. Congress, House of Representatives,* Program for the Great Plains, *iii–3.*]

Tue 25: 61°–94° Pleasant morning. Up early to get after heifers & dry cows. Oscar, Louis, Sam, Jim Warden & I had the dry cows in by 6:35 & soon had them weighed & loaded. 80 cows gross 1201 & net 1153#. Average per head $210. Oscar & Louis went down to Valley & helped hunt the 2's in the brush which has got mighty bad. By 12:30 they had 166 in the pen which with what had been picked up on neighbors made all but 6 or 8 head. . . .

Sat 29: 75°–105° Boys off to get in heifers & bulls to check on TB tests. We had that all done in fairly short order and weighed the 2 year olds as we did it. They averaged 989 plus which is not bad after all the chousing [*a term Watt used to describe the stress cattle experience when they are rounded up to be worked on or to be prepared for shipment*] they got the other day. . . .

OCTOBER

Thur 1: 48°–85° . . . Heard ball game. Chicago 11–Los Angeles 0. . . .

Mon 5: 52°–80° . . . Webbs & I left about 6:15 [*p.m.*] for Balance & Swing [*a square-dance club in Abilene that Watt belonged to*]. Back to Albany about eleven.

NOVEMBER

Tue 24: 37°–68° . . . Went in around 10. Took beef week dope to Albany *News*. To Joe's office & a man named Davies came to check windows at church for the outfit at Winona, Minn. (a lucky time). I signed a contract to put them in shape & put grandpa's name, etc back on for $420, a far cry from the $1800 wanted by Houston man who said they needed releading. . . .

DECEMBER

Fri 4: . . . Got organized and went in to meet Joe & Tom & John Matthews picked us up just after nine. He took us to College Station [*for Texas and Southwestern Cattle Raisers directors meeting*] . . . We were on time for part of the morning program then had lunch in their big dining hall. After lunch we had a nice tour of the animal husbandry projects. Back in time to get off for barbecue . . . D. Burns [*manager of the Pitchfork Ranch*] took us . . . There were about 400 there.

Sat 5: . . . Went to meeting of brand committee and could see cadet review fairly well while in there. It was impressive. To meeting from there. Tom [*Blanton*] made a fine statement on brand business & the way it has been handled. To beef council luncheon about 12:30. We left after prizes were awarded. . . .

Tue 22: 32°–60° . . . Tried to clean up tables & generally get organized for Christmas party . . . Total of 50 here for Christmas party [*the annual party that Watt gave for his ranch help and their families*]. . . .

1960

[By 1960, mass merchandising was having a major impact on the type of beef sold at the retail level. Supermarkets used beef as a traffic builder and guaranteed its quality; therefore, only young, fat carcasses that graded USDA Choice were ordered from the packers. Grass-fattened animals could not meet this specification, and feet lots became the fastest-growing segment of the cattle industry.]

JANUARY

Fri 1: 38°–50° . . . Starting year off with wonderful prospect for spring having such a season in the ground. . . .

FEBRUARY

[Even though moisture was adequate, prospects were dimmed somewhat by cold weather that prevented the growth of winter grasses. The stock shows, however, pleased Watt. He didn't enter cattle in the Denver show, which he described as "a regular reunion," but he was justly proud of his entries in the Fort Worth show.]

Fri 5: 37°–56°. Went down fairly early again . . . We cleaned up the calves, brushing & wet them a little. A lot of the family & others ate lunch at the Backstage, then back for judging. Jim Reagan went right along with it . . . Was done around 2 P.M. AV Champion Hereford; Pitchfork Reserve; TLB 1st in Class; Ft G C Co 2nd in Class; Spanish Gourd 5th. TLB Champion Angus. . . .

[Watt's fifteen yearling steers were champions in the Feeder Steer divi-

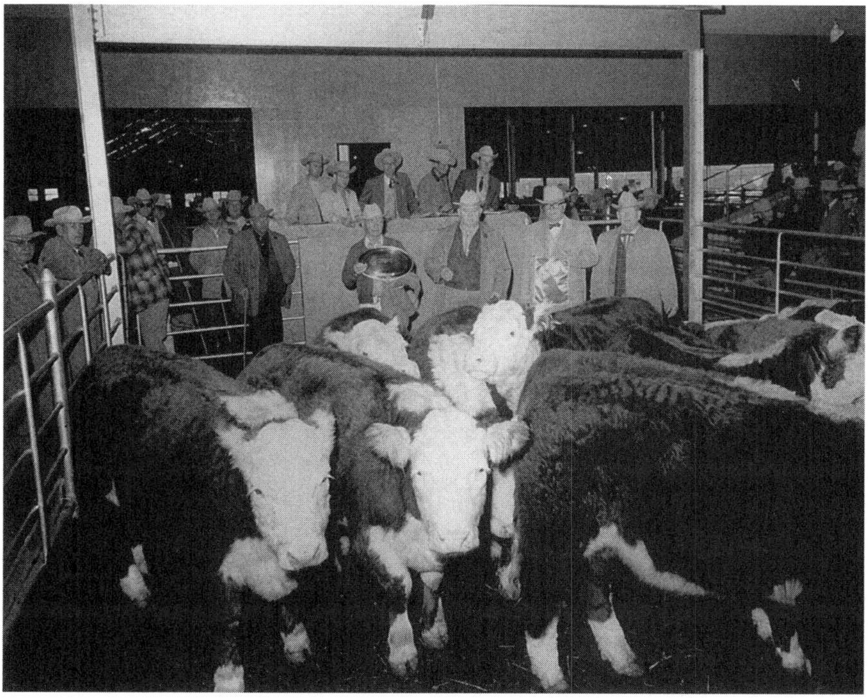

Champion hereford feeders, Fort Worth, February, 1960.
Courtesy Watt R. Matthews

sion of the Southwestern Exposition and Fat Stock Show. Held for the first time, this division reflected the feeder-stocker character of cattle produced in the area. At the auction the following day, the AV calves brought $31.10 per hundredweight, plus a $5 bonus provided by the Fort Worth Chamber of Commerce. Watt wrote: "Fine support and fine treatment by Ft. W."]

Sat 20: 30°–63° . . . I worked with Fortune & talked to Sy [*Seymour Freedgood, author of "The Specter at Lambshead Ranch,"* Fortune *(April, 1960): 123–30, 206, 210, 212, 215–16, 220, 222. The article stressed the adverse impact of selling part of a ranch to cover inheritance taxes. See April 27, 1959.*] Went in late for supper with Webbs,

Tom Blanton, Jrs., Ethel, Matt & Betsy there. We got manuscript ready to mail back to *Fortune*. . . .

Sat 27: 18°–56° . . . Left for town about 3 & picked up Ma Britt [*Lucile*] & little John at Tone's & took them to Episcopal church for little Penny's christening. Party at Tone's house afterwards which was nice. 23 there. Lucile & I home by 9 P.M.

MARCH

Tues 15: 42°–60° . . . Boys off to round Paint. Drove it the opposite way from the regular one which fooled the cattle. Nothing seen on looking it out which sets a record for a first round as far as I know. Wind got high with a lot of dust which made for a miserable day for man or beast . . . Ate our lunch across river to get out of wind. . . .

APRIL

Tues 5: 43°–89° . . . Billy Wilkerson was back to see Coxes, Mexicans, etc. for census count. . . .

MAY

Sat 14: 55°–105° . . . All of Blanton family, 5 of John A. Matthews family, & Joe and Louise Matthews out for birthday supper with us. Sister May's 80th.

Mon 16: 65°–97° . . . Talked to Harris about hauling the steer years to Colo. . . .

Mon 23: 70°–94° Up at 4 A.M. We had the steer years in and ready to weigh a little before six. Averaged 771 net. 397 head. Loaded 210 on 6 trucks which left just before 10. Turned 187 back in Road then they picked up 10 more in Valley which weighed 782 after a few hours in pen. . . .

Wed 25: 69°–98° We got 84 shorts & pony off about 3:30. Went in & had lunch with Tone, Press, Matt, & cattle buyers . . . Back here in time to see trucks off for Horse Creek Ranch [*in Colorado*]. . . .

Tues 31: 60°–91° Overslept and boys off for late start to bring in years. Had them in pen by about 6:20, however, but fuller than on May

23rd. The 210 that went off this time averaged 787 net as against 711 when 187 of them were weighed on 23rd. The other 23 averaged about the same when put in Road. They have no doubt gained some if not most of the extra 16#. These are the heaviest steer years we have had since we started weighing cattle about 1923. . . .

[*At the end of August, when the grass began to wane on Horse Creek Ranch, the steers were sold as feeders. They averaged 888 pounds, a weight that, Watt wrote, "is mighty good for years this early." Generally, steers weigh from 550 to 750 pounds off the range, the heavier animals being more suitable for full feeding of concentrates. These steers were in a feed lot for approximately 150 days and should have gained slightly over two pounds daily. After the excretory shrinkage during shipment, they averaged approximately 863 pounds at the beginning of feeding, gained another 350 during feeding, were slaughtered at just over 1,200 pounds, and probably graded Choice to Prime. See U.S. Department of Agriculture,* Finishing Beef Cattle, *1–5.*]

JUNE

Thur 2: 67°–96° . . . brought Jeep [*station wagon*] out which I miss when it is in for repairs. . . .

Tue 7: 68°–95° . . . We weighed fifty fat cows & put them in a dry pen to be ready for Abilene trucks, Average 1177. . . .

[*These cows were culled from the herd because they failed to breed, which explains their fatness. They were sold for slaughter at an auction market in Abilene. In the cattle industry, reproductive failure is the greatest source of missed income. See Faulkner, "A Calf from Every Cow,"* American Hereford Journal *56, no. 5 (July 1, 1965): 152, 156, 161–62, 166, 824.*]

Sun 19: 73°–104° We all went to church and little Lucile [*Wallace*] was christened. . . .

JULY

Mon 11: 74°–102° . . . Lucile had gone in and brought out J. C. . . . listened to Dem Conv. . . .

Herd bull with open A–Lazy V brand. Courtesy Watt R. Matthews

Mon 18: 67°–95° . . . after supper Tone, Chris & I went to brucuclosis (sp) meet at Court house. . . .

AUGUST

Wed 3: 75°–102° . . . Vet for Tecumseh job got here about 9:30 & Louis Cox went with him to show him way. Joe Brown & I followed a little later to make sure they got over river, etc. Joe stayed to chalk them. They finished with 142 a little before 2. We finished 322, T. B. & Bangs a little before 3. . . .

[*Watt was having the cows tested for bovine brucellosis, or Bang's disease. Since the passage of state laws for the establishment of disease-control areas in September 1959, Texas livestock owners were participating in an accelerated brucellosis eradication program. Community meetings were held to determine which action would be most beneficial for the county involved (see diary entry for July 18). Apparently ranchers in Shackelford and Throckmorton counties were blood testing every herd in order to become a Modified Certified Brucellosis Area. Animals testing positive were slaughtered, and those testing negative were issued certificates that facilitated shipment to other parts of the U.S. See Garrett and Wilbur, "What Is the Brucellosis Situation?"* Cattleman *46, no. 12 (May 1960): 26–27, 38.*]

Thur 4: 75°–103° Got report on Tecumseh cattle by 4 so we could let them out & all were clear . . . All AVs checked clear.

Sat 13: 64°–96° Another cool morning. Had to shut windows at my back. . . .

Thur 18: 75°–94°. Boys got early start to get heifers out of Road. Had them in pen just after 6:30 [*109 heifers*]. We had to put them thru the chute which took some time getting & making a list of the numbers on their legs. They were a pretty bunch of heifers. Average wgt 945 net which at 205 per head made them bring about 21.80 per hundred lbs. The trucks left here at 8:15 & got to Pool about 4 P.M. & unloaded in good shape Buster reported . . . went in & got check for shipment & banked it. Cattle sold O.K. Had visit with Roy & Mule. Out & to bed before nine.

[*On August 25, Watt sold 127 heifers for $200 and 14 heifers (10 percent of total) at $180 each.*]

Sun 21: 68°–102°. Bailey & Clarence had trouble with pickup helping some of Bailey's friends. Due to attitude of past few weeks, etc, plus such as this decided had better let Clarence go. As a matter of fact this place needs a house cleaning. . . .

SEPTEMBER

Thur 8: 67°–97° . . . Merle Thompson & student out & we went over Great Plains final plans & I signed it up.

[*Shackelford country ranchers who participated in the program received technical assistance and partial (50 percent) funding for building stock tanks and brush control management that reduced "water robbers" such as mesquite and prickly pear. They signed contracts agreeing to defer grazing for at least one season on pastures that received brush control management and to practice proper grazing on all pastures. Such grazing entailed taking half the grass and leaving the other half, in order to control water and prevent soil erosion. An adequate grass cover retains water that seeps back into the aquifer. Alan L. Heirman, District Conservationist, Soil Conservation Service, USDA, interview by Janet Neugebauer, September 14, 1992.*]

Fri 16: 65°–99° . . . Went up Hoover & helped pick out a calf to go to Abilene. Carrol left Lambshead with it around 12. . . .

Sat 17: 68°–91° . . . Met Matt, Patty & Gene Pickard at 9:30 & we went to Abilene to see stocker show and sale & see the calves sold for the Rehabilitation Center . . . They got started on the gift calves about 2:45 which was a tiresome wait. We left soon after 4. . . .

[*In 1960, Conda Wilie, a Coke County rancher, donated twenty calves in support of the West Texas Rehabilitation Center. Located in Abilene, the center never has charged for treatment or asked for government funds. Cattlemen, proud of their reluctance to accept federal aid, identified closely with the center. Thus, ranchers throughout the Southwest supported the annual Cattlemen's Round-Up for Crippled Children, which funded more than a third of the center's operating costs. See "Cattlemen Support Rehabilitation Center That 'Thinks Like a Rancher,"* Cattleman *52, no. 4, (September, 1965): 104, 106.*]

Tues 20: 69°–100° . . . Went to Bend, Hayford, & Farm to read meters. Saw smoke & phoned Richard from airstrip. It turned out to be in Lambshead. Oscar, Jack, Bill Jones (with Shackelford County truck) & I finally got it out even though it kept breaking out. Raymond Taylor brought out bull dozzier to go around it [*the bulldozer was used to cut a fire guard*]. . . .

OCTOBER

Wed 5: 60°–90° . . . Worked Road. Cut out 66 old cows to ship . . . Matt bought 50 of the old cows at 150 . . . Fine old cows. Practically all 10 with a few 11 years old. . . .

[*Cows reach peak productivity at seven to nine years of age. The rate of decline after that time is more rapid in some cows than others. Most authorities recommend a 15 to 20 percent replacement rate when the herd size remains constant. This would mean a complete replacement of all cows after five or six years. See Minish and Fox,* Beef Production and Management, *118–19.*]

Fri 7: 55°–82° . . . Left a little before 6 to go to Blanton's for supper and the Kennedy-Nixon debate. . . .

Wed 19: 54°–64° Cloudy & cool. Boys sawed wood all morning. . . .

[*Most rooms at Lambshead Ranch have a fireplace, and mesquite wood from the ranch produces a large amount of the requisite heat.*]

NOVEMBER

Fri 4: 51°–81° . . . Johnny Jones [*fieldman for American Hereford Association*] was out by one & I took him on tour of cattle until 4:15 To bed by 7 P.M.

DECEMBER

[*Watt wrote, "Nov started with winter annuals started & established as well as I have ever seen. A most beautiful mild fall." Good weather lasted through Christmas, which was spent with the Brittinghams at Reynolds Bend.*]

1961

[*At the annual meeting of the American Hereford Association (AHA) in October 1960, Watt was elected to the organization's board of directors. Entries about the work of the board during the six years he served add a new dimension to his diary.*]

JANUARY

Wed 4: 1°–55° . . . About ready to get off for Ft Worth, Dallas, & Phoenix [*to the Arizona National Livestock Show and a meeting of the American Hereford Association's board of directors*]. . . .

Thur 5: 33°–59° Had breakfast (7 A.M.) with Paul Swaffar [*secretary and general manager, AHA*], Earl Monahan [*president, AHA*] & Jack Van Natta [*director, AHA*]. We gathered at 8 A.M. and worked until 11:30 when we left for lunch at 1st Nat. Bank. From there we went to stock show then came back to work from 4 until 6, then got ready & went to chuck Wagon supper at Westward Hq. Back to Safari & Earl, Paul & Chas. Chandler [*vice-president, AHA*] met with some men until 11:45 & balance of us stayed near by. A long day.

[*Negotiations for purchasing the* American Hereford Journal *from Walker Publications, Inc., and plans for upcoming Progress Clinics, for breed promotion, very likely caused the meetings to be longer than usual. Fifty years ago, Herefords had surpassed Shorthorns as the dominant breed of beef cattle. Now other breeds and crossbreeds were presenting strong challenges to the Herefords. The AHA sponsored clinics where breeders, feeders, and animal science professors emphasized the strong points of Herefords and cautioned against fads. See "Plans for Clinic Programs*

Complete," American Hereford Journal *52, no. 3 (June 1, 1961): 10–11.*]

Fri 6: 28°–49° Sterling Nebbard took us (9) plus Gov Fannin [*governor of Arizona*] and 8 cow men, etc to breakfast at Safari, after which we met again until just after ten. They headed for stock show & Craig took me to airport for 11:25 plane . . . Decided to spend night with Lucile.

Fri 20: 28°–57° . . . had to rush to get ready to get into Mule's [*a friend*] for lunch & watch the inauguration which I enjoyed . . . Went by ASC and got lined up for some tree oiling for 1961 . . .

[*John F. Kennedy and Lyndon B. Johnson were inaugurated as U.S. president and vice-president. Regardless of party affiliations, most Texans watched with pride as a fellow Texan assumed the second-highest office in the nation.*]

FEBRUARY

Wed 1: 40°–70° Clear, mild breezy morning. Got 18 calves weighed, loaded, tied & off at 7:20. Average weight 700.8.

[*After getting odds and ends together, Watt followed the cattle into Fort Worth for the stock show. That evening the Matthews and Reynolds clan gathered at Lucile's house to celebrate Watt's birthday.*]

Thur 2: 37°–62° . . . picked up Jim Shelton & went to Texas Hotel where I got in taxi with Paul Swaffar, Roy Parks [*president, Texas and Southwestern Cattle Raisers Association*], R A McCann [*director of research, AHA*] & I went out to Meacham where Lewter came. Andy Duffle [*director of youth activities, AHA*], Earl Monahan [*president, AHA*], Don McCarthy [*director of public relations, AHA*], Glenn Bratcher, & Hershel Wood & Dirck (Ill feeders) joined us and we boarded [*Murchison*] plane for Lubbock & Lewter feed lots. Flew over ranch. They toured us thru lots then had real nice steak lunch at Country Club. Then back to lots where Glenn & men from St. Joe graded 53 herefords & 51 Angus steers on foot. The AHA men & Glenn Bratcher didn't come back to Ft Worth with us. . . .

[*These men spent the day at Lewter's feed lot at Lubbock, touring the facility and discussing his presentation scheduled for the Progress Clinics, to be held the following June. Durward Lewter operated one of the nation's largest feed lots, turning out nearly ninety thousand head of slaughter cattle annually. He was outspoken in his admiration of Herefords, stating that his records proved they returned ten dollars more per head than any other breed in his feed lot. See "Hereford Promotion Theme of Progress Clinics,"* Texas Hereford *10, no. 10 (July, 1961): 2–3.*]

Fri 3: 27°–57° Went down fairly early to help clean up calves. Tom & J F helped Carrol & me & we washed their faces, etc & finally put them out in sun to dry . . . The judging started at one. We rubbed up calves (Tom doing most of it & Lawrence Winkler also helped) until time for them to go in. They looked mighty nice & were champions even though they were pushed. . . .

Sat 4: 27°–56° Didn't get down to pens too early. Carrol had calves brushed up in pretty nice shape. Sale got going soon after nine. AV calves brought 34.25 plus 3 bonus; Pitchfork 34.30 plus 2.50 bonus. Quite a crowd of us gathered at Backstage for lunch. . . .

[*Watt's uniform, light-colored calves were champions of the carlot division. They averaged 677 pounds, and all were sired by CK Ranch–bred bulls. Lewter Feed Lots of Lubbock purchased the calves. See "J. A. Matthews Ranch Co. Again Shows Herefords to Feeder Championship,"* American Hereford Journal *51, no. 20 (February 15, 1961): 101; and "Southwestern Exposition and Fat Stock Show,"* Cattleman *47, no. 10 (March, 1961): 74, 76, 78.*]

Wed 15: 41°–78° Warm, foggy, damp, spring-like morning (a grass grower!). . . .

Thur 16: 47°–80° . . . Grass jumping! . . .

Tue 21: 36°–44° Got to Kansas City 8:50, 10 min early. Nice day there. Paul Swaffar met me then rounded up the other 5 directors on hand. We went to some big law offices where we spent the morning . . . I took 4:05 flight to Dallas. . . .

[*The main item of business was wrapping up the American Hereford Association's purchase of the* American Hereford Journal *from Walker*

Publications, Inc., which had published the journal for fifty-one years. Hereford Publications, Inc., a newly formed subsidiary of the AHA, took over publication. See "Hereford Journal to New Ownership," American Hereford Journal *51, no. 21 (March 1, 1961): 7*]

Sun 26: 36°–82° . . . Fine warm day. Heel flies had cattle in water a little. [*Cattle stood in water to avoid the aggravation caused by heel flies trying to lay eggs on the cows' legs.*]

MARCH

Sun 19: 40°–44° . . . Trying to get organized to get off to Ft Worth for Texas and Southwestern Cattle Raisers Association convention . . . Joe, Tom & I went (left) for Ft Worth about 2:15. Tom went on to town & met with Albert Gates [*chair, Brand Committee, TSCRA*] . . .

Mon 20: 37°–60° We went down for Brand Committee meeting at 9 A.M. Tom presented his case then things got a little heated for which I was sorry. It did have the appearance of a Committee packed against him I will have to admit . . . to Texas [*Hotel*] for Director's meeting. . . .

Tue 21: 34°–81° We went down for morning session. Heard Fred Dressler & others . . .

[*Dressler, president of the American National Cattleman's Association, warned the group that feed prices would be higher with a commodity-by-commodity farm program.*]

APRIL

Tue 4: 43°–89° . . . Got renditions ready and took them to Throckmorton as I went up to vote . . . Got election dope which was refreshing. The two wild candidates lost & the two conservative[*s won*], Tower & Blakely, 1, 2.

Wed 5: 55°–56° Boys off to round Overton. A good many visitors got there after we had them in pen & nearly separated. They topped out 65 of the bigger ones & 15 shorts & they looked mighty pretty. Joe got there with John & Jack Vanier & Jim Johnson before we were ready to brand. Others kept coming. I think 31 here for lunch. We branded 79 steers & let Momie Olsen have a club calf. Took Joe & Salina 3 on tour (Hayford, Long, Tecumseh, etc) after lunch then down to Joe's to supper. . . .

Wed 12: 38°–72° . . . I went in & met horse buyers . . . at 12. Showed them colts & sold them the snorty bay mare, her black year filly colt, the dun filly colt & the blue coming 3 yr old stud colt (mean) for a total of $240.00. Let them take Jodie & Peanut in place of Alkalie & if they get over $275 to send the excess to us. Clayton apparently gave them a skinning on Alky. . . .

Mon 17: 36°–88° . . . They rounded heifer years out of Trout & ran them freely (a discouraging day) [*the stress of running reduces the weight of cattle*].

Thur 27: 73°–89° Chilly morning. Boys off 4:05 to help Weaver get steer years in. They got in with them about 7 (in good shape). That was in spite of cowboys, however, as no amount of talking seems to convince them that it is necessary for some of them to stay in front of cattle. They (115) averaged 595# net per head & $156.37 per head. . . .

Sun 30: 55°–90° . . . Looks now like April will go out with no recorded rain fall which would be a record. Have only had a trace 2 or 3 times during month. . . .

MAY

Wed 3: 47°–85° Got to Kansas City a little ahead of time (about 8:55). Bob Day met me & took me up to office. We gathered about 9:50 & except for lunch down stairs & looking at IBM outfit, we were in session until after 5 (a long day) . . . to 10 P.M. train.

[*The newly installed IBM equipment, the first of its kind used by a breed association, electronically traced and compiled a bull's ancestry back to the first officially registered American Herefords. Records of nearly twelve million Herefords were in the data base, in preparation for issuing the three-generation pedigree certificates that became mandatory in July 1961. Breeders used this information to design the genetic makeup of future bulls and to speed troubleshooting when problems surfaced. See "Hereford Bull Sparks Electronic Brain,"* American Hereford Journal *51, no. 24 (April 15, 1961): 46.*

Sat 6: Oscar helping Howsley dock lambs, then took 2 horses in to have shod.

Thur 11: 93° [*high*] . . . When we got back for lunch (about 1:20) the shearing outfit was sitting around waiting for John to get back with strings & sacks which disgusted me considerably. They finally got these sheared by 5 P.M. . . .

Mon 22: 64°–92° We had 184 steer years drifted into pen soon after 5:30. Weighed them & sprayed 150 & are now (8 A.M.) waiting for trucks . . . Steve threw Carey off after opening Road pasture gate for no reason. . . .

Tue 23: 59°–73° . . . River came down late yesterday. Had stopped running in places.

JUNE

Wed 14: 74°–93° . . . John painting gates. Weaver & Carrol swinging trap gates. . . .

Mon 26: 63°–87° . . . Went over & got Clyde lined up on his road work. Colorado hay (Horse Creek) was here when I got back. JF had 180 bales & Chas 81 (our 1/2). . . .

Fri 30: 68°–92° . . . Getting shaped up to go to San Angelo . . . went to meeting of brand committee, which had a big turn out & lasted until about 4:30. . . .

[*At the quarterly meeting of directors of the Texas and Southwestern Cattle Raisers Association, members of the Brand Committee submitted proposals for possible improvements in current brand laws. Lengthy discussions were a prelude to a hearing in Austin on September 19. Several owners of auction barns formally opposed the renewal of TSCRA authority to inspect brands and other identifying marks at strategic marketing points. Most of their customers were small operators in East Texas who did not customarily brand their cattle and who objected to paying the required fee (eight cents per head) for inspection services. TSCRA won the day, with the help of law enforcement and government officials who testified that cattle theft was still prevalent in Texas and that no other agency was prepared to assume the duties performed by TSCRA inspectors. Authority, initially issued by USDA in 1943, was granted anew on*

January 1, 1962. See "New Authority for TSCRA Strongly Supported," Cattleman *48, no. 5 (October, 1961): 28–32, 43; and "TSCRA to Continue Brand Inspection Services,"* Cattleman *48, no. 7 (December, 1961): 7.*

AUGUST

Wed 30: 61°–72° Cool pleasant morning . . . I gave Butch & Joe lessons on being caught. Got hot & dirty. Got cleaned up & went to bank to see $42.00 check O.V. Houston had forged on me. To Soil Conservation Office & spent afternoon going over Great Plains program for Lambshead. . . .

Thur 31: 62°–99° Pleasant morning. Coyotes carrying on freely after day light. Rattlesnakes also on the move the past few days. Both good signs of rain which I trust we get.

SEPTEMBER

Sun 3: 73°–97° . . . Norther was moving in. We got home with dark clouds which got to showering before sun down. . . .

Mon 4: 54°–63° Rained a glorious steady rain all night. Could hardly have been better to order. A dry Aug & rain in Sept is much better than the other way around. By noon Lambshead had 3.20. . . .

Thur 21: 68°–92° . . . Went in for church committee meeting at bank at 11 to work on idea of sending truck load of relief stuff to Bay Town. . . .

[*On September 11, 1961, Hurricane Carla, one of the most intense hurricanes to strike Texas in recorded history, slammed into Port Lavaca. Only the evacuation of more than 250,000 persons kept the loss of life low along the coastline; 34 persons died. Loss of property, however, was valued at nearly $400 million. Aid came from across the nation. See Bomar,* Texas Weather, *71–72.*]

Wed 27: 62°–90° . . . County bladed road for us. . . .

OCTOBER

Mon 2: 48°–67° Rained practically all night & up to 6 A.M. . . . A wonderful way to start Oct. Country green & I believe more wild flowers than I have ever seen in fall. . . .

Mon 9: 62°–86° . . . Boys (all regular) off to round bulls out of William D. Reynolds . . . We accounted for 102 bulls 2's & up, which is 3 short the way I have it figured. . . .

Fri 20: 38°–78° . . . First frost. Did no damage.

Sat 21: 40°–85° . . . quit early so boys could go to class reunions, etc. . . .

DECEMBER

Sun 24: Beautiful, clear, frosty, cold morning. Went in for christening of Robert Scott Brittingham Wallace and song service which was nice. The kids looked mighty nice. Had a good turn out (92) . . . Bob [*Brittingham*] got out for church service [*from his home in New York*]. . . .

[*The year ended as optimistically as it had begun. Watt wrote: "1961 has been a banner year weather & range wise & I will probably never see another one to match it. With the bright dry weather we are liable to be headed for some dry years."*]

1962

[In 1962, Hereford leaders continued to focus on promoting their breed. Changes in eating habits allowed other segments of the meat-producing industry to compete intensely with beef. More important, Herefords were being challenged for supremacy by other breeds, whose leaders were waging effective promotion campaigns. Hereford raisers were updated on the strong points of their breed.]

JANUARY

Tue 2: 35°–62° . . . Humble geologist here for lunch. The drilling program starting with a well on Andrew near Overton. They have 23 located to drill on us. . . .

Tue 9: 18°–20° Cold bleak morning. Snowing some, but not much on ground . . . Didn't snow enough to make a measurable amount of moisture. John Reames & boy brought out 140 sacks Purina making 260 of 400 brought out. Moore brought 5-1/2 tons calf feed here & to Weaver so we should be fixed up for feed for some time. We kept a big fire going in cookshack which takes a lot of wood. Between checking in feed, etc, didn't get much done. After a good deal of phoning to bed by 8:30.

Tue 23: 15°–39° . . . Went over & checked on well. They set pipe on one on point near Valley pens. They will have this one finished in a matter of 36 hours or less which will make 6 down on us since 1-5-62. If they keep this rate up they will have the 23 down by April 1 which will be good. . . .

Thur 25: 52°–59° . . . In late. By Blanton's for quite a visit & got my new book *True Tales of the Frontier* which Otis has done a beautiful job on. . . .

[*Joe Blanton, nicknamed "Otis" by the family, arranged, illustrated, and published this book of excerpts from* Interwoven, *in commemoration of the hundredth anniversary of Sallie Reynolds Matthews's birthday. Joe, a grandson of Sallie Matthews, had edited her original manuscript for publication.*]

Tue 30: 36°–76° . . . Calves had little over 1/2 feed (didn't give evening feed) & put them in show pens for night. Have had syrup in water past few days. . . .

Wed 31: 38°–78° . . . Off with load 7:33. 19 calves, average 731.6. They stayed pretty clean but are wet . . . we left at 8:50 & got to Lucile's about 11 . . . J D & Ethel took me to show. Champion steer (black) had just been picked. I wanted AHA boys to get across & see the AV steers which were unloaded soon, but Hereford Heifer judging was still going on & they didn't make it before plane time. Cleaned up calves. . . .

FEBRUARY

Fri 2: 36°–77° . . . down fairly early again. Tone off earlier each morning. Carrol & James washed the calves faces, etc & we had them looking nice. Tone & Weaver had the Spanish Gourds looking nice too . . . They did the judging outside in the beautiful sunshine, which didn't take long. AV Champion Hereford; Spanish Gourds Reserve. Watt Cattle Co Champion & Res Angus, JAM Champion Crosses, TLB, Jr., Reserve. Sidleys, Bill Greens, Britts, TLB, Jrs., Jack Vanier & Jim Johnson, Milly & I went to Carter Museum afterwards. . . .

[*The Amon Carter Museum of Western Art, with one of the largest collections of art by Frederic Remington and Charles Russell in the U.S., opened in 1960. See "The Old West Comes Back to Life in the Amon Carter Museum of Western Art,"* Cattleman *48, no. 4 (September, 1961): 40–41.*]

Sat 3: 36°–83° Juddy [*Ardon B. Judd, Watt's brother-in-law*] took me by show grounds early on his way to Dallas. We got calves brushed up for sale which got started late on account of Cudhay's not being ready. AV brought 27.25 & weighed 745 gr; Spanish Gourds brought 25.10 . . . JAM Crosses brought 29 & TLB, Jr. Hereford Crosses brought 32 & his other loads 23.80 & 27.10. . . .

Wed 7: 25°–73° Partly cloudy, freezing morning. Red sunrise. . . .

Thur 8: 36°–85° . . . The Webbs & I went to Abilene with the Joe Bs, by John Matthews', then to Caldwells for dinner & they took all to the Van Cliburn concert which was good and a full house. . . .

APRIL

Sun 1: 35°–62° . . . Weaver came out & got the Jack which we will breed 3 or 4 of the little Mex mares to. . . .

Mon 9: 40°–78° . . . Went in late (around 5). Picked up JC [*Watt's grand-nephew*] & took him down & got him boots, hat, white Lees & blue jacket & he looked cute. Got mail, took some checks by bank, by Blanton's, Webb's, Couger's showing JC off. Taking him home then. . . .

Sun 22: 60°–83° [*Easter Sunday*] . . . rainy, cloudy, mild morning . . . I went to church (103) . . . It came a nice shower soon after we finished eating. Lambshead .66. . . .

Fri 27: 59°–84° Rained more in early morning hours. Boys off early to help Weaver get in steer years . . . They got the steers in in good shape & trucks had no trouble getting up hill with them. Cut out 8 & delivered 120, average weight 649 at 26¢. . . .

MAY

Mon 14: 55°–88° . . . Went in fairly early. Did a few errands then picked up Lucile & JC & we came out to ranch. Saddled Bald for JC & he rode a little while. After lunch I saddled Mack & took JC on a more extensive ride which he seemed to enjoy. . . .

Tue 15: 65°–89° . . . JC spent night with me. Lucile took JC in with her [*to John Brittingham's home in Albany*] & I later went by & put my stuff in her car & she picked me up at Ford outfit where I left my car to be undercoated, etc. She drove in [*to Fort Worth*] & I dozed. . . .

Wed 16: 68°–85°. Nice morning after a fine rest. Tom & Edna got in soon after 8 then Tom & I went to Bull Barn soon & registered for Hereford Progress Clinic . . . We had a full day until after 5 P.M. which was interesting & worth while. Got home in time to change clothes & get to social hour & dinner at Texas Hotel new layout which is nice & the party was nice with a big crowd. [*See January 5 and February 2, 1961.*]

Thur 17: 65°–83°. After breakfast Tom & I went back to Bull Barn. Had an interesting morning. Clinic over a little before 12:30. We went to Feeder Show lunch meeting Billie Bob had (about 38 there). Not much enthusiasm & I imagine show will probably be dropped . . . off for Albany soon after 5 with Tom & Edna. Went to party at Cook ranch.

[*Over six hundred cattlemen attended the clinic to hear animal science professors evaluate steers on the hoof, then evaluate the carcasses after the steers were slaughtered. Hereford people were pleased that the two rankings were so close. The use of ultrasonic measurement of the rib eye also was demonstrated, and Durward Lewter, Lewter Feed Lots, Lubbock, Texas, spoke on "Hereford Superiority for Feeders." See "Hereford Progress Clinic Big Success,"* Texas Hereford *11, no. 8 (May 1962): 147–48.*]

Tue 22: 69°–94° . . . to Ethel's for supper. Webbs & Craig also there . . . Home about 9:15 after going to sleep & running off road & thru Anderson's new fence. Damaged car considerably but I am extremely thankful not to be hurt or killed and want to try to show it by doing a better job for my Maker & my folks & my country.

Wed 23: 63°–100° Pleasant morning with a very light dew . . . John White & I took car in. Had to tow him on account of hole in radiator. Carrol & Melciadez fixing fence. . . .

Tue 29: 58°–92° . . . We shipped 26 cows to Ft. Worth. . . . I went back to Buzzard Peak to help Albert Speer load the cows & we had trouble. A cow got down and was dead before we could get the others off of her. She never tried to get up. . . .

JUNE

Fri 8: 63°–82° Boys looked out Culver but failed to find any steers. Tone flew it out & located 5. . . .

Tue 19: 69°–89° Quiet, partly cloudy morning. They got started spraying around 5:30. We went up & checked on spraying until wind got up too much to work. They didn't get to start again until 5 P.M. then worked until nearly dark. They have done something over 700 a[*cres*]. . . .

[*Watt was spraying 2-4-D to kill mesquite. The chemical could damage the pecan trees on neighboring ranches if it drifted with the wind.*]

Thur 21: 66°–95° Otis called me before six that they had taken Sister May in hospital about midnight. A stroke which they think is a light one . . . I went in. Poor Sister May is in bad shape, but I believe there was a slight improvement by evening. . . .

Fri 22: 70°–95° . . . Tom [*Blanton*] reported a fair night for Sister May. . . .

Wed 27: 66°–91° . . . They left for Ft. Worth with Sister May at 12 noon. Matt [*Blanton*] called me. She made the trip OK. . . .

JULY

Wed 11: 72°–102° Moved to porch for 1st time since summer of 1960. Cool by morn. . . .

Thur 26: 68°–82° . . . We had a nice gentle grass rain, but they had big rains around Albany. . . .

Fri 27: 69°–87° . . . Boys soaped & cleaned saddles during which the clouds were low & threatening. In afternoon they rode young horses. . . .

AUGUST

Fri 10: 66°–106° Same crew combining . . . They put up 3240# of maize off about 18 acres which is good for us.

SEPTEMBER

Mon 3: 69°–94° Sept getting off to a wonderful start with the second rain yesterday.

Tue 25: 64°–91° . . . Poor Sister May mighty low and left us at 9:45.

OCTOBER

Sat 13: 71°–91° Train got in[*to Kansas City*] about 10 AM an hour late. Got located in hotel then went down & watched the last part of the parade which wasn't much. Watched TU-OU game then to Vanier's room & had visit with John & Lesta. Then cleaned up & to Chandler's [*president, AHA*] room. Then all to Paul's [*secretary, AHA*] dinner party at KC Club which was nice.

Sun 14: 69°–92° To AHA bldg before 8 A.M. for our meeting at 8 which went on to 5:45 with a little while out for lunch downstairs. I was nearly down in back from sitting so long in that easy chair. To KC Hereford Club party at 6:30. Had a nice visit with a lot of people.

Mon 15: 64°–97° Breakfast at 7 A.M. with Billy Bob & BB jr. Back to room & talked to Susette & Ethel. Went out and watched judging. BB & BB jr & I went to Golden Ox & had drinks before they went into lunch then I went to Hereford Bldg. Had sandwiches then to meeting at 2 P.M. Directors gathered for little while afterwards & off about 5:30 to party in Chandler's room at 6 P.M. To banquet at 7. With the Adams & Chandler's until about 12 afterwards.

[*Watt was attending the American Hereford Association's board of directors meeting and annual membership meeting. The most important item of business was the overwhelming approval given to the issuance of a single certificate of registration for Polled Herefords and horned Herefords. See "Big 'Yes' Vote for Joint Registration,"* American Hereford Journal 53, *no. 13 (November 1, 1962): 28–29, 163.*]

Tue 16: 61°–79° Bill Adams [*incoming president, AHA*] & I had breakfast together. To AHA office at 7:30. There until 11:30 then to picking of champion steer (black) Lewter reserve. Chandlers and Gene Forrestals [*director, AHA*] had lunch with me at Golden Ox. I stayed in there until ball game over then looked at feeders (22 loads fitted) then to hotel. Had dinner with Chandlers & Bill Donnell after packing & checking out of hotel. Left them at table & went to station & got on train (10 P.M.) about 9:45.

Wed 17: 62°–71° . . . Joe & I went to PW & looked at Matt's corrientes. . . .
[*A corriente is a native Mexican steer that fails to achieve high quality because of poor breeding and environment. These cattle were fattened in a feed lot before being slaughtered. Because they often develop large horns without putting on weight anywhere else, they are popular with rodeo contestants. See "What Is a Corriente?"* West Texas Livestock Weekly, *April 18, 1963, p. 7.*]

Thur 18: 58°–81° . . . checked on haying (1190 bales, nice hay). Finished yesterday. . . .
[*Hay is an important forage for livestock. Dry feed is necessary for the digestive tracts of cattle to function properly. It helps move feed through the intestines and maintains the proper conditions in the rumen for the microbial action vital for the digestion of large portions of feeds. Approximately 85 percent of all hay is produced on the farm or ranch on which it is fed, rather than being purchased. Watt now plants Haygrazer for baling. See Ensminger,* Stockman's Handbook, *668–76.*]

1963

[Americans consumed a record ninety-five pounds of beef per person in 1963. Increased consumption was largely the result of providing consumers with a constant supply of meat they liked. Using feed lots guaranteed a uniform supply of quality beef throughout the year, and supermarket advertising made it America's favorite food.]

JANUARY

Wed 9: 42°–78° . . . Tried to clean up around desk a little more. Made some calls. Got packed up, cleaned up, and ready to start for Denver [*to attend American Hereford Association board meeting prior to National Western Livestock Show*] . . . headed for Wichita Falls. Train on time at 4:52. . . .

Thur 10: 54°–72° Got in at 6:30, on time. Temp 12° [*in Denver*] and a little snow. Got located in my room. Went to Paul Swaffar's room to meeting of Research Committee. Marshall Sellman, Chairman, Charles Chandler and I. Paul also there. The directors meeting started at 10 A.M. and lasted until 8 P.M. with a short time out for lunch in room next door. Dr. Russell & Dr. Sykes of Anderson clinic were with us and had presented a lot of pink & cancer eye data. It was a long, tiresome day, especially with a running nose & coming down with a cold. . . .

[An important project for association members was the research being done at M. D. Anderson Hospital in Houston, to isolate the virus that caused pink eye. The association contributed $35,000 for an electron mi-

croscope to be used in the research. See "Harmony the Keynote of AHA Meeting," American Hereford Journal *54, no. 13 (November 1, 1963): 24, 150–51.*]

FEBRUARY

Sat 2: 53°–58° We got up and got down to shed in plenty of time for sale . . . AV calves 21 brought 30.30. . . .

[*In the Feeder Cattle division of the Southwestern Exposition and Fat Stock Show in Fort Worth, the champion carload of Hereford steers was shown by J. A. Matthews Ranch and sold for $30.30 per hundredweight to Lewter Feed Lots of Lubbock.*]

Mon 11: 20°–25° Blizzardy morning. Ground covered with blowing snow. . . .

Wed 27: 39°–86° A mild blustery morning & we will probably have plenty of dust. Boys off to round MO . . . Branded 72 calves . . . We brought water truck over as precaution against fire. . . .

MARCH

Thur 7: 27°–63° Boys got fair start to round Long . . . We branded 144 calves (heifers 80, steers 64). Put 37 cows & 2 bulls in William D. Reynolds; 2 cows & calves to VN; 1 doggie looking calf to Lambshead doggie pen . . . The doggie calf balled for his mother & we will take him back probably . . . Cow kicked Joe. Knocked him down and bruised him. . . .

APRIL

Mon 1: 58°–84° Went to Muehleback [*Hotel in Kansas City*] & to bed. Up before 7, breakfast & to American Hereford Association office by 8. They thought I would not be in until 9 A.M. train & had delayed meeting until then. Had long day. Lunch at Kansas City Club. Albert Mitchell & Claude Mayer (of Steve Hart firm) with us. While they were going over the proposed tax situation I went to studio & had picture made they have been wanting. After 8 P.M. when we got out of meeting. Marshall Sellman, Charles Chandler, Bill & Dorothy

Adams & twins & I had drinks. Marshall & I went to station. Had a bowl of soup. I took 10 P.M. train. . . .

[*Proposed changes in the Internal Revenue Code were causing anxiety among cattlemen. Their greatest concern was the possibility that a capital gains tax would be levied on the appreciated value of land transferred from one generation to another at death. Albert K. Mitchell, chair of the National Livestock Tax Committee, and Stephen H. Hart, attorney for the committee, appeared several times before the House Ways and Means Committee to plead the cause of ranchers who opposed the new tax. The ranchers argued that it would force the sale of thousands of family ranches, because ranching operations generally have few liquid assets. Unlike securities, an entire ranch's value is diminished if part has to be sold to pay estate, inheritance, or capital gains taxes. See "A Look at Some Proposed Changes in the Internal Revenue Code,"* Cattleman *49, no. 11 (April, 1963): 26.*]

MAY

Thur 16: 71°–95° . . . Met Evan Easter at 3 P.M. & got lined up on putting up Hereford sign.

[*The sign, at the entrance to Lambshead Ranch, was part of the campaign to promote Herefords. The American Hereford Association furnished free billboard papers.*]

JUNE

Tue 18: 61°–86° Cool (chilly side) foggy morning. We have had as much muggy humid weather so far this June as I can remember so far but it has been a real grass & tree grower. . . .

JULY

Thur 11: 78°–99° To meeting [*in Denver*] at 8 A.M. with fieldmen, then into meeting of directors [*AHA*]. Went thru lunch at which time Bob Day was presenting his stuff. . . .

Fri 12: 77°–99° Went to show arena where they started [*American Hereford Association's*] Judge's conference at 8 A.M. Got hot there as day wore on. Had a box lunch which wasn't much. . . .

Sat 13: 76°–103° Bill Adams ate breakfast with me in my room . . . out to Swift & Co. for the carcass exhibit which was interesting. . . .

[*The conference stressed that selecting cattle to suit one segment of the industry could have detrimental effects upon other segments. Animals should reflect compromises among the needs of breeders, feeders, packers, and consumers. Carcass exhibits were held at every opportunity, to focus attention on differences in cutability of animals within the same grade. The retail value of heavily muscled animals was at least twenty-five dollars greater than that of animals carrying a lot of fat. Because the lean-to-fat ratio is determined by heredity, breeders could improve this important characteristic of their animals through selective breeding. See "Good Turnout for Denver Conference,"* American Hereford Journal *54, no. 7 (August 1, 1963): 28; and "Herefords Dominate PI Show's Carcass Contest with Four of Top Five Placings,"* American Hereford Journal *53, no. 23 (April 1, 1963): 58.*]

SEPTEMBER

Wed 11: 67°–102° Had a good deal I had planned to do around desk but feed & salt salesmen, etc., took up a lot of my time. . . .

OCTOBER

Fri 11: 55°–95° . . . John White planted a lot of my Rita Blanco plumb seeds at Bend & is planting some here today . . . A fire on Jim Nail [*adjoining ranch*] but they got it under control soon. . . .

NOVEMBER

Fri 8: 53°–63° . . . Harve bucked me off & got me mighty sore but I am thankful not to be hurt more. Took hot shower & to bed early.

[*Watt spent November 14–18 in New York, where he met his nephew, Bob Brittingham. They joined friends for a trip to Princeton, New Jersey, for the Princeton–Yale football game. Watt was a Princeton alumnus, while Bob was a Yale graduate.*]

Fri 22: 50°–65° Got raining in early morning. Lambshead .34 . . .We soon got the news of the tragedy to Pres Kennedy & Gov Connally. . . .

[*U.S. President John F. Kennedy was in Texas to patch up differences in the Democratic party when he was assassinated. Texas Gov. John Connally also was critically wounded. This episode was one of the great traumas of twentieth-century American history. See Kurtz,* Crime of the Century, *v, 3–23.*]

Sun 24: 28°–62° . . . After breakfast Carrol & I got figures together for cattle income for past 10 years. Some drought years were low but none showed a loss. . . .

[*Watt and Joe Matthews consistently practiced a light stocking program at Lambshead. Although the Soil Conservation Service recommended fourteen acres per cow in Shackelford and Throckmorton counties, the Matthews allowed twenty acres. Light stocking and an occasional lucky rain made it possible to go through the extended drought of the 1950s with a feed bill that was less than six dollars per head during the worst years. See Roger B. Letz, "Their Secret to Better Herefords,"* Cattleman *41, no. 3 (August, 1954): 38–39, 62–63.*]

DECEMBER

Sun 22: 23°–22° Ground white with snow early & a cold north wind. Snow made .03 of moisture. Roads glazed & I didn't try to go to church. Stayed around trying to keep warm. Cleaned up kitchen, opened presents, etc [*the annual Christmas party for the ranch workers had taken place the night before*]. Outside of kitchen, house was not in much of a mess. Took a rest after lunch but had to be on phone a lot. Richard & I went up to Bend about sundown and checked water heater, etc. He laid a fire in cookshack. Went to bed at nine & did a bunch of phoning.

Wed 25: 33°–79° A mild clear calm Christmas morning and we should have a fine day if wind doesn't get up. Opened packages, did phoning, etc. (always get a lot more than I deserve) and was late getting off to Bend. Tom Blanton & I went to White Flat & helped Joe & Louise bring John Matthews' family over. All of us arrived at same time. We had nice day. 9 Blantons, 9 Matthews (Joe's and John's family), 10 Brittinghams, Ethel, Katy Haven, Preston Van Slykes & I plus Richard for a total of 33 there. Ate early supper after quite a rest. Home & to bed at 8 P.M. Melciades gone again. A beautiful day in seventies. [*Although rainfall was slightly below normal—Lambshead received only 19.22"—1963 on the whole had been a good year. Warm weather and adequate moisture in November increased the prospects for winter ranges. The year ended with the cattle in good shape and a lot of calves on the ground.*]

1964

[With all the attention given to breed promotion and increasing beef consumption, many people overlooked the drastic reduction in screwworm infestations. Texas reported fewer than 300 cases in 1964, compared to 49,484 in 1962, when the screwworm elimination program was initiated. Each year, millions of sterile male flies were released to form a barrier several hundred miles wide along the border of Mexico and the U.S. Females, with only sterile eggs to lay in open wounds, ended their life cycles before breeding again. This program is considered one of the most important developments in livestock history.]

JANUARY

Wed 1: 24°–64° Ground about as white with frost as yesterday morning which was almost like a snow . . . It was a beautiful sunny mild day which was ideal for Texas-Navy game in Cotton Bowl. Tex 28–Navy 6. . . .

FEBRUARY

Tue 4: 31°–65° Lambshead 1.80 [*rain*] by 7 A.M. . . . All creeks have run I am sure & Leonard reports a lot of water caught in tanks. Two great rains and we already have had more than normal rain fall thru March. Worked around desk until noon. . . .

Wed 5: 36°–58° . . . The ground is mighty wet with hog wallows, etc., standing full of water which is a sure sign of a hide full [*a lot of rain*]. . . .

Wed 26: 23°–45° Cold, cloudy morning & we are in need of a warm spell while we have moisture. . . .

MARCH

Fri 6: 49°–82° . . . getting set for pinkeye work on heifer calves. . . .

Thur 12: 32°–73° . . . They had 69 dehorned when Dave Ballard & I got up there then we started the putting of viruses in the eyes & colored tags in ears of 5 groups of 50 each. . . .

Thur 19: 50°–66° . . . John Sykes took a picture of the eye treated on the 250 head. We put coral & linseed [*oil*] on all their heads & got along mighty well. Used Dave Ballard's head catcher & only caused one to bleed with it. . . .

[*Lambshead cattle were being used in field tests for pinkeye research being conducted by M. D. Anderson Hospital. See January 10, 1963.*]

Fri 20: 37°–49° . . . A blustery norther on & the equinox will beat 8:10 A.M.

APRIL

Mon 20: 68°–89° . . . helped serve meat at barbeque for Omar Burleson. Got rained out before speaking over. . . .

[*A native of Anson, Omar Burleson was first elected to Congress from the 17th District of Texas in January 1947. Considered a progressive conservative, his service on the House Ways and Means Committee with another Texan, George Mahon, was important to the state.*]

Tue 21: 62°–88° . . . Read *U.S. News* & took a rest. . . .

Tue 28: Boys off about 5:20 with Carrol to help Weaver get steers years in to deliver to Pick . . . Ready to leave for PW (5:30). Got over there early but they had a run (due to carelessness mainly). . . .

MAY

Thur 7: 70° [*low*] . . . A muggy windy day which had a pretty fair bank in NW by sun down. . . .

Fri 8: Started showering before 4 A.M. Lambshead .66. . . .

Tue 12: . . . Went to hospital meeting at 1, then to Dr. McCord at 2, then to bank meeting at 3, then directors of Cemetery Assoc met about 4:30. A full afternoon. . . .

Tue 19: 59°–87° Boys off 5:45 to round Paint. Calves bloomy & fine. . . .

JUNE

Mon 1: 49°–78° A real chilly morning for June 1. Temp on garden fence thermo 42°. . . .

Sat 6: 58°–98° . . . Went to Throckmorton & voted No. 1 in our box for Joe Pool the only race on ballot. . . .

JULY

Fri 10: 76°–107° Boys got a fairly early start to round heifers in Overton . . .We put 33 in field & sent 16 to Weigh Out. We watched them & they got along OK on the Johnson Grass. . . .

Mon 13: 59°–94° . . . Got horses (5) saddled & rigged up & all the Wallaces had a ride. Lucile & Rob on the same horse . . .

AUGUST

Mon 3: 76°–103° Up early and am getting off to Brownwood. Boys going over to DC to pickup balance of steers in there. Got down there in plenty of time after meeting Jean & Clyde on road & seeing Evan in town & checking with them on their jobs. I dreaded the trip to Brownwood but felt repaid & there was some good talks & I ate lunch beside Claude Maer (tax man) & got a good deal of information. Mozelle & I by Sedwicks for awhile. Out to Ethels and a snack with her. By Webbs & home.

[*Watt attended a conference sponsored by the Texas and American Hereford associations. Focusing on the role that Herefords could play in providing quality beef for consumers, animal scientists provided the latest information both on identifying animals that transmit desirable beefmaking characteristics to their calves and on methods of producing steers to meet the needs of feeders, packers, and consumers. A session on taxes was presented by Claude Maer, an attorney for the National Livestock Association's Tax Committee. See "Texas Hereford Round-up Conference Held,"* Texas Hereford *13, no. 9 (August, 1964): 2–3.*]

Mon 10: 72°–107° Boys off about 5:20 to round Valley. Days are very noticeably shorter. . . .

SEPTEMBER

Wed 9: 68°–98° . . . Went in about 4:30. Took my first long pants to get them mended, cleaned & pressed. . . .

Thur 10: 69°–99° John took 3 hogs and 7 wethers [*gelded male sheep*] in to be butchered & was late getting to PW & Weaver put out some salt & never did show up. Carrol helped with forms for scales. . . .

OCTOBER

Thur 1: 63° [*low*] . . . Cloudy, damp morning . . . met Joe & Louise at Ft. G. & went to the Field Day at the [*Texas*] Experimental Ranch with them which was interesting. There were over 300 there I think. We went to the Swenson's afterwards & had a nice visit & a good supper there. . . .

[*The highlight of this Annual Field Day was a presentation by Dr. Jan C. Bonsma, a visiting professor from the University of Pretoria, South Africa. His subject was "Judging Cattle for Functional Efficiency." Cautioning against relying entirely on production records to develop modern selection indices, he stressed the importance of combining visual appraisal of breeding stock with production records to improve production efficiency. See Jan C. Bonsma, "Judging Cattle for Functional Efficiency,"* Texas Hereford *13, no. 11 (October, 1964): 14–15.*]

Mon 5: 51°–74° . . . went in for the George Bush rally at 11:30 & his talk was good & I hope he can win. . . .

DECEMBER

Tue 15: 33°–63° . . . Worked around desk all morning with one thing and another including tally book which is out of balance with regular books . . . went to McCullough's [*bookkeepers*] to reconcile our calf accounts & didn't get out until 5:30. . . .

Thur 17: 21°–25° Norther on since around midnight & is around 20° now. . . .

1965

[For over a century, cattlemen believed that they could tell by looking how much red meat was on an animal and where it was located. This changed during the 1960s, when animal scientists stressed the importance of using production records in breeding and culling cattle. Feed lot owners supported the change by paying premium prices for animals with proven performance records.]

JANUARY

Fri 15: 30°–60°. Train got in on time—7 A.M. MST. Howard Miller & I came to hotel together. I was already registered in & he couldn't get in his room so I brought him up with me to shave and leave his stuff. To Committee (Research & TPR) at 8:30. Out about 10:30. To Fieldman 12:30. Then met until about 6:30. Then to dinner for directors, their wives, office men, etc. (21 total). Both lunch & dinner were mighty nice. A very mild warm day.

[Total Performance Records (TPR) was a three-phase program for herd improvement that was developed by AHA. It focused on Calf Performance, Feed Lot and Carcass Evaluation, and the Show Ring Register of Merit System. It was designed to raise the genetic level of a herd by identifying animals that were superior in growth and conformation from birth through slaughter, and also produced a desirable carcass for the retailer. The cost-price squeeze required cattlemen to increase the performance of their herds if they were to remain competitive. See John W. Jones, "Total Performance

Records," Texas Hereford *14, no. 7 (May, 1965): 19, 30–32; and John W. Jones, "TPR Program Is Ready for You,"* American Hereford Journal *57, no. 5 (July 1, 1966): 564, 861.*]

FEBRUARY

Mon 15: 31°–57° . . . R. A. & Rob & Frank Daws picked me up & we were off for Midland & Roy Parks funeral . . . Funeral at 2, 1st Presbyterian Church. Cow men from all over state there. . . .

[*Roy Parks was past president of the Texas and Southwestern Cattle Raisers Association and the American Quarter Horse Association and was a director of the American National Cattlemen's Association and of the Southwestern Exposition and Fat Stock Show. He had extensive ranch holdings in the Midland area.*]

Thur 18: 31°–53° Second mild morning since freezing rain on Tues which didn't freeze ground. Dr. Gordon came here for lunch after checking for TB on Spanish Gourd heifers which are going to Miss. We tested the new CK bulls for fertility, branded & tipped all except the 3 yr old herd bull. . . .

[*Fertility testing bulls shortly before the start of the breeding season identifies sterile bulls; however, semen tests do not identify bulls of lowered fertility. The young bulls Watt bought from the CK Ranch were premium animals that had been genetically selected to sire heavy calves of uniform quality. He intended to upgrade his herd with replacement heifers sired by these bulls. See Lasley,* Beef Cattle Production, 93.]

Wed 24: 16°–42° Cold, clear morning. My thermo about 14°. Picked up Mule & we were off for Guthrie about 9:45. Had fine lunch there [*6666 ranch*]. Plane flew in while we were eating. Charley Beaudouy, Frank Barber & Mickey Quinn were on it & ate lunch with us after which they plus us, Geo. Humphreys & Coon Jeffers took off for Meridian, Miss. . . .

Thur 25: 25°–65° Mule & I went out to yards & looked at heifers which had made the trip in good shape & were filling up pretty well. . . .

Fri 26: 31°–73° We went out to yards soon after breakfast which we ate about seven. Rigged up a fence & got heifers into shed & regular years. Richard got them cleaned up & looking nice after we cut them into 3 pens of 8 each. They didn't start sale until about 11. 28—6666 heifers averaged 218; 24 Spanish Gourd at 159. . . . out to airport & off about 1:15 . . . at Guthrie about 4:30. . . .

[*Because of reduced cotton acreage and low farm income, since the early 1950s the pattern of agriculture in Mississippi had been shifting from cotton to beef cattle. Top-quality heifers from Lambshead Ranch very likely went into a commercial herd. See Fatherree, "Revolution in Mississippi,"* American Hereford Journal *51, no. 17 (January 1, 1961): 132–34.*]

MARCH

Sat 20: 13°–47° The official first day of spring, coldest of whole year . . . A record low for this late in year. My thermomo was about 11°. . . .

APRIL

Thur 1: 48°–73° . . . Joe, Louise, & I left for Stamford (in their car) about 11:30 for the Swenson's barbeque for John Sellman (50 yrs. service). . . .

[*John Selmon came to work for the Swenson Land and Cattle Company in 1915. For fifty years, he was foreman of the Flat Top, one of the SMS ranches. Selmon died in 1981. See Doug Perkins, "A Century of Ranching,"* Cattleman *69, no. 3 (August, 1982): 59–69.*

Watt and Joe Matthews hosted the quarterly meeting of the board of directors of the American Hereford Association. Nine directors and several staff people attended.]

Fri 23: 60°–91° . . . got ready to get in for 2 P.M. meeting of *American Hereford Journal* directors at Joe B's which lasted until about six. . . .

Sat 24: 54°–89° . . . We got our [*AHA*] directors meeting going [*in the director's room of First National Bank in Albany, Texas*] soon after 8 & got done about 12:45. We then had a good lunch that Jean, JD, & Monroe had fixed. There were a total of 19 of us. Then Otis handled the projector while John Matthews lectured. We got to ranch about 3:30 (15 min late). Cattle demonstration [*conducted by the noted*

South African veterinarian, Dr. Jan Bonsma] over about 5. Got Fandangle started 7:45. . . .

MAY

Sat 22: 62°–84° . . . We had seen a total of about 334 calves. Sold 75% of them at 175. . . .

Mon 31: 62°–86° Raining at 4 A.M. Heavy thunder, etc. We waited until 6:15 to start after steer years . . . We got in with years about 7:20 & had them weighed before 8. Delivered 234 which averaged 730 & total of 514 averaged 724.74 which is good. We sold him 29 cwts at 23¢ & turned back in HP av 647 to be weighed when he gets them next week. Sent 14 to PW to go with Newell years. 4th truck off for Ft. Worth 5:25.

JULY

Thur 8: 77°–101° . . . Went up and checked on Victor who is doing well with his rock corral repair, etc. . . .

Tue 20: 73°–97° . . . went up river to fence & looked for some rolls of the old square barbed wire, but didn't find any. . . .

Wed 21: 69°–98° . . . Around desk lot of day working with tally book, etc. . . .

Thur 22: 69°–100° Boys off about six to round W. D. Reynolds to McFadden corrals. We had 57 bulls in there & I was afraid they were going to wreck them [*the corrals*] before we got them out and headed for Hayford. They did knock some of the rocks down.

Sat 31: 60°–98° Drew a sketch of the 4 rooms we are planning. Sallie [and] I did a little measuring and laying it off on ground. . . .

AUGUST

Fri 13: 62°–95° Got diary, etc., up thru year for birthdays, etc., as well as up to date then got birth dates on 1965 colts as well as breeding dates. This took most of morning. . . .

Mon 30: 72°–99° James & I put in good part of morning with colts. Taught all four of them to get in & out of trailer, etc. . . .

[*As soon as a colt is weaned and halter broken, it should be trained to load. The time and patience spent pays off later, because trying to force a frightened horse into a trailer can be very dangerous. See Jane Montague Vay, "Your Horse Will Load Himself,"* Cattleman *62, no. 4 (September, 1975): 58, 92, 94.*]

OCTOBER

Fri 1: 44°–78° . . . Took them [*Watt Reynolds & Bill Collins*] to Bend to see loaded pecan tree. . . .

NOVEMBER

Fri 5: 51°–72° . . . Got ready & off for Ft. Worth about 3:15 (without my little bag). Got on OK without it however. Lucile, Sally, Juddy & I had dinner with Joe & Mom & the Reynolds delegation. Then Watt & Dade took us to Assembly which was a mighty pretty party. Had visit with lots of old friends & a fine time.

Mon 8: 52°–65° Dark, mild morning. Has rained around 3 in near Abilene but none here yet as of 9:30.

Mon 29: 28°–65° First morning with freeze here at Lambshead. . . .

1966

[Despite the efforts of breed associations to increase production through genetic improvement of purebred herds, the cost-price squeeze encouraged many ranchers to use crossbreeding. Increased weight from hybrid vigor meant extra dollars. Traditional cow-calf operators like Watt, however, adopted a wait-and-see attitude.]

FEBRUARY

Tue 1: 22°–35° [*in Fort Worth for the Southwestern Exposition and Fat Stock Show*] Cold morning. Got on my coveralls (which kept me warm all day) and we got down to barn before noon (Clarkes & I) Tone early and worked with heifers & visited until judging time. AV Champion 20—Reserve 10—League Ranch Champion 10—Reserve 20. They sold well. 20 years at $210; 10 2's at $280; & 10 at $265. We sent 4 2's (averaged 841.62 at 24.90) & 3 yrs (averaged 451.80 at 25.10) to Farmer Kutch which did pretty well. Watt Reynolds & I watched rodeo from back stage [*the world's first indoor rodeo, the Fort Worth Stock Show Rodeo, started in 1918*]. Lucile had all family [*for Watt's birthday dinner*]. Six of us, Louise, 4 Blantons, John, Judy, Juddy, Tone & Clarkes. 17 total.

Wed 9: 48°–69° [*back at Lambshead Ranch.*] Mild morning with about .03 on top of the .23 yesterday afternoon. Took a rest & read most of morning. After lunch lay in sun on south side of house a couple hours trying to prevent my cold from getting bad or maybe getting me down. . . .

MARCH

Wed 30: 31°–79° Another bright, beautiful morning. Went over & checked on river which has been flushed up some 18 in or 2 ft. Did some phoning to Arab breeders & found that they ask high prices for fillies. We bred the Cutneck Blue mare (Annabelle). Bert Field, Mr. Morgan & son [*cattle buyers*] got here before 5. . . .

Thur 31: 41°–90° We left about 7, about 30 min behind Carrol & saw over half the heifers in Left Hand, but not as many as I had hoped for. They looked nice . . . Sold 200 of the heifers to Bert at $225 to deliver May 10. . . .

APRIL

Sun 3: 57°–73° Norther on. . . .

Mon 4: 45°–74° Norther has taken a fresh hold & is chilly. . . .

Sat 23: 56°–61° A day of big rain which lasted off and on all day & at times hard. Creek ran bold & thru & went around wrong end of dam on Lambshead as we lacked about 2 days getting the job done . . . We had a total of 3.62 for day by 4 P.M. after which it didn't rain any more. . . .

Thur 28: 54°–62° . . . we got off for Okla City about 12:40 [*for the opening of the National Cowboy Hall of Fame, of which Watt was a trustee*] . . . We had nice drive up. To cocktail party & dinner for Harry Jackson [*well-known Western artist, whose retrospective was the first one-man show at the newly opened facility*] . . . then to Cowboy Hall of Fame for showing of his art. Saw a bunch of friends & had good time.

MAY

Sun 1: 44°–64° Got up early & off about 6:30 . . . to 11:05 plane for Chicago. Margot & Allan met me . . . took me by hotel & I checked in then they took me to see their children & grandchildren . . . to Saddle & Cycle Club for a good supper. Margot & Allan dropped me at hotel & I had a visit with a lot of the beef folks—after that dinner.

Mon 2: 49°–67° To beef symposium which went on from just after 8 until after 4 and was very interesting They fed the whole group (about 150) a good lunch on the same floor. Had visit with Bill Adams and

Watt Matthews. A very dapper gentleman!
Courtesy Watt R. Matthews

others in bar then to our board dinner meeting [*AHA*] at 6. It lasted until about 12:15 at which time I went on to bed instead of going for coffee, etc. with a bunch of them.

Tue 3: 44°–75° Got up early (about 6:30) packed up & out to airport where I ate breakfast & phoned Margot before taking 9:10 plane for Dallas. Got there about 10:20. . . .

[*Watt attended the American Beef Industry Symposium, jointly sponsored by the American Hereford Association, the American Polled Hereford Association, the American Angus Association, and the American Shorthorn Association. Its purpose was to determine what was required in beef cattle to meet the present and future needs of the beef industry. The symposium was hailed as a unique "meeting of minds," because, historically, individual breed associations had gone their separate ways. The American Hereford Association board of directors also met at this time. See "Much in Agreement at Beef Symposium,"* American Hereford Journal *57, no. 2 (May 15, 1966): 16–17, 62.*]

Wed 4: 43°–78° Got diary, etc up to date. Cleaned up around desk a little but have a lot more to do. . . .

JUNE

Tue 21: 66°–87° . . . Carrol, Ralph, Richard & I went over to Bartholomew [*crossing*] & winched Fred Foreman's car out of river which was up about 2-1/2 ft (almost up to lights). Mighty lucky not to have washed Fred over when he waded out the shape he is in. . . .

JULY

Sat 2: 68°–100° Victor & I helped Ralph hunt the mares & colts. Not many over to ride. Visited with girls & rested on floor in Susette's room. Crowd all here for lunch. Bovine, Jack, Chauncy, Burns (who with Betty got here at noon) took Craig & Ethel's car to town. By Rodgers & Mules. Got flowers for Lucile which delayed us. All at Bend for fine birthday dinner & party. Total 42. . . .

Mon 4: 67°–98° Big exodus took place from fairly early until 1:25 at which time Jack & children, except Frances got off for Galveston. Got down to me. . . .

Mon 18: 74°–102° Got off fairly early. Matt, Graham, Bob Green, & I left Albany about 8 for 9 A.M. water hearing at Sands Motel. John Matthews joined us later. I don't believe we have any thing to worry about a lake on us in the foreseeable future. . . .

[*The Texas Water Development Board proposed a lake at Reynolds Bend on the Clear Fork of the Brazos. Watt protested, pointing out that damming the river at this point would create only a shallow lake with evaporation problems but would destroy valuable ranch land and historic houses. A site in the hills upstream could produce a narrower and deeper lake. The plan finally was abandoned because the river contained too many chlorides and sulfates to be suitable for city drinking water. See "Letter From by Matthews Blanton to the Texas Water Development Board," August 10, 1966; and "From the Water Plant War at Reynolds Bend,"* Abilene Reporter-News, *August 6, 1966, p. 4A.*]

AUGUST

Thur 4: 61°–96° Up early & off to Ft Worth 5:20. JD took me to 9:35 plane for KC . . . Bill & Dorothy Adams drove up behind my cab & I had lunch with them. Bill & I to meeting at 1 [*AHA board of directors*]. . . .

Fri 5: 61°–98° We met again at 8 then the Beechwood hearing started at 10. There were a total of 21 in the room inc 5 lawyers, a reporter & Dr. Stormonta [*from the University of California, Davis*]. After changing to a 5:30 plane I had to leave before our deliberations were quite over but had our minds made up. . . .

[*This hearing involved denial of registry to Beechwood Acres Ranch, Joplin, Missouri, and Circle M Ranch, Senatobia, Mississippi, for a bull whose blood type was incompatible with that of his alleged sire. The bull in question was sired by artificial insemination. See "AHA's Annual Meeting a Lengthy One,"* American Hereford Journal *57, no. 13 (November 1, 1966): 52, 168, 170–71.*]

SEPTEMBER

Wed 7: 63°–88° Another beautiful hazy fall-like morning with big dew. . . .

NOVEMBER

Tue 15: 41°–79° . . . Met Joe & Louise at Ft. Griffin . . . on to 6666 [*Ranch*] for lunch & the horse sale which was quite a show. From 1200 to 1500 people there. . . .

Wed 30: 31°–53° Fred Foreman was in cookshack when I got here (fairly late). He had brought the big Christmas cake plus one with no sugar, butter or shortening which he had made. . . .

DECEMBER

Thur 15: 30° [*low*] . . . Palo Casey out before lunch and had a conference & left right after lunch. I met him & Matt in Joe's office & everything in regard to division is about agreed on. . . .

[*Ethel Casey was separating her portion of the ranch from the main holdings.*]

Sun 18: Ranch full of hunters. . . .

[*Hunting is a profitable sideline for ranchers. By 1966, the better leases in Texas generated as much as two dollars per acre. Therefore, proper wildlife management had become as important as proper management of livestock. See Doug Perkins, "There's Gold in Those Hunting Leases,"* Cattleman *64, no. 2 (July, 1977): 42–44, 82–86.*]

Wed 21: Jean out & put in most of day cleaning my room which revolutionized it & I do appreciate having it clean for a change.

[*At the end of the year, Watt wrote: "Had a total of 27.04 [*inches of rain*] for year which made for a fine one & the 10th better than average year in a row even though one or two might not have quite had normal rain fall. . . . by the law of averages we are liable to be headed for a drought."*]

1967

[Many of the oldest and most prominent families in Texas are associated with ranching. Their ancestors depended upon courage, self-reliance, and fortitude to solve the problems of an earlier, simpler time. The colorful story of these rugged individualists is very appealing in our complex modern world.]

JANUARY

Tue 3: 23°–50° . . . Worked on diary all morning. Birthdays & summing up weather for each month of 1966. . . .

[Watt kept track of the birthdays of family and friends simply by writing the person's name in the blank space above each day's entry. This was a reminder to call them on that day.]

MARCH

Mon 13: 61°–94° . . . I went to Cattleman Committee meeting at 11 A.M [*at annual meeting of Texas and Southwestern Cattle Raisers Association*]. Out for late lunch which Joe, Juddy, Watt & I had together. To Director's meeting at 2, then at 4 P.M. to conference on minimum law which went on until about 5:30 & confused everyone. . . .

Tue 14: 59°–90° Juddy took us to hotel & meeting where we heard Gov Connally, Bob Poage, & others make some good talks . . . Then Jim took us to Med School (Baylor) where they were putting a valve in a calf's heart. . . .

[Gov. John Connally proposed establishing an Agricultural Development

Board to promote the use and consumption of Texas agricultural products, much as industry promotes its products. W. R. (Bob) Poage, chair of the Committee on Agriculture, U.S. House of Representatives, stressed the need to make complaining consumers understand that the nation's food supply could be endangered if low returns to farmers and ranchers forced them out of business. See "Governor Connally Cites Need for Agricultural Mobilization" and "Poage Fears Trouble from Low Farm Prices," Cattleman 53, *no. 11 (April, 1967): 32–33.*]

Thur 16: 35°–70° [*back at Lambshead Ranch.*] Worked with mail, diary, etc. all morning.

Fri 31: 62°–79° Some sign of rain & barometer still a little low. The truck got loaded & away from here early then picked up more horses at PW. I picked up Rodgers & Balls & we were off at about 7:35. Truck & trailers just ahead of us. We got down there by 11. After lunch we went out to the LBJ & unloaded horses & gear & practiced until 5 or after. My team didn't do well. We kept the horses at rodeo grounds in Stonewall. We all had supper together at Andy's Diner & had a nice time. A total of 68. Six of us hosts.

APRIL

Sat 1: 64°–84° Breakfast across street from Sunday House on Fandangle Assoc . . . The horse folks went to Stonewall & loaded horses about 12 & on to ranch & got to getting set up. Elizabeth Green & I went up & mingled with crowd awhile before show time. Met the Pres & Mrs. Johnson & saw several people I knew. Show went off O.K. We got loaded up & left Fredricksburg just after 6. Rodgers & I at Albany about 9:20.

[*The* Fandangle Sampler, *a shorter version of the* Fort Griffin Fandangle, *was presented at the Texas White House for President and Mrs. Lyndon B. Johnson, who were entertaining a group of Latin American ambassadors and U.S. officials.*]

Fri 14: 50°–84° Still pretty windy but dust has cleared. It will jerk what little moisture we got right out . . . Joe & Louise out late & we went up & checked on No. 16 well which was almost down to Swastika. Lucile & JD had got in when we got back.

MAY

Mon 15: 44°–77° . . . Carrol & Victor feeding heifers hay & cubes. . . .

Thur 18: 51°–94° We were after the heifers as soon as we could see. Hauled horses to back of Road before day light. Had them in pen before seven & weighed by 7:30. Average gross 821#. Trucks due at 8 A.M., but on account of Fed Vet they had to do a lot more cleaning of them before spraying them & didn't get here until about 2:35. We got them away with 250 heifers about 6. . . .

Sat 20: 56°–72° . . . Worked on my tally book & got it up to date. . . .

JUNE

Thur 8: 69°–95° . . . We got a fair start to round Left Hand & did pretty well considering how mean they were to round. We sprayed 141 cows, 138 calves, & 3 bulls back. Brought 3 cows & calves to Horse Pasture & 6 cows & calves to Weigh Out. One cow (sore eye) jumped out of pen into MK & her big steer calf ran thru fence into Stone Ranch. . . .

Fri 9: 69°–94° We rounded GT & the heifers worked mean & we really had to ride straight up to hold on to them.

AUGUST

Sun 13: 53°–90° Chilly morning. Slept cold. My thermo 54°.

Thur 31: 72°–78° Norther blew in before 5 A.M. which is a reminder that it is not long before the chilly winds will be blowing & unless we go to getting rain we are going to get caught in hard shape.

SEPTEMBER

Tue 5: 63°–74° . . . Out late. Met movie bunch coming back from Bend. They think they got some good shots. . . .

Wed 6: 64°–75° They were off for PW with horses by 6:30. I went in later & got there in time for the 1st shot around 7:30. Stayed until they were done . . . Had visit with Joe & Matt & came back & watched them work on the scene with a calf hung in a bush. After lunch they continued with that project while Dave, Weaver, Frank, Richard & Jones & I worked at starting chuck wagon scene at mouth of Paint Creek. To Ft. Griffin for some later shots.

Thur 7: 62°–78° Crowd for early breakfast. Left about 6 to get to mouth of Paint to set up chuck wagon scene. There were a total of 25 around including our bunch. Roy Matthews came out & was the cook. They were pleased with the set up. Lori & I came to cookshack about 11 & John & I fried up a bunch of fish for lunch which they seemed to like. They worked on Longhorns in afternoon & did small campfire scene late. . . .

[*Marlboro advertisements were filmed on Lambshead Ranch, and Watt's men were paid well for their performances. A cousin, Roy Matthews, was paid ten thousand dollars for his part as the cook. Watt allowed the cigarette company to film on his property, but he was opposed to smoking and did not appear in any of the ads.*]

Fri 8: 59°–84° Went in by 10. Went to Motel & saw Dave & some of the boys. Dave gave me money to give our boys. They were leaving about 11. . . .

Wed 13: 63°--84° Lucile & I cut some thistles for Houston folks to take. They got off before 9. . . .

[*Watt was referring to the eryngo (*Eryngium leavenworthii*), which is not a true thistle. This spiny perennial grows one to three feet high in dense masses throughout Central Texas. In September, the gray-green foliage takes on a vivid purple hue which is popular in dried arrangements. See Campbell Loughmiller and Lynn Loughmiller,* Texas Wildflowers, *231.*]

OCTOBER

Sun 1: 58°–86° Beautiful morning which we have been having a bunch of & country mighty pretty except for low tanks. . . .

Fri 20: 47°–84° Boys rounded Left Hand. Were late getting into Weigh Out pens, but had made a good round . . . We had a regular Roman holiday getting the big (ton) steer out of mule cattle guard. Chuck had all kinds of heavy equip there by soon after 8 & it took nearly 2 hrs. . . .

NOVEMBER

Tue 7: 39°–59° Got to raining in Albany about 4 A.M. but still none here. They had a total of .18. Such as this the last few years accounts for the hard shape we are getting in. Never did rain here. . . .

DECEMBER

Fri 15: 29°–30° Inch & half or more of ice, sleet & snow on ground this morning after a hard night on cattle. Melted up 1.89 of moisture which will do a lot for the vegetation if it can go in ground before a lot of it evaporates. Stayed around cookshack all day . . . Carrol took Charlene & kids in & brought Jean & a load of mail & packages out. She got tree ready & it looks pretty. . . .

Sat 16: 28°–32° Clifford Teinert came out last night & had the pig on early . . . Total of 42 for the party which was one of the best yet in spite of weather & elec. going off at 9:15.

1968

[*Ranchers were weary of the protests and riots that raged through the nation. They felt discriminated against because of adverse publicity about profiteering and affluence. Rather than expecting others to meet their demands, however, they reacted by trying to satisfy consumers. They increased efficiency through better breeding, improved ranges, and reduced labor needs.*]

JANUARY

Sat 20: 39°–52° Rained slowly all night for a total of 4.24 for spell. An all time high for Jan. Leonard drove around & checked a few tanks, read meters. There has been a lot of tank water put out not to mention running all the creeks & branches. I feel sure Lambshead has run thru. We had 4.35 by late afternoon. . . .

FEBRUARY

Mon 5: 35°–58° . . . was 2:15 when we got started branding. We branded 153 calves (16 keeper heifers, 65 dehorned heifers, and 72 steers). They had as much if not the most hair of any calves I have ever branded, I believe. . . .

Fri 23: 22°–37° Still about 15 inches of snow with us & according to forecast we may have it for a while longer. Didn't snow any more & sun got to breaking out now and then and to thawing. Partially clean by sundown & the snow mostly gone. The game department brought us 15 (9 does & 6 bucks) Mule deer from Kent. . . . Took them to

Stoneranch and turned them loose. We hope they will locate in Left Hand & Right Hand, but no telling what they will do. . . .

MARCH

Mon 18: 55°–66° Mild, cloudy morning. Grass should have grown all night. . . .

Tue 26: 52°–75° Got up & took Watt Reynolds, Dean Krakel [*director of National Cowboy Hall of Fame*] & Wilson Elmore to 7:30 breakfast [*at Texas and Southwestern Cattle Raisers Association meeting in San Antonio*]. Afterwards Dean & I had a visit with Helen Campbell & Mrs. Furd Halsell. Then to meeting which was a big crowd. Ben Carpenter made a wonderful talk. Went to Animal Health Committee meeting at 2 P.M. Big crowd there on Bangs (continuation of panel from morning session). . . .

[*Traditionally, the president's report at the Texas and Southwestern Cattle Raisers Association annual meeting consists of his view of the cattle industry and administrative activities of the preceding year. Ben Carpenter, however, deviated from this pattern by directing his remarks to the social and economic changes of the decade. His plea for a return to the standards and mores of earlier generations reflects the concern many Americans were feeling about the upheaval of the 1960s. Recognizing the scientific and technological benefits that people enjoyed, he blamed excessive government spending for the inflation that caused housewives to demonstrate at the grocery stores. See "Address by Ben H. Carpenter, President, Texas and Southwestern Cattle Raisers Association at Its Annual Membership Meeting, March 26, 1968,"* Cattleman *54, no. 12 (May, 1968): 28–29, 90, 92–94, 96, 98.*]

Wed 27: 57°–76° . . . To meeting Cow-Calf panel. Was good. Gov Connally made a fine talk. Went to directors luncheon. . . .

Thur 28: 58°–70° . . . turkeys struting & grass rising & it looks like spring is finally really here. . . .

Fri 29: 56°–76° . . . The last two mornings have been warm & mild. Grass growing weather . . .

Sun 31: 58°–76° . . . Joe & Louise here. They went in soon after. We rested a little then took trip to Davis & MO, checked cable, etc & back to the Joe B's for supper. Heard Johnson take himself out of race.

[*Dismayed by his growing unpopularity due to the Vietnam War, President Lyndon B. Johnson announced that he would not seek or accept his party's nomination for another term.*]

MAY

Sun 5: 51°–75°. . . . To church. The preacher was a cute little girl & she did a good job. . . .

Mon 27: 56°–79° Cool morning. Went in & met Louise at 9:45 & she took me to Hardin-Simmons University Commencement which was nice. Nancy Green got a B.A. & Bob Nail a Dr. of Human Sciences. We went to lunch in Petroleum Club with Bob Green family. . . .

JUNE

Sat 8: 65°–88° We rounded the heifer years in WO & not having been handled since being weaned they were pretty bronco & several ran off. We also missed several in the bad brush. We put 272 in Weigh Out & 1 in WO (short about 33). . . .

Thur 27: 55°–90° . . . Richard & Victor got up the buffaloes . . . We put the big bull & cow with youngest calf on truck, but the bull wrecked the rack & he & calf got out. When put back in pen he wrecked it so we only used cow & calf. It was a pretty float . . . Bob, Alice, & I met Gov & Mrs. Connally & party. They held the parade up about 30 min. Show went off well in 2 hrs & 3 or 4 min. Full house.

[*Governor and Mrs. John Connally attended the Fandangle Parade and the performance in Albany.*]

JULY

Tue 2: 64°–84° . . . Picked up Alice & we were off for Ft. Worth soon after 4:30. By for a visit with Browns before going to Harry Jackson & Poqzeba show at Carter Museum which was nice. . . .

[*The Jacksons came out to Lambshead for a visit.*]

Preparing for the Fandangle parade. In stagecoach (left to right)*: Bob Owen, Reilly Nail, Joe Blanton; leaning on stagecoach* (left to right): *Bob Nail, Matt Blanton, Bill Blanton; on horses: Tom Blanton* (left), *Watt Matthews. All were Princeton graduates. Courtesy Watt R. Matthews*

Thur 11: 66°–91° . . . Checked on the haying. Jack has baled over 4800 & they were going to have around 4000 in barn by night. . . .

NOVEMBER

Mon 11: 30°–55° . . . Got the sad news of Bob Nail's death [*of a heart attack*] before supper which is a terrible jolt to Albany & the whole community & a sad, sad deal.

Tue 12: 27°–71° Another cold morning. . . . Got to Alice's soon after 1 or 1:30. Had a visit with them then took Alice by funeral home & to Nail's where I put in the rest of the day. . . .

Wed 13: 45°–78° . . . Went to the church by 1 & people already gathering. They filled educational bldg & about 100 outside I understand. George Walker did a fine service. . . .

Wed 27: 37°–43° Still misting & we have had 2.21 so far. A great Nov rain. Our total finally got up to 2.84 and some of the gauges 3 or more. For a single Nov rain I am sure this has been one of the biggest if not the biggest ever recorded. It is a great thing for the country & changes the prospects for winter. . . .

DECEMBER

Sat 14: 18°–56° We went to the D. Burns for a while before they took us to breakfast at a motel. Mrs. Murry Chappell, Miss Snyder, & Carl Anderson there also for a total of 12. Currie took me to Tech & showed me the collection of old ranch records, those of L H Hill, Texas books, etc. He then showed me the Library which is something. . . .

[*Watt was in Lubbock to attend a planning session to establish the Ranching Heritage Center that now is located on the Texas Tech University campus. Before the meeting, he and Dr. William Curry Holden visited the Southwest Collection, a history research center on the campus, and the library. The papers of Louis Hamilton Hill, an Albany rancher, are housed in the Southwest Collection.*]

Tue 24: 18°–67° . . . No one here which is unusual for Christmas Eve.

1969

[The decade of the 1960s was a profitable one for the cattle industry. One of the outstanding food stories of the twentieth century was the growing demand for beef; during the 1960s, per capita consumption of beef increased by 30 percent. Cattlemen responded with increased production through feed lot finishing of younger animals, and research brought disease better under control. Cattlemen had been waiting for years to share in the nation's growing prosperity.]

JANUARY

Fri 10: 24°–40° . . . The Arkansas (Hope) Sheriff, DA & another man came out to hunt. They brought me a gallon of moonshine. . . .

MARCH

Thur 27: 39°–73° . . . We all less John plus Lucile went to Ft Griffin and watched the crew uncovering ruins. . . .

APRIL

Thur 17: 50°–65° Dry norther on and on cold side. . . .

Wed 30: 45°–80° . . . to the Bob Green's at 6:30. Bob showing us his irrigation project which is quite a deal. There were about 45 at the party including a lot from Abilene.

MAY

Tue 13: 57°–81° Boys including Evan, Antonio & Pete Jones off about 7:15 to round WO. They made a good round. I only knew of 2 back but boys looked out pasture. Never did find them. We had a long hard day. Tipped & sprayed 299 (short 3), bled 272 for bangs & all tested OK for which I was thankful. Sprayed 15 bulls. Pete & I went back after he finished testing & turned them out at dusk. Back ate a snack & Pete left & I went to bed. I really hate to have to punish & up set those heifers to such an extent.

Fri 16: 61°–75° . . . Terry Moberly out & I hired him to start to work Monday & he will live over there after he marrys June 20th. . . .

Thur 22: 60°–88° Another fine morning with a lot of dew. Boys rounded Lambshead as the river stays pretty deep. Sprayed 144 cows (1 crip known back). 134 calves & 7 bulls back. Took 7 cows & calves to Valley & 3 cows & 13 calves to VH. They looked mighty fine & calves are beginning to get some bloom on. . . .

JULY

Sun 20: 72°–103° . . . watched moon walk. . . .

[*On July 20, 1969, two American astronauts made their historic landing on the moon. As he made the first human footprint on the moon, Neil A. Armstrong, the civilian commander, declared, "That's one small step for man, one giant leap for mankind." A hundred years earlier, Watt's parents had left footprints on another frontier—the ranching frontier in northwestern Texas. Imagine what a giant leap it must have been for Watt to span the distance from the horse-and-buggy days to the space age. See "Men Walk on Moon,"* New York Times, *July 21, 1969, p. 1.*]

AUGUST

Fri 22: 71°–104° Frank & John took our fire rig to Green's & fought that fire until about 4 when they got it under control after burning probably 1000 or 1200 acres. I had left a little ahead of them. They then went to one on Jim Nail (started by lightening?) that probably burned 200 acres. Rusty brought his rig to it & Weaver & Terry also went. I was headed there but they got it out. I came on up to Clifford's camp at Burkett Bend. It rained .30 at Frank's road. Lambshead .04.

SEPTEMBER

Wed 3: 69°–87° Worked around desk. Clifton Caldwell & Ronald Thomason [*a well-known Texas artist*] got here for a late lunch. . . .
[*Tom Blanton died September 23.*]

OCTOBER

Sat 11: 69°–78° Evan cut on broom weeds in Hayford. . . .
[*Dry broom weeds are a problem during grass fires because they ignite quickly, break away from their roots, and travel with the wind, spreading fire in front of the main blaze. Watt Matthews, interview by Janet Neugebauer, September 19, 1991.*]

Wed 15: 42°–81° Went to Caldwell's at 9 for a brush control tour which was good. . . .

NOVEMBER

Fri 14: 39°–49° Linda brought her Texas history class (21) down in a bus. We met them at river to see them across then I made round of houses—Hayford, Stone Ranch, etc., with them. Girls had hot chocolate & cookies here for them to have with their sack lunches. They went back to Throckmorton by Putnam's. . . .

DECEMBER

Thur 18: 47°–65° Another mild morning. Went to Dr. Hardwick at 10:30. He gave me a good report. Did some shopping for Christmas party at Nail's which took considerable time. . . .
Tue 23: 37°–67° . . . Fixed up bonus checks for men & wives. . . .
Fri 26: 31°–66° Clear freezing morning & should be a nice day. Didn't get off to Throckmorton until after 12. The riders & hunters had all gone. Had a nice lunch with Zada, Eleanor & Ivy. We then went to Bishop Radio Store & I got a portable Jap TV. . . .
Wed 31: 23°–36° . . . We took a smoked turkey, sliced ham & beef steak, etc to old kitchen & snacked up there & saw the new year in with a jolly party. The Bill Rogers got in by 8 P.M. Had fires going in old house [*the B. W. Reynolds house at the Bend*] except old fireplace.

1970

[*Texas cattlemen remember two events from 1970. One was a harbinger of things to come, the other a recognition of leadership. For the first time, the grand-champion steer at the Southwestern Exposition and Fat Stock Show was a Hereford-Angus cross. At the annual meeting of the National Livestock and Meat Board, Dolph Briscoe, Jr., was elected chair of the board. Briscoe represented the Texas and Southwestern Cattle Raisers Association.*]

JANUARY

Fri 2: 34–46° . . . Got my deer and turkey count up to date. 64 bucks, 63 does and 65 turkeys killed during season. . . .

Tue 13: 32–38°. . . . (After supper) did some reading in book (*Ranch on the Ruidoso*) then some phoning.

[Ranch on the Ruidoso *is Wilbur Coe's account of settling his family in Lincoln County, New Mexico, and establishing a ranch there. Coe had been a lawman in Shackelford County before moving to New Mexico.*]

Thur 22: 28–62°. Visited with John P and C. We took a short late round. Got back in time for nearly all of Nixon's talk. A S Jackson got here in time for a late lunch with us.

Sat 24: 26–79°. Got a few odds and ends done and got off (to Washington D.C.). We were off for Love Field about 8:35. The 12:50 plane got off about 1:30. John Burns and RB [*nephews*] and Nancy [*RB's wife*] met us at Dulles airport. RB and Howard Wallace [*RB's brother-*

in-law] brought me to hotel (Shorem). University Club for dinner. [*Watt and Joe attended the 73rd annual convention of the American National Cattleman's Association in Washington, D.C. The Shoreham Hotel was convention headquarters for more than thirteen hundred cattlemen, who packed the meeting rooms to hear speeches by administration leaders, congressmen, and beef industry leaders. Members approved proposals to: launch a comprehensive program to increase consumer awareness of the value, quality, and uses of meat; pursue ways to increase the export of American beef and beef products, as a means of improving the U.S. balance of payments; establish an office in Washington, D.C., in addition to the Denver headquarters; and increase public understanding of the role the $20 billion cattle industry played in the American economy. See "It Was a Capitol Convention,"* American Beef Producer *51, no. 10 (March, 1970): 10–12.*]

Sun 25: 52–72°. Joe, John and I to meeting at 1:00. Stayed thru all of it.

Mon 26: 31–74°. Chris Schenkel [*a national sportscaster and a Hereford breeder*], Eliz. Green [*of Albany*], Bob Day [*director of public relations, AHA*] and I had a visit in bar across and down street. Later Joe B, Greens and I sat together at President's luncheon where Chris was speaker. We later made a trip to RB's office which is nice. He joined us later for Texas Congressional reception which was pretty to me. Afterward Joe B, Greens and I went to Congressional dinner Vice Pres Agnew was speaker. RB was hot. Greens and I to Rotunda.

Tue 27: 33–78°. Went with Eliz and Birdwells [*Albany folks*] on White House tour which enjoyed. Joe, Greens, Bob Britt and I called on John Burns in his office then to RB office. . . . All went to RB for dinner. Total of 13 adults with Wallaces.

Wed 28: 41–80°. Packed up and checked out. RB picked us up. To Dulles for flight. Got gun [*a hunting rifle*] on plane without any trouble. Nice flight Dallas. Stopped by for short visit with Lucile. Off to Albany 3:40. Took cleaning to shop and got mail.

Thur 29: 37–50°. Had stack of mail to go thru. Took good part of the morning. Did a bunch of phoning. RB called to see if I had fixed our new gun which I had not. Carrol and I fixed it after lunch.

FEBRUARY

Tue 24: 49–52°. Rain and mist continues which is great. Met Paul Swaffar at Joe's office about mid morning. Took him up to D [*the Davis Ranch, which the Matthews leased to run AV cattle; Watt referred to them as D cattle*] and Rusty and Buddy led us around in South pasture calling up D heifers. We finally saw 62 head of them. Back to town for lunch and fixed up a contract for the bred D heifers at 225 and the open AV & D heifers at 200 with 10% out of both bunches. Paul and Mrs. Freed in Albany when we got back. I brought them out here about 3. After Paul [*Swaffar*] had left. Showed them about 1/2 the years in Road and corral called up about 80 those in Valley. Really got to moving around and kept it up until bedtime. A total of .15 hear at Lambshead & country mighty muddy.

MARCH

Mon 16: 45–60°. [*In Corpus Christi for Texas and Southwestern Cattle Raisers Association annual meeting.*] Watt [*Reynolds*] & I had breakfast with Bill Green & Birdwell. I went to Agriculture Research Committee meeting at 9 AM and it was interesting. (After lunch) to Director's meeting at 2 which was a short one. (Evening) to Western Round party at Exposition Hall which was fun.

Tue 17: 32–58°. (After breakfast) To meeting for a while. Went with Elizabeth Green to rent a car for trip to King Ranch . . . got with Val Lehman in his car [*wildlife conservationist at King Ranch*] & he took us to big house for coffee and showed us it then on C. Very interesting—short tour. (Flew home.)

APRIL

Fri 3: 36–75°. . . . Off to Abilene & West Texas Historical Association dinner with Louise. A man talked for 45 min and bored everybody to death. . . .

Mon 13: 44–68° Worked on lists. Did some phoning. Census takers here at noon and we gave them a total of 14 houses 8 of which are empty. . . .

Mon 20: 54°–81°. Clear mild breezy morning. Boys rounded Weigh Out

& Carrol hauled the buffaloes and longhorns to Bend. The buffaloes gave some trouble and 8 got over in Gentry (adjoining ranch). They got 6 back at Hayford. . . .

Wed 22: 58°–89°. Cloudy & mild. The buffaloes showed up in Cem Trap [*enclosure around the family cemetery*] for which I am thankful. They failed to find the dun longhorn. . . .

Thur 23: 66°–83°. . . . Found 3 buffaloes in the Davis. They came back on us in the afternoon & I hope will stay. . . .

JUNE

Fri 26: 70°–104°. People leaving & coming a good part of day which kept up plenty of confusion & no time to rest . . . Didn't get to Green's until about 6:30. Lady Bird had been there a few minutes. . . .

[*Watt brought Lady Bird Johnson to Lambshead for a tour of the ranch before they attended the* Fandangle *performance in Albany.*]

AUGUST

Fri 14: 70°–100°. Weaver worked the little mules. Jim rode one of the young horses & helped Sally & her girls get saddled up. Jack, John & I took a round checking on horses, Clyde, etc. . . . After lunch we had a nice shower. Lambshead 1.15, Hayford a trace, Overton 3, Ft Griffin 1.50 . . . Started a fire near bluff down Lambshead but rain put it out & a bunch of others in various places but didn't rain any on MO to put that one out & it burned a relatively lot of acres plus the hayshed at field.

Mon 17: 73–102° . . . Took Pick up to see MO calves & check burned country which think 2000 acres will catch. Back & a Fandangle Committee meeting about 7 P.M.

Wed 19: 73–100° Went to Bend and checked on houses, etc. Boys left early to go to fire on Green's South ranch that started about 3:30 and finally burned 2000 or more acres probably. Then about quitting time they called about one on LG Davis & Ackers & they broke down on way but it was out by then. . . .

Fri 21: 69–92°. We had a wonderful rain during night. Lambshead 1.40 (1.79 for yesterday & last night). . . . 5.56 total with the 3 in. Fri & .19

on Wednesday MO 1.60, YL 1.81, Brushy 3.1. Leonard & I took an early round checking on rain.

SEPTEMBER

Mon 21: 67–86° River ran thru ranch. About 2' rise from up Anson & Rotan way. Juddy with me to Farm, Hayford & Bend to read meters & check on mowing. . . . I went to Hospital meeting at 1. Only lasted about 20 min for shortest yet.

OCTOBER

Fri 2: 58–87°. Put in most of morning getting organized for trip to Lubbock. . . .

Sat 3: 58–88°. Up around 8. To museum . . . I was late getting up to meeting [*first annual membership meeting of the Ranching Heritage Center, Texas Tech University*] . . . Bob Green made a fine talk at dedication meeting later. Big turn out for lunch sampler which went off great . . .

[*Bob Green, an Albany rancher, paid tribute to the courage, industriousness, honesty, and humility that made ordinary people extraordinary during the free-range era. He commented that it was appropriate to have this museum on a university campus, where young people would be reminded of these qualities when they saw the restored buildings of pioneer ranching families. See Robert Green, "The Free Range Era of the Cattle Industry,"* West Texas Historical Association Year Book *46 (October, 1970): 204–10.*]

Tue 20: 41–80°. To Valley before daylight. The 178 years there were all hauled up here & weighed before 11:00. There were 4 in pen added to them for a total of 182 & a total delivery of 672. They averaged 710 which we were pleased with after the summer we had. . . . They handled fine & were a beautiful bunch of years.

Thur 22: 62–86°. John Matthews picked up Joe, Palo, RB, & me at White Flat strip at 10:30 & we were at Guthrie in 20 min. Jim Arnold took us to Pitchfork tour. Joe & I went from there to Hdqtr with Frank Chappell & Dub Waldrip. Visited with cowboys at wagon then ate lunch with the brush control boys. Several talks afterwards. John made a good one. Over at 3:15. Back to plane. . . .

Sun 25: 49–89°. Joe & Louise took us to turkey dinner at colored church which was good. A big crowd there.

NOVEMBER

Tue 3: 31–54°. First freezing morning here. Left fairly early for Throckmorton. Was the first to vote by fifteen minutes or so. . . .

Wed 4: 33–55°. Boys off to round Paint. Tried to meet Ike at Buzzard Peak but never did make connection. Got news of Carrol Putnam's death when I got back. Rushed over there [*adjoining ranch*] and helped put his body in ambulance. Margaret & Jay Miningham were the only ones there when I got there. To Buzzard Peak after lunch. 109 cows back to Paint, 1 cow known back, 4 cows to Road & 117 calves (including 2 unbranded) to Pen. Cleaned dust out of Bronco and tried to stop places where dust getting in. Bill Cougar helped me with part of it.

Sun 8: 48–77° I went to funeral home at 1. Funeral at 2 & Rodney Williams had a fine service [*Putnam's*]. Burial at river by John Larn lot (a beautiful spot. Our whole family there except Sallie).

Fri 20: 30–73°. Chilly morning (my thermo 28 degrees) after a blustery day yesterday. Boys looking out Left Hand. Frank helping Putnams. They got 5 calves out of Putnam's & 1 out of Left Hand. Off for San Antonio. Hertzog party.

Sat 21: 45–82°. We all had breakfast together (some of us dragging in a little late). We all went to the Hertzog program and stayed until noon break. We got off soon. Made stops in Boerne, Kerrville & Fredricksburg.

DECEMBER

Tue 15: 43–65°. Had a few sprinkles of rain before daylight. Valley .05; Lambshead .04. Soon cleared & got to getting hazy soon & by 5 P.M. we had a full fledged sandstorm that I believe was the worst since the fifties. We really haven't had a bad year since the drought broke in 1957. . . .

Sat 19: 35–44°. Terry knocked at 5 AM and told me about the Moore [*oil*] rig being on fire. (Two Halliburton men ate breakfast with all). . . .

Wed 23: 24–43°. Cold norther on. Tried to get Christmas checks ready for boys & due to hunters, visitors etc was all day getting it done. Joe out later & looked at heifers went by fire (where they had a big lot of equipment & later got it out). On to Bend & back for lunch.

Thur 31: 30–63°. They had a lot of hunters out. Harry Moore meant to leave before 4 A.M. but lights out & had to wait for daylight. Met Pick at Ft. Griffin & we went to Mrs. Bob Daws funeral at Woodson at 2:30. I didn't know anything about it until nearly noon but was real glad I went & I was an Honorary Pall Bearer and sat with the Pall Bearers. Jack & Betty Eleston got here about noon. He & Tom came in late with 4 or 5 quail.

1971

[Dry weather and poor pastures forced an unusually large number of cattle into feed lots; Texas, for the first time, became the nation's leading cattle feeding state. Watt sold as many animals as possible to protect the range. Knowing that cattle can be replaced easier than grass, he often said, "It doesn't do to abuse the land. You have to keep it in the best shape possible."]

JANUARY

Mon 4: 19°–31° Cold morning & norther continued all day. Put in day around cookshack & JOS [*one of the rooms in the headquarters compound*] working on mail, diary, birthday books, etc. Seemed mighty calm with the cookshack not full of hunters & company at breakfast & a good part of morning. . . .

Thur 21: 46°–63°. . . . Chuck [*Jacobs*] & I checked on acreage in 5 new leases to be drawn up around new [*oil*] production out here. . . .

FEBRUARY

Wed 17: 40°–80° We put out bulls all over except Long & Davis. They look well & I hate to put them off feed & on such slim pickings . . . to Historical Survey Com meeting in court house at 7:30. Home & to bed by 9:30.

[Because most bulls lose between two and three hundred pounds during the breeding season, many ranchers condition their animals with a high-protein supplement of cottonseed cake for about a month prior to the season. Successful breeders must be strong and vigorous but not too fat.

Fat can ruin fertility. Watt also was concerned because the grass was not as plentiful as it should be during the breeding season. See Fowler, Beef Production in the South, *372–75.*]

Thur 18: 43°–76° Carrol took 5 bulls (CK) to Long pasture. Average weight 1688. . . .

Fri 26: 50°–67° . . . Girls [*Lucile & Susette*] have worked all week polishing brass, copper, etc & getting the houses all ready for 117 women from the Ft Worth Woman's Club due here Monday. We branded the 118 calves in 46 minutes. Got in before 5 & had fairly early supper & early to bed.

MARCH

Mon 1: 37°–63° Boys rounded Stone Ranch. Sprayed & tipped 313 2 year heifers & there were 16 bulls, 4 of which had to be tipped in a fiz. . . .

[*The horns of young bulls were tipped to prevent damage to each other during territorial fights.*]

Wed 17: 37°–83° . . . Bad wind out of little E. of So. Got fire going on Sloan's & Caldwell's. Our outfit from here & Davis went. They didn't get home until 1 A.M. I drove Lorene, Betty & Jim Law out late with food & cakes. I got home around 10.

APRIL

Thur 1: 54°–57° A blustery norther on. Dudes [*visiting relatives*] didn't do but little riding except 3 little girls in late afternoon. They surged all day however with trips to town, Jackson tank, etc. . . .

[Surging *is Watt's word describing people who are always on the go.*]

Mon 12: 61°–90° Boys got in a total of about 441 steer years from Gober to Road. Due to not being in front of them they got to stringing out & running & some ran off which was all uncalled for & depressing. Wind blew hard all day stirring up a lot of dust which did not help matters any. . . .

Wed 28: 50°–88° . . . Went by Caldwell's and took Jeanette to the birthday luncheon for Dr. [*Rupert*] Richardson [*history professor at Hardin-Simmons University in Abilene, Texas, and a founding member of the West Texas Historical Association*]. We met Clifton & Shirley [*Caldwell*] there & they took J. home. . . .

Thur 29: 53°–84° . . . The south & west sides of this place look mighty sad & if we don't get some good rains we will have to loosen up more. . . .

MAY

Sat 8: 55°–83° Boys tied the calves. John drove the old bronco in & I brought him back around 1. He driving. Ordered a six passenger pickup & left the bronco to be sold. . . .

Thur 13: 43°–75° My thermometer about 36° & we had a little bit of frost. . . .

Tue 25: 53°–95° Ronnie Browning out & they cut [*gelded*] six colts (4 3 year olds & 2 2s), wormed 9 horses & cut 4 buffaloes. Carrol & Rusty took the wild buffalo cow to Abilene Zoo & got a nice bull calf which will be 1 year old in Oct. Dan Meyer (commodity broker) was here for lunch. . . .

JUNE

Thur 3: 71°–91° . . . Back to City Hall to meet with Social Security man & got lined up on S.S. . . . Got copies of my 1970 & J. A. Matthews Ranch Co. '70 income reports, copies of Matthews and Brittingham Co., old Poll Tax receipts & my birth certificate made after lunch & mailed to him. . . .

Thur 17: 69°–97° Thirteen riders [*visiting grand-nieces and grand-nephews*] got off after so long a time. Got a horse bogged in a tank & it is a wonder some one didn't get hurt. I am always thankful when they get back whole. . . .

Mon 21: 66°–89° . . . Got to Paul's Valley, Oklahoma at 11:35. Betty's house. Betty with us to hospital. Mighty sad to see Susette in such pitiful shape. We had a fine lunch at Betty's with her & Chauncey [*Susette's daughter and son-in-law*]. . . .

Tue 29: 67°–94° They (dudes inc) 13 total rounded Road & left 15 cows & 12 calves & took the balance 61 cows & calves to Stone Ranch. The kids with long hair & no hats are a pretty discouraging lot as prospects for future cow men. . . .

JULY

Mon 5: 69°–105° . . . I cleaned off my porch & I will have it ready to sleep on as the past two nights have been hot.

Sat 10: 67°–102° . . . To Nail ranch late for pool party. Had been going on since about one & was quite a splash.

Fri 16: 74°–105° River has stopped running. . . .

Sat 17: 36°–104° . . . I went over Gentry & it is a sad sight with the river not running. Covered with [*prickly*] pears & very little grass (bone dry). . . . I pulled a cow out of the mud in tank at Nail point. . . .

Tue 20: 64°–80° . . . I went on to west side & down river & country is mighty hard. It is hard to tell what to do. . . .

Wed 21: 66°–94° . . . Boys got horses together. Ronnie Browning, Wayne & grandson out & vaccinated a total of 105 horses & mules. A lot too many & we would have got rid of a bunch of them Sat if we had not been caught by the quaranteen. They will get the horses at the Davis Ranch & MO tomorrow. . . .

[*In late June, Venezuelan equine encephalomyelitis, known as VEE, crossed the Mexican border for the first time. Transmitted by mosquitoes, it affects the central nervous system of horses, mules, and donkeys, and causes an upper respiratory illness, with high fever, in humans. Secretary of Agriculture Clifford Hardin declared that a national emergency existed threatening the horse industry. On July 13, the Texas Animal Health Commission decreed a quarantine restricting to the premises all equine animals which had not been vaccinated with VEE TC-18, an experimental vaccine. USDA-paid veterinarians were assigned to vaccinate horses without charge to the owners. By the end of July, over three thousand Texas horses were dead or sick. Rodeos, horse shows, and other activities involving horses were canceled throughout the state. See "VEE Strikes Texas Horses,"* Cattleman *58, no. 3 (August, 1971): 22–23.*]

Sun 25: 60°–95° . . . We toured Okla City a little then off for Paul's Valley. I was very depressed there as Susette is mighty pitiful. Betty had a fine brunch. . . .

AUGUST

Mon 2: 60°–84° . . . Fred & Nancy Carpenter, the Caubles, Roy Eubanks, & Rodgers out for a late supper with us after a sing song. . . .
[*Fred Carpenter was the field representative for the Southwest Collection at Texas Tech University. Later he returned to interview Watt. In the interview, Watt traced the history of Lambshead Ranch and described the historic homes that have been restored on the ranch. See Watt R. Matthews, interview by Fred Carpenter, October 14, 1971, Oral History Files, Southwest Collection, Texas Tech University, Lubbock, Texas.*]

Thur 5: 62°–85° . . . A woman after labor statistics was here for lunch, but had to send her to McCulloughs [*Watt's bookkeepers*]. Got to A Ave [*an auction in Abilene, Texas*] about 2 just as our cows started to sell & they averaged 178 plus. Good for 13 yr old cows. . . .

Fri 6: 64°–85° . . . We had the best shower we have had since May. Drove up to Road tank where it stopped Clyde. Lambshead .69. . . .

Sun 15: 66°–87° Had slow rain from early morning on. We had a total of .31 for the day. Hayford 1.10, Road 1. That country thru there is going to improve a lot as there has been a shower for 4 days in a row for a total of about 2.50 inches. . . .

SEPTEMBER

Mon 6: 69°–99° . . . at Joe's office. Roy [*Matthews*] came by & told me Susette had died at 5 P.M. By his house then supper & visit with Ethel.

Wed 8: 68°–94° . . . Got organized to go to Paul's Valley. . . . Ann & Otis & Edna here by 2 P.M. & they, Sallie & I were off for Paul's Valley by 2:30. . . .

Thur 9: 66°–91° . . . To house before 10—in church by 10:45. Back by Motel from cemetery then to house soon after 12. Ann & Joe B flew back to Abilene with John, Judy, & Louise. Susan Brown took Ann's place with us & we left about 3. Came by Gainesville, Decatur, etc. Looked at Ft. Richardson, the court house, the old Waggoner house, the old oak tree at Graham, etc. Here just after sun down. Had rained in spots along. .03 here.

Wed 15: 64°–92° . . . Picked up Pick [*Gene Pickard, a local cattle buyer*] just after 9 & to MO to look at calves. He bought the steers at 38¢ [*average net weight was 483 pounds per head*]. . . .

OCTOBER

Mon 4: 59°–75° Golden glow beautiful & about at its peak. . . .
Mon 11: 49°–85° The Golden glow still profuse & beautiful. . . .

NOVEMBER

Mon 29: 30°–62° [*Watt sent four boxes of mistletoe home with Lucile, and she shipped it to her family.*]

DECEMBER

Mon 6: 31°–55°. Boys rounded in the bulls from Road . . . We cut out 20 to ship (average weight 1490). They are all fat & in fine shape. . . .

Tue 7: 29°–42° . . . Left soon after 9 to go to Abilene. By A Ave [*auction*] & saw about 10 of the AV bulls sell that left here about 8 . . . got check for bulls that sold high as the moon. Av $400 & 1 brought $500. . . .

[*December was warm and damp, with 2.18 inches of rain. Christmas was celebrated at Reynolds Bend with the traditional large gathering of family and friends. The day was a balmy 78°. Annual rainfall, 23.58 inches, was below normal, but it greatly relieved the droughty conditions that existed through July. Most of the tanks were still low and some pastures had not fully recovered, but Watt wrote at the end of the year: "Going into New Year in relatively good shape." The high humidity and warm weather that prevailed through the fall helped the range.*]

1972

[There was great disagreement about beef prices in 1972. American housewives complained that they were the highest since the early 1950s. Cattlemen responded that, during those twenty years, wages and ranching expenses had doubled. They also pointed out that an hour's wage in 1971 would buy 3.3 pounds of beef, compared to 1.7 pounds from an hour's wage in 1951.]

JANUARY

Tue 25: 23°–60° Ronnie & Fed Vet out checking on heifers & found they have some type of scabbies [*scabbies mites are very small parasites that cause mange*]. Fed. boy was going to take some mites to Austin for further study. It is bad luck & we are puzzled as to how it got in here. We haven't even bought any new bulls for around 4 years. . . .

MARCH

Fri 3: 31°–62° Boys off fairly early to round Tecumseh after which they rounded the Hitson. Don Boaze's brother (a vet) & Joe Underhill (an inspector) got over there with John White when he brought the lunch. They did a lot of scratching & came up with some live mites. They now say they will have to be dipped twice which is discouraging. We sprayed 87 cows, 77 calves, 7 bulls back in Tecumseh. Branded 77 calves (& 18 heifers, 22 dehorned heifers, 37 steers). Sprayed 67 steer years Hitson to NT. Back by Buzzard Peak where we are rushing to get vat ready. Five Mexes working. Left there after 5. . . .

Sat 4: 37°–60° . . . With a lot of help from inspectors, Bert & others, Evan, Terry, Rusty, Carlos, Louis, Louis Cos & I had vat ready to go right after lunch and got along fine with dipping & had a fine successful day. . . .

[*The next three months were spent dipping cattle. Scabbies must be reported and animals are quarantined until they are dipped twice, at ten- to fourteen-day intervals, in an insecticidal solution. Most cattlemen prefer to use a lime-sulfur solution to control the disease. A federal and a state veterinarian kept a close watch on the cattle at Lambshead Ranch throughout the year. See Ensminger,* Stockman's Handbook, *926–27, 958–59.*]

Fri 31: 32°–66° [*Good Friday*] Fair sized frost. My thermo 32°. Mesquites are out but I don't believe they are going to be hurt. In fact, I don't think any damage to speak of. . . .

APRIL

Wed 12: 64°–101° Boys rounded Tecumseh & looked out DC as they came thru. Dipped 87 cows; 72 calves & 5 bulls. Tecumseh to VH & 4 cows; 3 calves & DC to VH & 1 calf to Stone Ranch. May Cox, 4 Hungarians, Bob Day, Hop Dickenson, AHA & C. T. Barnes of Holstein Assoc got here about 2:15. Beth & J went on the tour with us. We saw a little game, turkey, deer & 1 coyote. Finally saw a lot of cows & calves. Rodgers & Teinerts out for supper (buffalo steaks which were good). Bill Cauble & Roy Eubanks here on way home from Bend.

Thur 13: 73°–101°. Boys off early to get heifers in. They were slow getting their cuts out after which we went to WT where boys had 60 that we got 54 more out of to make them 225. Max & Co. left before 1 P.M. for Love Field. Joe out & stayed until about 2. It was about 4 before they finished bleeding the heifers. . . .

[*A team of Hungarians was in the U.S. to purchase 425 commercial Hereford heifers and 20 registered Hereford bulls to strengthen their nation's beef herd. Lambshead Ranch furnished 225 of the heifers, which were flown aboard Trans World Airlines in a series of "jet barns" specifically designed to handle cattle shipments. The remaining cattle came from South Dakota. These cattle, the first major shipment of U.S. beef cattle to Hungary, went to two large cooperative farms. See "U.S. Hereford Exports Boom as Hungary Purchases 445 Head,"* American Hereford Journal *63, no. 2 (June, 1972): 8–9.*]

JUNE

Thur 1: 53°–87° . . . Saw Pablo and Heilda. Paid him $50 & told him we got things cleared up about his shooting the wet back & no charges would be filed. . . .

JULY

Tue 25: 67°–100° . . . Got to work on my commodity records right after lunch & worked at that until about 4. . . .

AUGUST

Tue 1: 68°–99° . . . Took Joe out past Overton to see Longhorn trail drive . . . We checked on drive. They just got into side [*of*] Overton to camp.

Wed 2: 67°–100° River has stopped running at all crossings . . . Supper at Greens. Fandangle meeting at 7:30. Went off well. Lorene & I by Green's after it was over. Trail drivers were having square dance on street when we got out.

Thur 3: 66°–95° . . . Trail drivers camped at Dillingham for night. . . . [*On July 1, a herd of Longhorn cattle left San Antonio on its way to Dodge City, Kansas. Sponsored by the Historical Performance Society, the drive followed the old Western Trail as closely as possible. After bedding the cattle down for the night, trail hands were entertained in towns along the way. See "Cattle Drive Reached Albany Wednesday; Bed Down for Night,"* Albany News, *August 3, 1972, p. 1.*]

Tue 15: 67°–89° Up about 4:30 to get organized to go to MO. They didn't [*get*] in with the cattle [*until*] a little after 8, then got the cows & heifer calves after that. The 94 steer calves delivered, average 483.9# at 49¢. $237.14 per head. The 33 dehorned heifer calves averaged

413.6 at 47¢. $193.77 per head. Ronnie Brown out later & tested a bunch of the old cows. Carrol & Hoss got off for Dalhart a little before 12. Rested in Joe's office & didn't eat lunch. Visited with him & others later. . . .

Wed 16: 62°–93° Went over & checked on river after getting diary up, etc. . . .

[*The fall of 1972 was a busy time. Watt, John Brittingham, and Cliff Teinert purchased three Longhorn bulls from a wildlife refuge at Lawton, Oklahoma. After they got the bulls to Lambshead, work was started on a house at Hayford crossing.*]

OCTOBER

Fri 13: 60°–92° Worked practically all morning at my desk and while I didn't get it cleaned up it is in much better shape. . . .

Sat 21: 44°–70° . . . Rained practically all day. Had the road soft & sloppy. After dark it rained 1.40 more which packed the roads but didn't run much water. Lambshead Creek has not gone across lower crossing. A total of 3.33 for day & 4.02 for the 3 days. Second greatest October rain I have any record of. . . .

Sun 22: 49°–73° A beautiful clear morning & mild. You can almost see the grass greening up. . . . Watched ball game. Oakland beat Cincinnati (7th game). . . .

Tue 24: 34°–59° My thermo near 35° here in this hole. A little frost on the shingles. . . .

Tue 31: 36°–43° Raining more this morning & country getting mighty wet. Starting with the 19th we have had about 7.70 of rain as of 7:30 this A.M. Rained enough by midnight to put that total for Oct to 8 inches . . . Went to Hayford just before noon & it poured rain. That tank was almost full & the most water I have seen in it in a long time. The cistern was running over. . . .

NOVEMBER

Thur 2: 38°–70° Wayne, Rusty, Buddy, & I left before 9 for the Dudley bull sale [*at Comanche, Texas.*] They had a nice lunch (cowbarn) at

11 & sale got going before 12:30. We got 6 for MO which with the Edwards bull av 1342.85. . . .

Fri 3: 36°–71° Worked about desk. Went to Hayford just before noon. They are slowly coming up with the chimneys. Checked on the river which was about 4 ft deep. I am thankful it didn't get out in the bottoms. By the camp & those roads held up pretty well. . . .

DECEMBER

Mon 4: 24°–54° A cold cloudy morning but sun came out before very late & it turned into a fine day to work which we had a lot to do. We weighed & branded 384 calves out of Road & Weight Out. Those out of Road averaged 553 & the 49 Lambshead calves av 583. With the 108 Davis calves they have averaged net 531. They got all but 8 moved to MO pens. We have never had a finer more beautiful set of calves I believe & I am only sorry it is such a bad job of dehorning. Went to camp late & ate supper with John Curtis, Sue & Tom Lipscomb. Home & to bed at 7:30.

1973

[Extremes characterized 1973. An energy crisis rocked the nation, while people heated and air-conditioned more space in buildings and cars than ever before. Housewives boycotted beef, while expenditures for overseas travel and recreational items such as campers and swimming pools broke all records. The Food and Drug Administration banned the use of diethystilbestrol (DES) in cattle feed and the same week approved its use in the "morning-after" contraceptive for women. Americans lost a president, saw the value of their dollar diminish, and finally let go of the idea that consumerism could go on forever unchecked. After blaming each other, they blamed inflation.]

JANUARY

Thur 4: 27°–25° . . . Boys rounded Gober. We brought 82 head to Wn. They averaged 474 & look nice. We will probably pick sixty odd out to take to Ft. Worth Show. . . .

Sun 7: 24°–26°. Rained, sleeted & snowed during night enough to melt up .49 for the 2 days so far. Did very little more sleeting or snowing during day & evening. Spent the day in JOS & got my weather records up to date & worked on income matters a little plus being on phone a lot. Very little supper & to bed about 9:45.

Wed 10: 12°–22°. Still no relief & more snow predicted for this eve & night. Still no more than a trace of moisture since Sunday. Doc Breeden got here at noon with his tractor. He, Jim & Matt took the big trailer to farm & got a load of hay & took it to the 3 YL calves &

calves in WO. Terry & G took a PW load to the cows (young) in Hitson. Jean & Dudley went with me to Bend & fed Longhorns. We took Carlos to Hayford & got a bunch of turkey feed which we put out in there, Burkett Bend, Mouth of Paint & Bend. Worked on water. Spun in ditch several times. Got to snowing before 6. To bed about 8.

Thur 11: 13°–27°. About 2 in or less snow here. Moisture .20. YL & Albany 5 or 6 in & Abilene 8 in. Boys all at work putting out hay. . . .

[*Watt, Joe, and Louise left for the Denver stock show on Sunday, January 14.*]

Mon 15: 29°–71°. Got up fairly early. Phoned the ranch & made other calls . . . Joe & I out to the Hereford & steer judging. I really liked the job the steer judge did & what he had to say. . . .

FEBRUARY

[*Good rains got everything running, including wet-weather springs.*]

Fri 16: 22°–45°. Got to Jenkins pens a little late for lunch. Helped finish topping out heifers. We branded 173 calves (28 tipped heifers, 56 dehorned heifers, 89 steers). . . .

MARCH

Mon 19: 54°–70°. Watt [*Reynolds*] & I had breakfast together [*at Texas and Southwest Cattle Raisers Association annual meeting in San Antonio*]. Then I went to Animal Health Com meeting at 9 & Agri Research Com meeting at 10 which took up all morning & when we got to the Ann Armstrong luncheon everything was running over & we had to eat in dining room. Back for her speech which was great. Directors meeting at 2. Ranch Hdq party in Helen Campbell apt at 5 then to big party at La Villita at 7 for a full day.

[*Anne Armstrong, special counselor to President Nixon, spoke about beef prices. Her comments encouraging women to seek the best buys in supermarkets instead of boycotting them were received warmly by TSCRA members. See "Ninety-sixth TSCRA Convention Sets Attendance Record,"* Cattleman 59, *no. 11 (April, 1973): 21–23, 140.*]

APRIL

Wed 4: 38°–58°. Wayne, Terry & Jim worked on fences & gates. Put a gate in NE corner of Jackson trap which we have needed for some time . . . Glen Key & I checked on some road work for Bob Snyder to do. Evan & Carlos about to get work on his cabin done. Bert got 2 Mexes & cut brush on road to highway, gathering cans etc. . . .

Thur 5: 33°–66° . . . After supper I worked on arranging class mates checking on what they have done, etc. . . .

Sun 8: 33°–44°. Had .14 shower about 12:40 A.M. Temp 31° at 7 A.M. A bad day in the making. Had a little snow later in the morning but only a trace of moisture from it. . . .

Tue 10: 23°–53°. My thermo down to 32° by 10 last night & was 22° around 6 A.M. . . .

MAY

[*Watt hosted a reunion for Princeton University's Class of 1921. A large number of his classmates and their wives spent the weekend at Lambshead Ranch, where they enjoyed the daily ranching activities, a barbecue supper, and the* Fandangle Sampler *at Reynolds Bend.*]

Mon 7: 55°–80°. Boys got the cattle in out of Road & after breakfast we gathered the crowd at corral. We weighed & dipped the 52 cows & 2 bulls then branded the 52 calves (tipped heifers 14; dehorned heifers 16; steers 22). They seemed to enjoy it. We had lunch then in a strain getting Hendersons, Bush, Luke, Shorty, Ty Wood off with JD in crew cab for Love & Halseys off with Bert in yellow pick-up. Balance rested & later took a tour which they seemed to enjoy especially seeing the houses. Had a jolly evening & good late supper after a lot of Fandangle songs, etc. 60 here.

Tue 8: 50°–89°. In a stir with an early breakfast. Bus got here about 7:40. Matt had met it at high way & led it up here. Thirteen boarded bus here & Max E. brought 6 from Motel & put them on at cut off. . . . [*This group flew out of the airport at Abilene, some in their own Lear jets.*]

Wed 9: 52°–95° . . . Rested & looked up data on the 24 classmates & 11 wives we housed & fed. One more (Tom Thash) stayed at Breckenridge. Bill & Lois Kirkland also housed four a total of 43 . . . I will ever be thankful for the break we got in the weather over the weekend.

Sun 20: 60°–91° . . . Got organized to go to LBJ Ranch. Bill, Liza & I left Albany about 1:45. Fredricksburg about 4:40. To party at ranch at 6 & enjoyed it.

Mon 21: 60°–100°. We had breakfast about 8 then drove around & saw some of the restorations. Met Harry & Louise Moore & followed them to LBJ. We looked at cemetery which is beautiful, then went thru the replica of the house LBJ was born in. It is attractive and interesting. We then went up & looked at the cattle which were not impressive. Had lunch then to sale [*dispersion sale of the LBJ Hereford herd*] & I thought they sold high. Left Fredricksburg about 4:25. Albany before 8. Home & to bed about dark.

Thur 24: 56°–96°. Boys got late start to work at MO. Got off late & was hurrying in daze & ran thru the fence across lane from PW & really wrecked my cab. I will ever more be thankful the balance of my days for not getting hurt. . . .

JUNE

Sun 24: 61°–95° Carl & Paul Meeks flew in about 9:30. Alvin & I showed them heifers & the 50 calves until about 12:30. A bunch here for dinner. Meeks left soon after. . . .

Tue 26: 63°–93°. Had the steer years in pen by 6:45. Weighed & dipped by 7:15. Cowboys left for Overton as soon as weighed. 117 years averaged 619 & $328.19 at 53¢. Got off fairly late. . . .

JULY

Mon 30: 67°–80°. Off fairly early to go to MO. Poured rain on the way to Albany. . . . Started after cows & calves. Late on account of light rain early. Got to raining straight down while they were separating & we had a wet sloppy weighing & delivery. Had trouble getting the trucks to and from chute. 120 steers averaged 470.6 at 65¢—$305.50 average after knocking off $130 for some heavy ones (3 or so). 50 heifers averaged 407.98 at 60¢—$244.79. Sent 46 cows (4 MO included), 21 steer calves, 12 dehorned heifer calves, 3 unbranded heifer calves, 1 unbranded bull calf, 1 sharp horn 3 year heifer, 1 2 year heifer—a total of 85 to A Ave late in day. . . .

Tue 31: 63°–81°. No more rain last night or this morning. Lambshead had 1.33 for total of 4.36 for the 4 days past. A great July rain & a great way to start Aug. We were mighty dry here. Went to hospital meeting at 1:30. Picked up Roy & to A Ave in time to see MO cattle sell (which they did higher than a kite). Thru in time to make it to Dr. Devening by 4:45. Back by A Ave & picked up check—2540.02 for the cull cows (46) & cull calves etc. . . .

AUGUST

Mon 13: 69°–95°. Settled (final) with Pablo on Culver pears. A cost of $15.39 per acre. We have had a pear crew going for the past 18 or 20 years. . . .

Fri 24: 68°–103°. To Tecumseh fairly early before Paul's Valley folks left. Men only ones up. We weighed 91 calves to Pick 85 averaged 463.2 at 71¢; 6 averaged 575 at 68¢. 30,302.16 total for 91 average 332.99 per head. 6 bull years (4 at 500; 2 at 400) to Ira Stark $2800. 8 cows, 3 bulls, 4 steer years, 3 steer calves, 1 dehorned heifer calf, 9 unbranded calves to A Ave net $7368.60. $40470.76 total. . . .

Fri 31: 72°–95°. They got the cows & calves in Road in pen by around 8. Separated & weighed & loaded . . . Mack Tiner & Wilcox bled 76 cows while Ronnie tested them (for preg.). They had no reactors for bangs I am thankful to say. Second truck got away after 4. A total of 195 calves averaged 430.47 at 71¢—$305.64 per head. . . .

SEPTEMBER

Mon 24: 67°–94°. Got cows & calves in from Road fairly early. Weighed 91 steer calves to Gene at 71¢ which is above the market now. They averaged 436.7 # & $308.52 per head. . . .

Thur 27: 52°–74°. No cow work. Frank & Buddy not here. Wayne riding, bal working on school house. They got the school house done by noon & got started on the benches. . . .

[The Matthews family rebuilt the 20' x 14' one-room ranch school on its original foundation in Reynolds Bend. Thirteen children from families living up and down the Clear Fork had enrolled for the opening term in the fall of 1888. Joe B. Matthews had been one of the pupils. Complete with hitching post, pot-bellied stove, benches, and blackboards, it stands today as a symbol of the family's commitment to endeavors that enhance the area's lifestyle.]

Sun 30: 51°–83°. We are winding up a beautiful green cool Sept with a beautiful fall-like day. Had even 5 inches of rain for month & Hayford & spots had over 8. . . .

OCTOBER

Sun 14: 56°–70°. . . . We watched ball game until late. NY Mets finally beat Oakland in 12th inning. . . .

1974

[The year opened dry. Lambshead had received only a half-inch of rain since the preceding fall. The grass could not grow, and by May the river was about to stop running. Drought, an unwelcome but regular visitor in the Southwest, was sneaking in.]

JANUARY

Tue 1: 11°–34° . . . No company & spent the quietest most restful New Year's Day I can recall in many years. . . .

Fri 4: 11°–44° . . . Alice & Don Ferguson out about 3:30. I took them on tour of Hayford, Mouth of Paint, Burkett Bend (which looked a little sad), Bend, Cottonwood Crossing, Reynolds Crossing & Dug Out. Saw about 300 turkeys, 25 or more deer, 1 bob cat & a beautiful bald eagle. They stayed & ate a little snack. To bed early. A very restful start into 1974 so far.

Mon 7: 17°–67° [*At Lucile's house in Fort Worth.*] After a morning visit we all went to town by way of bank where I cashed my S S check then they let me out at R C Co. [*Reynolds Cattle Company offices*] They had been thru with their stock holders meeting at 10 A.M. Had been over about 15 min when I got there just after 10:30. We had a nice director's meeting which was over before noon. Watt Reynolds took us (REH, Jr, John Reynolds, Pete Peeler, Dick Hughes & me) to Ft. Worth Club for lunch. Back to office & I enjoyed looking at minutes of the early day meeting of the Matthews Land & Cattle Co under which the R C Co. operated first. . . .

Tue 8: 46°–79° Ben Peacock started work. . . .

Sun 27: 37°–73° JD took Tone & me to bull barn by 8. [*Southwestern Exposition and Fat Stock Show*] Judging started about 8:35. A fine bunch of heifers (a little over 700 head). 6666 Champion & Reserve AV 2 years . . . A lot of Albany folks at Back Stage for lunch. Val Bumgart one of judges with us. Sale at 1 P.M. & it went well. AV 2s 565, years 500, MO 520 & 440. Party at Backstage. Fed 126 & all went well.

FEBRUARY

Mon 11: 24°–75° We turned the 7 new 2 year old CK bulls into Lambshead. Drove around W. D. Reynolds & those bulls look well. . . .

Fri 22: 30°–64° Pick out & we weighed him 100 steer years (shorts) at 54¢. Average weight 454.25 . . . Carl, Vivian & Jim Rodgers got here for lunch. Frank & Rosemary Wardlaw [*Frank Wardlaw was the director of Texas A&M University Press*] got here a little before 3:30. We took a tour & after 6 getting in. Guests getting in before we got dressed. Party went well. Total of 34 plus John & Jean.

MARCH

Thur 14: 41°–79° . . . signed a deal for government to shoot coyotes & bob cats out of helicopters. . . .

Tue 26: 43°–74°. . . . Picked up Joe & to MO. They bled 97 cows & bulls & all checked neg for which I am thankful. . . .

Wed 27: 45°–89° Jim Boyd of the AHA came out and we showed him the heifers in Road which he seemed to like pretty well. I then took him on a tour of MO, Bend, Burkett Bend, Hayford & by Farm to see CK year bulls. He left a little after 1. Didn't get to do much around desk which I am in dire need of doing. . . .

APRIL

Sat 20: 62°–88°. . . . went to Anson for Burleson celebration.Real good. The Teagues, Bob Poage, & Clark Fisher came here for night. Retired after getting here a little past nine.

Tue 30: 60°–67°. . . . Fire Fighters Feed went off well in spite of about .10 rain & Buddy Rodgers getting the beer there late. 50 or more there.

MAY

Sat 11: 57°–84° . . . Sampler went off well to big crowd. More than they could feed (probably over 600 including cast, etc of 100).

[*Watt's annual party at the Bend included a performance of the* Fandangle Sampler.]

Tue 21: 62°–96°. Boys rounded Culver. We stayed around here while I did some phoning, etc. They barely had time to get their cameras set up before they came in with the cattle. We sprayed 156 cows, 155 calves & 3 bulls back. . . .

Wed 22: 69°–98°. While boys were working Valley Garnet Ken & Jeff Brose & I went to Bend & they interviewed me & took all kinds of pictures in cemetery, etc. Evan brought horses to Bend for Joe & me. After he, Louise & Helen got there we got on the horses & they took pictures (moving & still) of us. . . .

Sat 25: 55°–91°. Got diary up to date. Went thru mail & was on phone a lot. . . .

Thur 30: 72°–99°. Cow work going on in every direction. . . .

JUNE

Sat 8: 64°–107°. Boys looked out MO & got 7 heifer years. Had to let one back to her calf. . . .

Mon 17: 65°–104°. Worked at cleaning off tables & desk & got most of magazines out of the way. . . .

JULY

Wed 24: 77°–104°. Boys got a bull out of cattle guard between Culver & Road. I went on although there I saw plenty sad sights. A bunch of the tanks are in bad shape & if we don't get some good rain by fall we are going to be in real tough shape. . . .

Tue 30: 73°–87°. Hartsell Ash, Wayne Webb, Moran and one other man

Watt making an entry in his daily diary. This was done in the cookshack each morning. Courtesy Watt R. Matthews

here early before John White got here. We showed them the years and 2 year heifers. Got back here about 10:30 & ended up selling Webb the dehorned heifers at 33 & 33.25 for the horned heifers. Throckmorton County trapper & man waiting on me & I signed a deal for them to use cynide guns. None of them stayed for lunch. Went up and checked on Taylor fence which was done at noon except for stays. . . .

AUGUST

Tue 6: 64°–82° . . . Clifford went to Abilene with me & did the driving . . . we checked on pumps at Phantom which were moving 400 million gallons per day into lake Phantom. We came into Albany & I phoned Bill Weems & he stopped the pumps. . . .

[In 1938 a reservoir was built on Elm Creek, a tributary of the Clear Fork of the Brazos, to impound water for the city of Abilene. Permits issued by the Texas Water Commission allowed a specific amount of water to be pumped into the reservoir when certain stream flow conditions prevailed. During a dry year, such as 1974, municipal demand was high and apparently the city water officials were slow about turning the pumps off. By the same measure, ranchers downstream needed the water and wisely kept a watchful eye on the operation. This incident illustrates the problem posed for Texans as growing urban areas make increasingly stronger demands on the water that agriculturists traditionally have used.

Nice soaking rains in the fall produced an abundance of winter annuals that carried the cattle into spring in very good shape. Watt wrote, "We really dodged lightening & I will always be thankful."]

1975

[Watt always claimed that his nationally recognized herd of white-faced cattle reflected the inherent qualities of Herefords rather than anything he had done. Cattle people who knew him recognized that Watt's progressive ideas had played a major role in the development of his herd and the promotion of the breed.]

JANUARY

Fri 3: 28°–47°. A light freeze & frost but ground not frozen which is good. Finish going through my bank statements & decided I had better use income tax I paid for '73 as an estimate for 1974 tax. I was thinking it would be less but the royalty account is near twice as much which will offset a lot of the lower receipts for cattle. . . .

[Throughout January, Watt's men prepared the calves for the stock show in Fort Worth. He drove in with Ethel and Joe on Friday, January 24, in time to ride in the opening parade through downtown. The AV calves placed sixth and eighth in the feeder division, the MOs placed fifth.]

Mon 27: 50°–62°. Up pretty early. Tone & I to Hereford show (WRM) by 8:30. Had my picture made with the Champ & Reserve. They had a little ceremony before they named the Champ bull & gave me 2 plaques & a metal bull which are nice & appreciated even though not deserved . . . Had a little rest before Lucile, Sallie, and Joe, Tone & I by Millie Diller's room. A visit with her, the Sargents & Kent Dawkins. By Ft Worth Club cocktail party then to THA banquet. Lucile with me at head table. Got another plaque.

[*The highlight of the week occurred on Monday, when the Hereford division of the Southwestern Exposition and Fat Stock Show was designated the "Watt Matthews Register of Merit Hereford Show" in appreciation of his years of work with the breed. Hence he was photographed with the champion animals. Later, at the annual membership meeting of the Texas Hereford Association, he received an honorary life membership in the association. The plaques he received are among the treasures adorning the walls of the headquarters house at Lambshead.*]

MARCH

Fri 21: Temp 58°. We got the 2 baby markers [*historical markers on unmarked graves*] plus the Butterfield Gap marker all set before lunch. Domingo went with us (Evan, Juan & me) after lunch & we set the Relay Station marker, cleaned up the road by it & the graves near by & shaped up the rocks stacked over the 3 graves a bit. Killed a little rattle snake (2nd for season) . . . To Baird Chamber of Commerce banquet with Bill & Elizabeth [*Green*]. Cp. John White the speaker. Party at the James Snyder's later . . . To bed just after 12.

[*The Butterfield Overland Mail route crossed Lambshead Ranch. During the 1850s and 1860s, travelers were happy to reach the Clear Fork Station because they could bathe in the river. Watt marked this historic route with a stone monument on a hill called Butterfield Gap. See Ormsby,* Butterfield Overland Mail, *48; and Greene,* 900 Miles on the Butterfield Trail, *152–53.*]

APRIL

Mon 14: Temp 48°. Started work on picket cabin. . . .

[*A picket cabin is a form of log construction made by planting logs vertically in the ground instead of stacking them upon each other. The space between is filled with a weatherproof material such as cement. In frontier times it was filled with mud. The Spaniards used this building technique in their early Texas missions, and later it was used on frontier military forts, including Fort Griffin. Building a picket cabin on Lambshead was Watt's way of preserving part of the architectural heritage of the area. This cabin consists of a very large bedroom–sitting room and bath. In*

December 1993, Watt moved from the bunkhouse into the picket house. The sitting room was large enough for his nurse-companion and family to gather for an evening toddy.]

Thur 17: Temp 61° . . . saw Clifford Teinert & me on the ABC news then took a tour. The flowers are beautiful. The sweet peas the greatest I have ever seen.

MAY

Sun 4: Temp 58° Foggy. Stayed foggy all morning & kept us guessing about the weather. Lucile, Sallie, Beth & John Burns went in for church. Some of us here toured & checked on things at Bend which was cleaned up & looking nice. Had forty odd here for lunch. Had no time afterwards to do much resting. The 2 buses from Cowboy Hall of Fame got here around 5:30. 62 people besides the drivers. Otis, S. A., Millie & A. S. Jackson had met them at Ft. Griffin & went with them to Bend by dugout, school, etc. Party & show went fine. Fed 456 & food fine.

[*Watt was presented a Wrangler Award for his lifelong contributions to Western heritage. He could not attend the award ceremonies in Oklahoma City, so the other four recipients joined the group that came to Lambshead. They, and other guests from across Texas, were treated to cocktails, dinner, and a* Fandangle Sampler *performance at the Bend. The weather was perfect and the wildflowers magnificent. Watt wrote the following day, "the flowers are out more & most beautiful. I hate to miss a day driving thru them." See "Hall of Famers Bring 'Wrangler' to Matthews,"* Abilene Reporter-News, *May 5, 1957, p. 6B.*]

Tue 13: Temp 60°. Fine cool morning. Louise brought Joe to Ft Griffin and he & I went to Tordon demonstration on Swenson Ranch by Dow Chemical (Prickly Pear Control). . . .

Fri 16: Temp 45°. Beautiful chilly morning. Boys rounded Road. We shaped up 126 cows (average 1075), 2 2 year dehorned heifers (860), 1 unbranded heifer year (720, 5 calves (averaged 338). Turned 126 steer years back in Road (averaged 701). Gene Pickard & Hartsell

Ash [*cattle buyers*] both here. Ended up selling the steer years to Hartsell at 37¢. Carrol & Terry moved the balance of the stuff to Breckenridge after lunch. Junior Dunlap & Bob Creel had taken 101 of the cows before lunch. . . .

Sat 17: Temp 49°. Beautiful morning . . . Juddy went to Breckenridge Stock yards with me. The 126 cows averaged 1032 & 228.15 per head. One had a calf over there. They only lost 43# which was good. . . .

Tue 20: Temp 63° . . . We got the mesquite mantle up [*in picket cabin*] just before time to quit yesterday & it is going to look nice. . . .

JUNE

Thur 5: Temp 70°. Boys off early to round heifers in Stone Ranch. Gene Pickard out. He, Henry & I started to Buzzard Peak leading Bob Crest & his truck. Met Carrol with a load of heifers so Henry & Pick got in with him to come back here & start weighing. After all the cutting, weighing back, etc., 203 heifers averaged 601. On truck, loaded at noon & got off for Ill. The other 2 trucks didn't come. . . .

Fri 6: Temp 70°. Trucks still not here at 9 A.M. Terry & Carlos looking out to Buzzard Peak again. Wayne gone to Ft Worth. They got 2 heifers one of which was unbranded. Trucks got here around 11. Loaded the 2 of them after lunch. Add 3 more heifers (1 unbranded) for a total of 206. . . .

Wed 18: Terry & Wayne took in the buffaloes (3) & the water truck [*for* Fandangle *performance*] . . . Lucile, Helen Howard [*from* Fortune *magazine*] & help (4), Fran Holden, Margaret Watkins & Betty Rhea Moxley [*from Ranching Heritage Center*] all got in just after 5:30. It was 7 & after before we got off for Sally Ann Harrison's where we ate. Helen, Fran, Margaret & Betty went with me to rehearsal. We left at Ft Griffin scene.

Thur 19: Temp 74°. After a lot of delays, etc finally got Helen, Fran, Margaret & Betty & Juddy off on a tour. We ended up at Bend for lunch. Only 11 there beside help. Sallie met us there. Back here by way of dugout. Between tickets, etc, had no chance to rest much. The 4 girls & I left for town about 6. By Cotter party, by church &

Ethel's. Supper at Sally Ann's & to show. It went off well (for first night) in 2 hrs.

[*The* Fandangle *went off well the next weekend, too, with the stands packed and people sitting on a nearby hill for each performance.*]

JULY

Tue 8: Temp 76° . . . Dudley drove me to the edge of town soon after lunch. Got to bank a few min after it closed & cashed my SS check. . . .

Wed 9: Temp 76°. A feed man came so while he was taking up my time took a tour & checked on yesterday's shower at Bend, etc. . . .

Sat 26: Temp 71°. Left here at 5:30 A.M. They got the MO years in soon after 7 except for 3 in Horse Pasture which they got in after we weighed the main bunch. Thru before 5:30 but trucks not there. 104 head averaged 722# at 40¢—average $288.89 per head . . .

[*Matt Blanton died, and family members began arriving for the funeral. Watt and Matt had been roommates at Princeton.*]

Mon 28: Temp 74° . . . We all got off for funeral just after 9. Church full & some standing outside. A nice service. We all had lunch at Patty's [*Blanton*]. . . .

SEPTEMBER

Fri 12: Temp 51° . . . All of us except J. D. & Chuck to Joe & Louise's for Joe's birthday party which was real nice. 35 there.

Mon 22: Temp 47°. Big dew & fine fall morning. Carlos cut wood [*mesquite*] while Domingo & Juan cleaned out cattle guard going out of Lambshead. After lunch Juan & I took the wood to camp & did some work on the road. . . .

OCTOBER

Thur 2: Temp 36° in this hole. Pete's [*Peeler*] car had plenty of frost on it when he started it up. The yellow pickup that was also outside had frost on it but I couldn't see any on the grass or the roofs, so it shouldn't hurt anything. I believe this is the earliest frost I can recall. . . .

Fri 3: Temp a little below 36°. Can see frost on the grass in this hole this morning. . . .

Mon 6: Temp 44° . . . A bus load of Abilene High School kids 2 teachers & a driver (total of 52) got here about 10:30. After showing them houses, tack room & shop here I led them by dugout, William D Reynolds camp, Bartholomew & school house. Didn't get thru Reynolds house & cookshack on account getting late & kids so hungry. To Burkett Bend where Bill Cauble & Bob Echols had fine hamburgers. Some of them ate over 3 & they were big ones. . . .

NOVEMBER

Thur 27: Temp 30°. Clear. RB took Dudley out & he got 2 nice gobs! 8# & 20#. Had a good Thanksgiving with 31 family plus John, Jean & Juan here. Had 3 turkeys plus a brisket for the Matthews. People were leaving thru afternoon . . . Had supper around 8 & I went to bed around 8:30.

DECEMBER

Thur 25: Temp 30° [*Christmas Day was spent with seven Blantons, ten Brittinghams, seven Caseys, four Harrisons, Alice, Susie, John White, Jean, L. A., Friday and Watt—a total of thirty-five people.*] . . . Nearly cleaned up 1 wild turkey plus 2 geese around 10 lbs. . . .

[*Finishing up odds and ends for the year included paying taxes and making final charitable donations. The New Year was welcomed in at a party with friends.*]

1976

[Throughout the year, celebrations were in order for the Matthews family. In addition to the many public ceremonies spawned by the U.S. Bicentennial, 1976 was the centennial anniversary of the wedding of Watt's parents, J. A. Matthews and Sallie Reynolds.]

JANUARY

Wed 14: Temp 25°. Beautiful clear quite morning . . . The young folks from Ranch Headquarters (Andrea Holman, Lisa Sasser & Tanner Laine) got here about 2. I took them to Gentry. They took pictures & measured barn. Took them by Hoover, Hayford, Mouth of Paint, Burkett Bend, Bend & showed them the houses & Dugout when we came back. Saw a lot of game & got here just after sun down. Had fairly late supper & to bed.

Thur 15: Temp 27°. 33° by 7 A.M. Carrol led the barn crew to farm & they stayed & measured, etc. They were back here for lunch & left for Albany & Lubbock soon after. . . .

FEBRUARY

Wed 11: Temp 45°. Got whole crew together to get the barn down. Had John White come up & fix lunch & bring it to us. . . .

Fri 13: Temp 44°. . . . Carrol, Butch & Domingo left in truck at 4:15 to join Evan in Albany for trip to Lubbock. They were in edge of Lubbock by 9:39. Got unloaded before they ate lunch & back to Albany by 5:20, which was a fine trip. . . .

[*The Reynolds-Gentry barn was moved to the Ranching Heritage Center, Texas Tech University, for restoration and inclusion in the outdoor museum. Mart B. Gentry had been linked to the Matthews and Reynolds families in business and friendship as early as 1868.*]

Mon 16: Temp 55°. Got my cattle sales book up for 1975 & in bal with Jim Cotter [*Watt's CPA*]. . . .

MARCH

Thur 4: Temp 38° real early. 58° at 6:30. Wichita Falls 41°—Abilene 55°. Boys in taking down old shop the White Tank Co. is giving to use on Gentry barn. John took lunch in for them. . . .

MAY

Fri 14: Temp 51°. Wayne took Domingo off with him for no good. I jumped him about it at noon & he asked for his time. Domingo went in with him after lunch to go to Del Rio or some where down there, but I imagine he will be back when his money runs out which shouldn't be long. . . .

Sat 29: 58°. Boys off to work Tecumseh . . . Went to a sale at 19. I got a pair of OK spurs, a well bucket, wagon wrenches, & 4 old eye hoes. . . .

JUNE

Fri 4: J. D. took me to Dallas–Ft. Worth airport for 8:30 plane & got to Newark about 12:30. Sally & John [*Wallace*] met me & brought me to Princeton [*for reunion of the Class of 1921*] in time to hear the last of Pres. Down's talk. Ate a little snack then to council meeting Heinie then brought me & others to Treadway Inn. Got located in my costume [*tuxedo*] & did some visiting. Back to Stephenson Hall for class dinner & meeting. To bed by 10:30.

Sun 5: Had breakfast with Otto Reimer, Brant Henderson & Wally Todd. Rode up to Princeton with Otto & drove around the place a little. Memorial meeting at 10:30. To Art Museum then lunch at Prospect.

Geo. & Jo Finney were at table with Otto & me. Alumni Parade & meeting next which was impressive. . . .

JULY

Fri 2: 74° . . . LeRoy [*Denman, of San Antonio*] took D. Burns, Cliff & me to place where parade started & we got on our horses for around a 3 hr deal. It wasn't too hot however as a cloud was coming up in N. & NW. It forced the activities indoors which was too bad. We didn't get away ahead of storm & had to turn back to near Lubbock & by Midland, etc. Let Cliff off at Stamford. John Burns & Calene picked us up in Breckenridge. Albany, Lambshead in Ethel's car. 12 o'clock.

[*Watt was in Lubbock to ride in the final part of a trail drive of Longhorns from San Antonio to Lubbock to celebrate the U.S. Bicentennial and the opening of the Ranching Heritage Center at Texas Tech University. Lady Bird Johnson delivered the opening remarks on Friday, but Watt's group had to leave early because they were traveling in a private plane and the weather was stormy. On Monday, July 5, he and Watt Reynolds went to Midland for the opening of the Nita Stewart Haley Library and J. Evetts Haley Research Center. The opening coincided with Haley's birthday.*]

Tue 6: We had breakfast, a visit with Evetts, the Holdens, Washingtons [*friends from Lubbock*], Carl Hertzog, & Tede [*Elizabeth Olds, a friend from Washington, D.C.*]. Left at 9 & others were leaving for library where they were having a panel. Curry [*Holden*], Carl [*Hertzog*], & Don Ornduff [*AHA*] were all on it & I would [*have*] liked to hear them but we needed to come on. . . .

Thur 15: 67°. We had a big day working & selling dehorned heifer years. Sold 128 to Emery Mills at 36¢, 9 heifers & 8 baby calves at $192.00. Average $179 per head. We got the 128 loaded out about sundown. Hartsells, Emery & son Larry, Evan, Richard, Terry & Buddy all ate supper here & cleaned the steak, etc John cooked about like the bunch cleaned up the lunch yesterday.

Fri 16: 67°. Boys off to round Weigh Out. We cut off 168 calves & sold them to Hartsell at $61 [*hundredweight*]. They averaged 223# & were about 115 heifers to 53 bulls. Carrol, Evan, Juan & Carlos helped Hartsell haul the calves & the 36 years home. . . .

AUGUST

Mon 16: 69° . . . Took in Republican Convention at some time. Didn't get to bed until 11:30 or later.

Wed 18: 76°. . . . up until after 1. Bored with convention.

SEPTEMBER

Tue 21: 54°. First day of fall. Is fall-like & we are going to start it in good shape. . . .

Thur 23: 57° . . . John [*Bennett*] & I watched Pres. debate [*between Jimmy Carter and Gerald Ford*]. I didn't get to bed until after 11:30.

Mon 27: 60°. . . . John & I left for Abilene soon after lunch. We went to Rehab sale first, then to see Dr. Rupert Richardson [*history professor at Hardin-Simmons University*] at 3:30. Got information on Thomas Lambshead [*first owner of Lambshead Ranch*]. . . .

OCTOBER

[*Watt, Watt Reynolds and others from Albany were in Lubbock for the annual meeting of the Ranching Heritage Center. The Reynolds-Gentry Barn was dedicated at this time.*]

Sat 2: . . . We got everything loaded & all to ranch & looked around until time for dedication which went well. [*See January 14.*] Then lunch after which Watt [*Reynolds*] took off for Rita Blanca. Annual meeting, etc which got Sampler off about 45 min late & got to sprinkling a little & bunch of crowd got on porch. Show went fairly well. . . .

Wed 20: 28°. A very thin ice on wash pot & a white frost. Other than Johnson grass, tomato plants, & wild vines nothing seemed to be hurt at all. Jim & I went with Evan to feed the little bulls & saw all the buffaloes. . . .

NOVEMBER

Mon 1: 34° by my thermo. Wichita Falls 40°, Abilene 39°. Lowest average temp on record for Oct for all stations heard from. Worked on mail most of day. . . .

Wed 3: 45°. Disappointed with election & sorry for Ford. . . .

Fri 12: 27°. Unpleasant cold dampish day. Allie & I got to MO in time to drive around & show Allie 4 of the concrete dams. The 2 big ones after the prongs get together are full & going over. . . .

Sat 13: 24°. 3" or more of snow. .28 of moisture. Had quit before daylight. Started before 9 P.M. Got to a total of about 4.5" & .43 moisture. RB got 129# 7 pt buck in W. D. Reynolds. . . .

Sun 14: 17°. Clear, cold morning. Abilene 15°. Had low of 14° in Abilene & it is the earliest big snow on record & several other records. . . .

Tue 16: 30°. Cloudy. Quite a spell for mid-Nov. We had 07° Thanksgiving morning 1911 which was a hard spell & a hard winter, but no snow that spell, but this one keeps hanging on. . . .

DECEMBER

Wed 8: 26°. Should be a nice day. We moved 295 steer years from Stone Ranch to Valley. Put 25 in Lambshead corral to go to Weigh Out (11 Longhorn crosses & 14 shorts—average 666. The 11 Longhorns 800). . . .

Fri 24: 24°. Wichita Falls 33°. A lot of surging back & forth. . . .

Sat 25: 34°. Had tree about midnight & to bed soon after 12. Got organized & to Bend before 10:30. Dick Wood [*minister*] here & we got the crowd in Reynolds House & service started about 10:40. All seemed to like it. We didn't start eating until about 1:15. There were 91 there (87 direct descendants & in-laws plus Alice Reynolds, Bob Harding, Ruth Jones & Dr. [*Rupert*] Richardson). A total of 30 great, great grandchildren there including their wives & husbands. A good many from away left after dinner. JD & Friday brought tamales down here & at least 35 or more had supper here . . . .

[*Traditionally, Christmas at Lambshead was celebrated in the Barber Watkins Reynolds home in the Bend of the Clear Fork, where Watt's par-*

ents, Sallie Reynolds and John A. ("Bud") Matthews, had been married on December 25, 1876. The unusually large crowd on this day was there to celebrate the one-hundredth anniversary of that wedding.]

Fri 31: 39°. Still nice morning so far at 8 A.M. Stayed nice all day & I think got a little above freezing for a high. Worked around desk all day. Got my tally book up to date & am anxious to see if my sale figures agree with Jim Cotter . . . John Bennett ate supper here & he & I watched Texas Tech–Neb ball game. A good one N 27, T 24.

1977

JANUARY

Sun 2: 24°. We got no sleet, rain or snow. Ground covered in Albany & heaviest south of Greens & I didn't try to go to Gail Dudley's funeral He died about 2 Friday. . . .

FEBRUARY

[*Watt was ill with the flu while he was in Fort Worth for the stock show and his traditional birthday party at Lucile's. This really cramped his style!*]

Tue 1: 24° Lambshead, 20° Ft Worth. Another day in bed. Temp down nearly a degree & better but still feeling pretty poorly. Family got to arriving for birthday party thru afternoon. A total of 36 here including Emily, Wyldon and Riley, beside me. A bunch came up [*stairs*] to see me. John Burns [*a nephew*] brought his little book which is delightful.

[*The book,* Summers at Lambshead, *had been written "In affectionate memory of Sallie Reynolds and John Alexander Matthews, at the one hundredth anniversary of their marriage" (see December 25, 1976). In this book, John H. Burns shares memories of his summers with nieces and nephews, who also return to Lambshead Ranch to renew their spirits. Initially* Summers at Lambshead *was published privately; later it appeared in the journal* Persimmon Hill. *Burns continues the family tradition of recording his experiences. He too keeps a daily diary.*]

Thur 17: 32° 50° before 9 A.M. . . . I went to the Krick [*a nationally recognized weather forecaster*] weather meeting in Throckmorton at 2. . . .

MARCH

[*Texas cattle people had their own celebration in 1977. It was the one-hundredth anniversary of the Texas and Southwestern Cattle Raisers Association. In 1877, a handful of cattlemen—including Watt's father, John A. ("Bud") Matthews, and his uncle, George T. Reynolds—organized the Stock-Raisers Association of North-West Texas "to work for the good and common interest of the stock-raisers of North-West Texas." Many changes occurred during the following century, including changes in the nature of ranching and the name of the organization, but the organization's goal remained constant. By 1977, the fifteen-thousand-member association still was working for the good of all ranchers, and it was doing so from a position of strength and prestige. See Clarke,* A Century of Cow Business, *13–14, 265.*]

Mon 21: . . . Met Millie, Jane & Jack Irwin there then to luncheon [*at TSCRA annual meeting in Fort Worth*]. Ronald Reagan the speaker. Corburn fed 1800 (a sea of tables). Women had something after lunch. . . .

[*Ronald Reagan, the former California governor, spoke about the need to control government interference in the free enterprise system. See "Ronald Reagan: On Free Enterprise,"* Cattleman *63, no. 12 (May, 1977): 34, 70–82.*]

Tue 22: . . . to convention. One of the most interesting sessions I have ever attended. John White & Dolph Briscoe & the new Com. of Agric Reagan Brown spoke. . . .

[*John White, deputy secretary of USDA; and Reagan Brown, commissioner, Texas Department of Agriculture, spoke to the group about their efforts to make agriculture profitable. Texas Gov. Dolph Briscoe emphasized his efforts to protect the state's energy resources. See "Centennial*

Convention Draws 2,478 Cattlemen to Cowtown," Cattleman *63, no. 12 (May, 1977): 21–23, 108–12.*]

Sun 27: 54° Rained all night off & on some times hard. Had total of 3.01 by 7 A.M.—3.10 by noon which ended it. . . .

MAY

Tue 10: 50° . . . We [*Watt and Lucile*] went to town & met with Joe, his John, Sally Ann & Juddy in Joe's office at 2. Signed up deeds & gave checks for dif in land, etc. Louise not there to sign & John the deed to 1/2 Tecumseh for Betty & Chauncy & to send on to Susanne & Warren. A sad sort of day. . . .

Wed 11: 54°. Wet morning & cloudy. Worked around desk. Joe called 5 or 6 times as he was confused about what all went on yesterday. . . .

[*Joe Matthews separated his portion of the family ranch from the rest, incorporating it into his own estate.*]

Mon 16: 64° . . . went to hospital meeting at 1:30 (My last as I resigned due to all members having to be residents of district when & if they vote one). . . .

JULY

Tue 19: 70°. Nearly the whole country in a bad heat wave. . . .

Mon 25: 80°. Put in morning working with mail & stuff around desk also part of afternoon. Evan took water truck in & had something about it fixed. Having some hot days & feeling a little draggy. 109° in Dallas & 108° Ft. Worth yesterday 98° Abilene. My thermo 100° this aft (the first time I have seen it that high). We have had a better than average summer so far. . . .

Wed 27: 74° . . . Did some road work on way home [*from one of the pastures*]. Lightening hit right in ahead of us & set grass. Buddy Putnam's son-in-law was coming the other way & we had it out by the time it burned 10' x 10'. . . .

Fri 29: 68° Carlos & family left for Lubbock after 5 yesterday. He is after papers for citizenship. I wrote a letter & talked to the Consul. Worked around desk. . . .

AUGUST

Fri 5: 69°. Judy [*Matthews*] called about mid-morning to tell me Louise found Joe dead in bed this morning. Have been on phone a lot of the time since. Dick Wood out & ate lunch with us. Went to bank before 4. Got hair cut then to funeral home & picked out coffin. Evan by & picked up outside box which cost $75 & worth about 10 . . . To Ethel's & ate with Anne & Otis. . . .

[*Joe B. Matthews died, at the age of ninety-four, in Chautauqua, Colorado. Named after his grandfather, Joe B. had been a vice-president and director of the American National Cattleman's Association, an honorary vice-president of the Texas and Southwestern Cattle Raisers Association, a member of the board of directors of the Southwestern Exposition and Fat Stock Show, an elder of the Matthews Memorial Presbyterian Church in Albany, chairman of the board of First National Bank of Albany, and a Shriner.*]

Sat 6: 73°. Rusty & Buddy got here early with the [*air*] compressor & with Evan, Terry, Carrol, Carlos & wets. There were eight digging. We didn't get back here until nearly 6. John Burns got here at noon & went back to Bend with us. Family got to arriving before long after having supper at Louise's. . . .

Sun 7: 73°. Had so much going on I didn't [*get*] in for church. We visited around cookshack most of morning. All to Docia's for lunch . . . We then went by funeral home. Then back here. Lucile, Sally & I left 4:45. By funeral home & to church. It got [*to*] running over. Then Sunday school room full & some outside. Nice service & everything went fine at cemetery. People impressed with cemetery.

[*Many ranches have a family cemetery. The earliest grave in the cemetery at Lambshead is that of three-year-old Anne Caroline Matthews, the first child of John A. and Sallie Matthews. At the time of publication, the most recent grave was that of Lucile Matthews Brittingham, who died on January 30, 1995. She was buried 114 years after her sister.*]

Tue 9: 75°. Evan cleaned up flowers etc at cemetery. He & wets spread the black soil in low spots, fixed fence, etc in cemetery yesterday. . . .

Wed 10: 72°. . . . Sallie, John Vandiver & I took the 7 deeds to Throckmorton to be recorded. . . .

Thur 11: 75°. . . . Dick Wood out about 6. Louise & Frances by later & I went to cemetery with them. They went on back to town. Dick ate supper with us. . . .

Wed 17: 76°. . . Louise gave me a bunch of Joe's ties, shirts, a pair of gloves, thermometer & radio.

Wed 24: 75°. Went over & checked road, cemetery, etc. Joe's grave has settled some more & we are going to have to put more fill on soon. By corrals & they had made quite a showing. Grass got a fire while they were here for lunch & Chuck's men put it out for which I am mighty thankful. We could have lost some equipment especially the winch truck. Watt [*Reynolds*] got here at noon. I went over to check fire damage which there was little. . . .

Fri 26: 76°. Ellen called that Graham [*Webb*] died at 4:30. Louise called a little later . . . I had been to Bend & by corral job. Fire got going for third time during noon & burned up 35 or 40 posts which should not have happened. . . .

OCTOBER

Tue 11: 48°. To Clifford's at 9 . . . Lubbock just after 12. Lunch after finding the Presbyterian Church. To D. Burns funeral at 2 . . . Clifford [*Teinert*] sang at church then again at grave side service in Lamesa at 4:30. By Mamie Burns sister's house afterwards. Back to Albany a little after 9.

[*For twenty-three years, D. Burns had been manager of the Pitchfork Land and Cattle Company. In addition to ranching, he and Watt had shared an interest in the Ranching Heritage Center, Texas Tech University. Burns had been the first chairman of its board of overseers.*]

Sun 16: 43°. Tony checked all my suits he had made & is taking my last coat back to make it smaller. Ordered a new one (suit). . . .

NOVEMBER

Wed 9: 36° . . . Carlos brought the news that young Watt [*son of John Matthews*] had died [*the result of an airplane crash*] when he brought lunch down. A mighty tragic, sad deal. Didn't get in until about 5 & was on phone a lot. . . .

Thur 10: 24° in this hole & plenty of ice around. Frost big around river. Frank & Richard helped Carrol feed calves, etc & balance plus Rusty B, Marshall Clements (with their air com) & Louise's Carlos concentrated on getting Watt's grave ready. Started a little before 8 & finished about 2:30. Met boys with box as I came home & they had to make grave a little over 7 ft long which was easy. It was already 7 x 3. John White brought lunch up & John & Betty joined us. Lucile went back with me before 4 & quite a crowd already there. Getting toward 4:30 when they had funeral. John & family went home by Louise's. Lucile, Mary Ford, Glenn Reynolds left after supper here with family & several others. Clifford had brought a sirloin strip.

Sat 19: 31° . . . Carlos & I added a bunch of dirt to Watt's grave under the sod. . . .

[*November ended on a happier note than the earlier months of 1977. The Matthews clan attended the wedding of Tom and Dot Brittingham's daughter in Nashville, Tennessee, and remained for a family celebration of Thanksgiving.*]

DECEMBER

Wed 14: 24°. Cookshack about to get full of hunters by 6:30. Counting our boys had a total of 14 for breakfast. . . .

Sat 17: 39° . . . Party went well [*the ranch Christmas party*]. Had 2 geese, 19 ducks. A total of 44 & all seemed to enjoy it. Blue Jean started having puppies just as guests were arriving & caused a big stir & a lot of confusion. She finally had 4.

1978

[Even though Texans have learned to take the weather in stride, 1978 made a big impression. It started off with a drought, and the dry, clear air allowed winter temperatures to drop very low. This was hard on the cattle and the grass. During the summer, ovenlike winds burned the ranges to a crisp until the drought broke with a bang in August.]

JANUARY

Wed 11: 22°. Cloudy & no rain or sleet yet for which I am glad as it would be plenty hard on the cattle and they are not in shape to take too much. I don't believe my thermometer has been above 32° since Sunday afternoon, the 8. Put in most of day trying to get desk & tables cleaned up but didn't seem to get much done. . . .

Wed 18: 24°. RB & Sallie called. Juddy died 12:30 A.M. Have been busy on phone since . . . I am thankful to be home. Rusty had gone out & I didn't get him until later. He got over with airhammer about 11 & we went up & got started on grave after lunch. Then Evan & I went over & checked air strip over & cut a little brush & back to cemetery. . . .

Fri 20: 13° . . . visited with folks here until about 10. Went to cemetery & we got the tent up & stove in & going. Carlos had a fine big fire laid in the road & we lit it up at 11 & it was great to have. People got to coming then. I believe we had at least 100 & eighty odd stayed for lunch. Didn't get above freezing all day but much more pleasant than the past 2 days & wasn't bad at all. The Houston folks got there by 11:45 & we didn't miss the 11:30 too far. Everything went real well.

People got to going in every direction around mid-afternoon & ended with Sallie, Sally Ann, Susan Brown, RB & family, John Burns & me left. We sat in picket house & visited & had a late supper.

[*Ardon B. Judd was the husband of Watt's sister, Sallie. Sallie stayed at Lambshead for two weeks, then went to Fort Worth with Watt for the stock show. Ethel, Sallie, Lucile, and Watt had some good visits in Lucile's home before Sallie returned to Houston with her daughter, Sally Ann. Watt was an administrator of Juddy's estate. This was a sad duty because Juddy had been more than a brother-in-law; he had been a dear friend. Years later, Watt was still reminiscing about the good times and laughs they had shared.*]

MARCH

Sat 4: 14° . . . to Green's & to [*Albany*] Chamber of Commerce banquet. We [*Watt Reynolds and friends who were visiting*] picked up Millie [*Diller*] on way in. Much to my surprise & gratitude I received the Cornerstone award. Senator was the speaker.

[*The Cornerstone Award is presented each year by the Albany Chamber of Commerce for outstanding civic contributions.*]

Sat 11: 44° . . . Mexicans finished spading up the garden in afternoon. Put in the onion plants & a few other things. . . .

MAY

Thur 11: 66°. . . . Watt Reynolds & I to Golden Spur gathering at TSCRA office at 1:30. To Watt's afterwards & had visit & rest with him. . . .

[*Watt Matthews presented a bronze replica of the National Golden Spur Award to the Texas and Southwestern Cattle Raisers Association, one of the sponsors of the award. See January 20, 1966, and September 22, 1978.*]

Mon 22: 61°. John Birdwell got here from Lubbock just after 8. Erving and Dolly Turner went with us to look at the steer years. When we got back Lucile & Sallie went with us to see the dugout & houses.

Sold the years with a 13% cut. There is a remnant of 2's among them. John left for home around 3. Glenn & Grace Leech were out for lunch with us. . . .

Fri 26: 75° . . . John & Genene Birdwell got here about 5:30. I took them on a tour of the houses. Louise Matthews, Billy & Liz Green were here when we got back & had supper with us fixed by Jean.

Sat 27: 72°. Lot of activity from 4:30 on. Boys had cattle in pen by 6:30. 371 steer years averaged 451 at 75¢; 56 years averaged 544 at 69¢ or $375.36 per; 12 years averaged 669 at 60¢—$401.40; 3 crossbreds 540 at 50¢—$270; 9 3 year old steers averaged 985 at 56¢—551.60. Total—451—average 479.63 or $348.36. Total check $157,110.36. We had them weighed out & dipped soon after 9:30. Rested them a couple hours & had 4 trucks loaded before 1. Birdwells followed Buddy home to look at MO years & then home. Fifth truck got away for Muleshoe by 2:30 [*to Coyote Lake Feedyard, Inc.*]. Other 4 to Quemado, NM. Cleaned up and rested. . . .

JUNE

Fri 2: 64°. We had .51 more rain by noon here but it rained a trash mover on Rocky & the shed of Cottonwood Creek Tank. It didn't fill up but caught a big lot of water . . . Evan took OK spur and put it on bus for Fran Holden. Chg. $4.70. . . .

[*Inexpensive, mass-produced spurs stamped "O.K." were used by cowboys before custom-made spurs became the mark of a good hand. Those manufactured by the August Buermann Company of Newark, New Jersey, were the most popular. Even though this cheap spur lacked respectability for many years, it is now a collector's item. Today this working cowboy's spur, or its replica, is awarded to people for outstanding contributions to the cattle industry. This "O.K." spur, donated by the Matthews family, was gold-plated and placed on permanent display in the Ranching Heritage Center at Lubbock, with the name of each year's honoree engraved on a plaque. See "Mystery Spur . . . the OK,"* Western Horseman *33, no. 12 (December, 1968): 112–13; and Pattie,* Cowboy Spurs and Their Makers, *3, 33–34.*]

Thur 8: 62°. Evan went to Abilene to get material for Overton corrals. Richard & wets on house tank fence. Carrol & Juan & Isidro put in part of support for cat walk. Carlos & I finished the lick logs & put one here by cookshack & the others in Bend. . . .

Fri 9: 54°. Beautiful sparkling wet morning. Boys got in with 12 of the buffalos after I had left here about 9:45. Clifford & I left Albany at 10:30 for Bob Masterson's funeral at Paduca at 2. He sang cowboy's prayer. We had lunch at Aspermont. Holdens, Denhams, & Millers there. Buried him on the ranch on a hill hard to get to & we didn't try to go. J J Gibson [*manager of 6666 Ranch*] had invited us to go with them in a 4 wheeler which it took to get there. Back to Albany about 5:30 after a stop at SMS office. . . .

Tue 20: 72° . . . Ann & Donna Martin here after 4 for a visit. She said she made me 52 shirts over the years . . . To bed before 6. Throat sore.

JULY

Wed 5: 76°. River has been stopped running about everywhere on ranch for past 3 or 4 days. Has run all year up to now. I don't believe it has failed to run for more than 10 months total time since Feb '57. . . .

Wed 26: 72° . . . There was a good looking cloud in NW & N as I came out [*from Albany*] & looked like we couldn't miss getting some rain but didn't which is a droughty discouraging sign.

Thur 27: 68°. Evan not out. Richard & John's grandson going to ride Left Hand. Valentine & Juan painting Valley pens. Carlos & Isidro building gates. They rode in W. D. Reynolds. Let the dogs follow and Dusty's horse stepped on Trey's foot & has him crippled. . . .

AUGUST

Wed 2: 73° . . . Cloudy & pleasant all day. Came a little sprinkle late in afternoon. Gulf stream brought floods to Hill country & some nice clouds to us.

Thur 3: 68°. Started a nice gentle rain soon after 12 A.M. We have had 5.5 up to 8 P.M. with seldom a let up. Boys cleaned things up & did a few things around shop but didn't get much done. Watt Reynolds got in from Rita Blanco before 5. We took a drive down Lambshead (poured out 3.20 at Valley pens). Went down Rocky but was a little afraid to cross it so we came back. We ate a snack & Watt to bed at 7. I watched the King Tut show & went to bed soon after 8. Pouring rain. Otis reported over 8 inches & I told him they were in for a flood.

Fri 4: 66°. Poured rain all night & is still doing it. 8 ins. I got in Bronco early & took Watt Reynolds, Juan & Valentino to higher ground as creeks 2nd highest on record. I was mighty glad for daylight to come & creeks to start falling. Creeks came between well & house June 1901 & 10. We were not here June 10, 1910. By 10 we had over 19 inches from around 6 yesterday. Total since 12 A.M. yesterday 24.86 inches. Other gauges wouldn't hold enough. Phones out and hemmed in by creeks. We couldn't get any news out. I knew folks would be worried & we tried our best to get news out on these CBs, but couldn't. Stuck in mud a good part of the day. We checked on river late. A sad, sickening sight. About 5 ft deep in Reynolds house. Within 5' or 6' of Hayford. Sid Merchant & pilot picked up Carrol & Charlene around 3 (in chopper), then checked on us. Later John Matthews & pilot, then later Henry Musselman in P.M. & Larry & J. Nail & M. Farley in pickups. Clifford & Co in plane over earlier.

[*During the first week of August, tropical storm Amelia triggered torrential rains throughout Central Texas and westward to the Rolling Plains. Floodwaters caused a record-breaking rise on the Clear Fork of the Brazos, and parts of Shackelford County received over twenty-nine inches of rain in as many hours. The rainfall sent a twenty-foot wall of water down Hubbard Creek into Albany, where six lives were lost. See "Albany Folks Recall Terrifying Hours,"* Abilene Reporter-News, *August 20, 1978, p. 21A.*]

Sat 5: 64°. All hands worked on creek crossing & bad places in road to help Watt to highway. When we got there we all went to Ft Griffin & saw river which looked like an ocean. I went on into Albany & looked at things which are devastated. Watt got turned back at Hubbard & was here from 11 on. Had lunch and long rest at Ethel's. Got some groceries, stopped for a visit with Pickards—boy & Jane Key gone & no doubt dead. Watt in bed when I got here at 7:30. To Bend &

checked on things. River back in banks & a lot of damage, but much less than expected for which I am very thankful. I am mighty thankful to be alive.

[*Friends and family came to help with the clean up. Restoration of the Reynolds house at the Bend took over two months.*]

Wed 23: 66°. . . . Water was 58" deep in Reynolds house, 5.5' in cookshack. Lacked 6 or 8 inches going over top of cabin, turned mobil home (pretty well anchored) over, way over top of wagon shed.

SEPTEMBER

Sat 2: 66°. . . . to Hayford, Burkett Bend where we put up a flood mark. . . .
[*On Friday, September 22, a delegation from Albany attended the first Golden Spur Award and Prairie Party at the Ranching Heritage Center in Lubbock. Watt's old friend, Albert K. Mitchell of the Tequesquite Ranch in New Mexico, was the first recipient of the award that is given annually to a person who has made significant contributions to the beef cattle industry. During the weekend, Watt and Bob Green attended a meeting of the Ranching Heritage Center's board of overseers, and the* Fandangle Sampler *was presented at the Prairie Party.*]

Fri 29: 58°. Carrol & the 4 Mexicans worked at Bend. Carrol got the sand out of road around river bottom & Carlos & boys did a fine job finishing up the Wagon shed. You can hardly tell anything has happened to it & I am highly pleased. . . .

OCTOBER

Tue 10: 57° . . . Watched NY-LA ball game a while before going to bed.
Sat 14: 36° . . . Went up to Bill Swenson's funeral at 2 P.M. . . .
Wed 25: 55°. . . . Planted a bunch of buckeyes and chinaberries along new rail fence at Bend. . . .

NOVEMBER

Fri 17: 30°. Wichita Falls 30°. Abilene 36°. Wash pot didn't freeze over, but a little very thin ice on the water. Not a very big frost, in fact only a little on the grass & not too much on roots . . . Finished reading 1951 diary. . . .

Mon 27: 37°. Norther blowing & we should have our first hard freeze in the morning. . . .

DECEMBER

Fri 15: 32°. Wichita Falls 27°. Abilene 40°. . . . Carlos & I got Christmas trees off cedar point after lunch. . . .

Wed 20: 56°. Was 72° at 9 last night and 62° at 4 A.M. . . .

1979

JANUARY

Mon 1: 13°. Wichita Falls 14°. A rough finish of 1978 & beginning of '79. Went to town in Bronco by soon after 11:30. Roads covered with snow, sleet, & ice, but no trouble. Worst part in Albany. By bank and P.O. . . . home before dark. Temperature never did get above low twenties. Record low Jan 1 in Wichita Falls & a number of places.

Tue 2: 6°. No water this morning & I imagine the main line is frozen some place. They got the water going to the heifers in NW water lot but don't have it coming to houses yet 2:10 P.M. . . .

Thur 4: 25°. Ground (bare) & roads still white. Grass has showed thru the sleet, snow & ice from the start. I think the cattle will come thru pretty well. . . . We put out turkey feed (corn) around Mouth of Paint, Bend, & W. D. Reynolds as we came back for lunch . . . Did some thawing for about 2 hours before sundown. We had a high of 40° or more but it only reached 34° at Wichita Falls. . . .

Tue 23: 30°—5 A.M. 25°—7:30 A.M. . . . to cabin to hear the President's state of the Union speech & later comments.

FEBRUARY

Sat 17: 14°. Enough snow to make the ground white, but very light . . . Got my sales all on my book, but I don't bal with Cotter [*Watt's CPA*]. Watched the Welk show all the way thru without an interruption which is the first time that has happened in the not many times I have seen it. Below freezing all day.

MARCH

Tue 27: 40°. . . . Telephone men showed up & it looks now that we may get an underground cable here, Farm & Bend by end of year which will be great. I had about given up on anything coming of it.

APRIL

Wed 18: 58°. Dot Brittingham & 4 guests took a ride. Found a man in Butterfield that claimed to have been high jacked in Abilene & put out in this area. I took them up & got him. Our sheriff & deputy down & checked on him. His wife over & got him. . . .

JUNE

Tue 12: 50°—Overton; Wichita Falls 59°—San Angelo 50°. A mighty cool June so far as well as a chilly spring after an icy cold, hard winter. Cattle came thru in fine shape without feed. . . .

AUGUST

Fri 31: 74°. . . . Evan started on John Burns' house yesterday. . . .

SEPTEMBER

Mon 3: 72°. . . . watched horse race. Anne Tandy's horse 2nd & won $177,000 plus. . . .

[*Anne Tandy, granddaughter of Samuel Burk Burnett, managed the Burnett Estates ranch operation in northwestern Texas, which included the 6666 Ranch. Horses from this ranch are world-famous.*]

Wed 12: 62°. Up just after 4:30 . . . They had the steers in pen at 7:25. They were mighty pretty & not a single case of pinkeye. The 349 averaged 734. Cut out 24 2 year olds average 898 & 18 longhorn crosses average 738.8 at 68¢ & 75¢. The 307 straight Hereford years averaged 713.09 at 80¢ . . . the 6th truck had left by around 10:30. All left before lunch. . . .

NOVEMBER

Tue 6: 36°. The 2 Toms [*Tom Charlton and Tom Parrish from Baylor Oral History Collection, Waco, Texas*] got rigged up & had me on video tape for over 2 & 1/2 hrs which was a bit tiring. We quit just after 12. . . .

DECEMBER

Tue 11: 60°. Boys got calves out of Road. Ronnie out & gave heifer calves Bang shots & we also gave blackleg, etc. [*The calves were then moved to winter pastures.*] . . . Wind got out of north soon after lunch & we had a dusty, disagreeable afternoon. Heard the news, ate a snack & to bed at 6:45. . . .

Wed 19: 40° . . . Put in most of day getting organized. Made contract with Tom Edger to build shop & shed for $15,500. His bro Earl & helper got started on east chimney. Burns & Barbara Densmore got here about 6:30. Party went well [*ranch Christmas party*]. A total of 45.

Sat 22: 50°. Was busy trying to get some stuff ready to mail & got the sad news that Lucile had fallen & broken her hip . . . Off for Ft Worth & there by 5:30. JD after & MO [*a nickname for Sally Wallace*] with him to get Tom, Dot, & Bo [*a nickname for Bob Brittingham*] at DFW later. By hospital, Lucile & home.

Sun 23: 40°. Bo & I up fairly early. Having a real nice rain. He & MO to hospital, Tom & Dot later. JD took Watt Reynolds & me later . . . Lambshead for supper & night.

Fri 28: 44°. Worked all morning trying to get everything that needs to go thru bank before year-end, also checks for taxes for Carrol to take to Throckmorton then back here for lunch & checks to Abilene & to bank. . . .

1980

[The decade opened with challenges that would have far-reaching effects on ranchers. USDA shifted aggressively from a "producer" to a "consumer" food policy that cast beef consumption in an unfavorable light. Industry-sponsored research countered by pointing out the nutritional benefits of beef. Then environmentalists entered the arena. A golden era of ranching was passing.]

JANUARY

Tue 1: 26°. Beautiful frosty morning. Bunch of hunters. Temperature got up to about 66° and we had a fine mild day. Wyldon called me that Anne Tandy had died. . . . [*See September 3, 1979.*]

Wed 2: 35°. Up fairly early. Jean & Clarence here by 7:30 They Sallie & I off at 7:40 for Ft Worth. At Lucile's house by 10:10. Watt Reynolds there just as we arrived. Clarence & JD then took Watt & me to Anne Tandy's 11 o'clock funeral.

[*Watt visited with Lucile before returning to the ranch.*]

Mon 7: 24°. Put in morning on mail & reading Fran's manuscript on Lambshead [*Lambshead before Interwoven*] which is really interesting. Tom, Edgar & helper got here at noon with forms & some material for shop & shed. Left about 1:20 for Cecil Weaver's funeral at 2. To cemetery with Nancy Green & Millie. By Millie's on way home. Here 6:15. Finished the manuscript. Talked to Anne Phillips [*Anne Tandy's daughter*] & to Fran twice as well as several others. Turned out to be a pretty day—on chilly side.

Watt receiving one of the many phone calls that daily come to Lambshead Ranch. Courtesy Watt R. Matthews

Sun 20: 34°. Mist still going on. Got to .15 by 9 P.M. for the 2 days. Didn't go in for church. Stuck around cookshack working on papers, etc. Watched LA-Pittsburg Super Bowl in late afternoon & early evening. P. 31—LA 19. To bed fairly early after a snack.

FEBRUARY

Thur 7: 47°. Maria's last day. Quit on account of food stamps cutting down or off her pay. . . .

Thur 14: 45° . . . to the Bill Green's for dinner & John Connally on TV [*from*] 9 to 10. . . .

Fri 15: 50°. . . . Betty & Chauncy got here for late lunch. She worked on curtains for John's house all afternoon . . . We watched winter Olympics after supper.

MARCH

Sat 1: 12°. Chill factor –26°. Bitter, cold, (hard wind) blew all day. Very little work done except stoke fires. Carrol & Val. fed heifers. Pete Jones out & got elec going in cookshack. . . .

Mon 10: Lambshead 36°. [*Watt was in San Antonio for the Texas and Southwestern Cattle Raisers Association annual meeting.*] Up fairly early. Talked to Terry & things seem to be going OK there. Bud, Kent & I had breakfast together after which we went to Agricultural Research Committee meeting which went on until after 11. Got Millie & to luncheon. Sat with the whole Reynolds delegation (John, Leona, Susan, Dick, Pete, Mary Fru, Mary Joe, WWR III [*Watt Reynolds III*] & Tom) plus a fellow from El Paso. To directors meeting at 2. Visited with Reynolds boys. Millie & I to St Anthony Hotel at six for a drink with Helen Campbell's party. Then a bunch of us to Institute of Texas Cultures for a fine big party. Fine food, drinks & dancing.

Tue 11: Lbs 48° . . . To meeting in time for start. John Armstrong made a fine speech that I wish every one in the country could have heard. John Tower also good as well as the preacher & Gov Clements.

[*Armstrong spoke about the spreading threat of Communism. Tower agreed and stressed the need for a strong national defense. Tower also targeted spiraling inflation. Detente was dead, and Middle Eastern problems were causing a lot of anxiety for Americans. See Armstrong, "The President's Message," and "Tower Speaks on Defense,"* Cattleman *66, no. 11 (April, 1980): 132–33, 164, 166, 168, 170, 172, 174.*]

APRIL

Wed 2: 56°. . . . Rained enough after we got to branding after lunch to get the hair too wet for us to brand for about an hr. Cleared off with not enough rain anywhere on this place to do any good. Lambshead .03 & about such around. . . .

Sat 12: 40° . . . Got news that Calene [*family nickname for Mary Casey Lasater*] died about 11:30 last night our time. Went in & spent the day (most) with Ethel, Palo & Docia & others . . .

[*Watt had visited Mary when he attended the National Western Livestock Show in January. He had written: "Had a visit with Calene who is in poor shape & a mighty sad situation." See also January 18, 1952.*]

Sun 13: 42°. Did some phoning, etc. Still raw, not raining . . . a good many callers during afternoon & early evening. Got started on trying to charter a plane or 2 to take us to service for Calene at 11 Wed in Simla [*Colorado*]. . . .

Wed 30: 62° . . . Tom Perini & helper came by late on their way back from the Bend where he took his chuck wagon. . . . [*He was making preparations for approximately five hundred people to be fed at Watt's annual Fandangle party the coming weekend.*]

MAY

Sat 3: 49° . . . The Pres and Regents here by 5:45.

[*The president and regents of Texas Tech University were honored guests at the Fandangle party. Texas Tech President Lauro Cavazos had grown up on the King Ranch, so he and Watt shared many interests.*]

Sun 4: 58°. Up only fairly early. Myra in for breakfast soon & Larry Cavazos next. Myra off for DFW by 7:30 & I took Larry on a tour. Back around 8:30. The Hardwicks & Kelseys here soon to pick up Larry & they were off by 9. . . .

Tue 6: 60° . . . Cutter Bill crew here taking pictures of their models & our boys inc. Jack Pate on porch of Picket House. . . .

Wed 21: 57° . . . Carrol moved gravel in on holes & low spots after he, Evan & David fixed the longhorn head over the gate [*entrance gate to headquarters area*] in the right position & secure shape. . . .

JUNE

Fri 13: 67° . . . Bob Lapham with [*Abilene*] Reporter-News got here about 11:30. I took him on a tour after lunch & he left about 3:30. Rested awhile & read the *Wall Street Journal*. . . .

Mon 23: 69° . . . I got a bale of division orders ready to mail. Carrol & David took them in when they went after winch truck. . . .

Tue 24: 112° high in Wichita Falls for all time high for June. . . .

JULY

Tue 1: 78°. Sallie & I left about 9. By bank & drug store. Picked up Frances & off for Abilene . . . Took old Miles City saddle [*a family heirloom that was made in Miles City, Montana*] to shop to be restored & home. . . .

Wed 2: 81°. Put in most of morning working at getting calliope hauled to Stamford & someone to fire it. . . . [*For the fiftieth anniversary of the first Cowboy Reunion and Rodeo at Stamford, Texas. See July 3, 1957; and Seagraves, "Cowboy Reunion, Texas Style,"* Cattleman *67, no. 4 (September, 1980): 138–45.*]

AUGUST

Mon 4: 78° . . . We staked off Sallie's house about 2:30 or 3. Evan & Val. then went to Bend & got some lumber. Sallie & I to Bend late & ate supper with that bunch. Missed 100° in Wichita Falls for 1st time in 43 days.

Thur 7: 74° . . . John White worked some on taking down old wood cook stove but left soon after lunch & didn't get much done. . . .

Fri 8: 68°. We had a lot of activity getting stove moved out of corner & into fire place until we can move it out when new one comes Wednesday. . . .

Tue 12: 78°. They got the jams off the door & the old stove out long before they got here with the new one after 12. Have roamed around a lot before getting here without any fittings to hook it up with & had to make 2 trips to Albany. Didn't get done & away until after 6. . . .

Sun 24: . . . DFW at 12 [*Watt was returning from a session with Carl Hertzog and Curry and Frances Holden in El Paso concerning the design of* Lambshead before Interwoven]. Dot had got in from Nashville & we came on to Lucile's in a taxi. . . .

Mon 25: 69°. . . . Went to Bend about 5 checking on things. Back by McFadden crossing, etc. River still running a little from the 1' rise that finally got in on us about a week ago. . . .

SEPTEMBER

Wed 10: 66° . . . Talked to John Matthews twice after going to bed—re: getting pumps stopped at Abilene. [*See August 6, 1974.*]

Thur 25: 65°. [*Watt went to Fort Worth with his sisters, Sallie and Ethel.*] All to see Watt Reynolds (except Lucile) after 2. They took Sallie to get blood tested & I stayed & visited with Watt, Watt III & Tom which was a sad affair going over things he wants done. [*Watt was dying.*] Tom took me back to Lucile's & we got off a little before 5. Lambshead before 8 in a shower which made 1.24 for day.

Sun 28: 50°. Poured rain from late in night to 8 A.M. by which time we had four more inches for total of 11.60 for the 5 days. Creek rolling big. . . .

Mon 29: 56°. Rain still coming at a steady lick . . . River was nearly 32' at Ft Griffin late in afternoon when Carrol & Rodney checked it. John V couldn't tell me much about the river at Bend so I went up & checked it just before dark & found it 5' or 6' below the Valley & showed to have dropped about 1'. This was good news to Martins who are staying in town. The flood water from California Creek & Paint Creek has not got down here yet.

OCTOBER

Sun 5: 56°. Valentino & I took a circle around Lambshead, Gober, part of Valley, Culver & Butterfield. All the tanks we saw have run around & the country looks great. . . .

Thur 9: 60°. Watt III called me just before 4 A.M. that Watt had died about 3. . . .

[*Watt W. Reynolds was born in Albany, Texas, in 1889, the son of William D. Reynolds and Susan Matthews Reynolds. A Yale graduate, Watt was a director of the Texas and Southwest Cattle Raisers Association and a director of the Southwestern Exposition and Fat Stock Show. In 1974, he became president of Reynolds Cattle Company, with offices in Fort Worth. As president, he oversaw a vast commercial Hereford and Angus operation.*]

Fri 10: 58° . . . off for Ft Worth at 9:30. Lucile's at 11:50. Heavy [*Watt's nickname for Bob Harding*], Andria & I went to funeral home. They had Watt looking nice. He showed to be pretty thin. Lucile had a big crowd of family for lunch. The funeral cars (4) picked us up at 2:30. Gathered at Lucile's after funeral at which there was a fine turn out. We then went to Watt's house where there were a lot of people & a lot of nice food. . . .

NOVEMBER

Thur 13: 52°. John Birdwell (young) out by 6:15. Showed him the steer years when Evan & Valentino got them called together. Did get them sold to Hartsell for Lane feed lot Dighton, Kansas. 72.50 for the Herefords; 70 for the Longhorns [*crosses*]. . . .

Fri 14: 42°. Boys had years in pen before 8 . . . Cattle were all weighed & made ready to go before 12. Four of the 5 truck drivers had lunch before leaving for Lane feed lot, Dighton, Kansas . . . a total of 27 for lunch. 356 Hereford years averaged 639 at 72.50; 58 Longhorn crosses averaged 607.55. . . .

Mon 17: 30°. Six inches of snow which made a lot of moisture (.85). With the leaves still on nearly all the trees it had a lot to stick to & broke off a lot of limbs. Stamford and places nearby had 12". . . .

Thur 20: 28°. Pot frozen over & a big frost.

Tue 25: 32°. . . . Clarence out with John V & they got us a couple of gobblers & 2 nice shoates for Thanksgiving. . . .

Thur 27: 32°. . . . Folks got to gathering . . . for a total of 29 not counting John White. A lot left soon after eating & some didn't leave until the *Sound of Music* was over at 10. A partly cloudy, chilly day.

DECEMBER

Wed 3: 24°. Boys rounded Weigh Out. Turned 87 cows, 30 baby into Left Hand. Turned 38 cows back in Weigh Out to make sure they were not cut off from young calves. Hauled 57 calves, 18 heifer years here. Carrol stepped on round rock by loading chute fell & hurt his leg. They think no bones broken but kept him in hospital for night. John V, Clarence & I cleaned dugout up built fire & changed chairs, etc. Evan & Valentino took Swag & Sleepy to Bend harnessed them & schooner out of shed for the TV folks due right after lunch but didn't get to dugout until about 4 and the schooner job wasn't done until after sun down. All hands after dark getting in.

[*Cow work continued until all the culls had been sent to an auction in Abilene and the keepers put in winter pastures. Activities then focused on Christmas preparations. Hogs were butchered, trees were decorated, and bonus checks were deposited for the hands.*]

Thur 25: 14°. Heavy & I visited for quite a while [*in the cookshack*] before any of the family got to showing up. It must have been around 11 when we had the tree. Didn't eat until about 2. I believe we had a total of 44 inc help. Some went home, some toured & some hunted afterwards. Louann out late for a total of 26 here for supper. Most of us to bed early.

Wed 31: 40°. . . . I got all the year end things cleared thru bank fixed checks for boys, grass leases etc before day was out. John Burns got in for lunch. Sally Ann, Edna, Frances, Millie, Dudly, Tom Caldwell, Louann & the 4 Kochs here for supper & the year out. A total of 17 of us & a real nice evening. Connie played for us then she & Louann played *Fandangle* songs & popular music which was good.

Epilogue

Watt Matthews wrote regularly in his diary until May, 1993 and sporadically until September, 1993. Several factors influenced the decision to end this edited version in 1980. As an octogenarian, Watt began to ease into the winter of his years by keeping his activities closer to home. He continued to manage the ranching operations, even branding calves until well into his nineties, and his active social life would have exhausted a much younger person. He did, however, relinquish to a younger generation his advisory role in the beef cattle industry. Thus diary entries after 1980 tend to repeat earlier ones that described life on a Texas family ranch.

Watt always declared that his primary goal in life was to hold the ranch together and pass it on to future generations in better shape than he received it. An important step in that direction was taken in 1981, when he banished the "Specter at Lambshead" (see February 20, 1960) with articles of incorporation. Those descendants of J. A. and Sallie Matthews who still had a financial interest in Lambshead Ranch became stockholders of the Matthews Ranch Company. Their annual meeting is held at the ranch in early March—often on March 2, the birthday of John A. Matthews.

Passing the ranch on to future generations in better shape than in which he received it also meant preserving the material culture of a Texas family ranch. As early as the 1950s, Watt and his sister, Lucile Matthews Brittingham, began restoring the historic houses located on the ranch. Other family members joined eagerly, until every historical site on the ranch has been restored and recognized with appropriate historical markers. The family's interest in preservation also included restoration of other historical sites in Shackleford County. Today the Matthews name is synonymous with historic preservation in Texas. In 1990, Watt received a National Preservation Honor Award from the National Trust for Historic Preservation.

During his life, Watt Matthews received practically every honor that could be given to a cattleman. In fact, the first time he was inducted into the Great Western Hall of Fame, National Cowboy Hall of Fame, he turned the award down, urging successfully that it be given instead to his mother, Sallie Reynolds Matthews. The honor came his way a second time, and he was inducted in 1990. Numerous news articles, magazine articles, and books have focused on this man and his way of life.

In the 1980s, Watt started using Angus bulls on Hereford cows to produce black calves with white faces, called "black baldies." Feedlot owners paid premium prices for this cross because of its excellent gaining ability. Watt's herd later grew to include Brangus and Santa Gertrudis bulls, as well as Longhorn and Angus. Crossbreeding had become the hallmark of a good cow-calf operation, just as purebred sires had been a generation earlier. John Burns, a nephew, described the herd as "quite cosmopolitan."

"Quite cosmopolitan" always has been a good description of life at Lambshead Ranch, but never more so than in the 1980s and 1990s. When business records were tallied, it was confirmed that more than a thousand plates of food were served in the cook shack most months. In addition to cowboys, cattle buyers, wildlife people, and salesmen, people from all walks of life came to visit this man who walked comfortably with "kings" but never lost the common touch. In the spring of 1995, Watt entertained a group that included the son of Prince Rainier and Princess Grace (Kelly) of Monaco. They came to see the restoration of historical houses. Later that summer, a retired factory worker from California stopped by to meet the man he had read so much about. All were greeted with the same "How you do?" Each visitor took a seat in the cook shack, and the conversation began. Watt always listened more than he talked, but from time to time he would add, "Bueno." A fitting comment on his life.

Appendix A

Honors and Awards Bestowed on Watt R. Matthews

Watt Reynolds Matthews, after graduation from Princeton University in 1921, lived all his life on Lambshead Ranch. The honors and awards he received are for his accomplishments in four areas: historic preservation and restoration, conservation of land and wildlife, contributions to the development of the livestock and cattle industries, and cultural development and achievement.

1962	Meritorious Achievement, Princeton University
1967	Elected trustee, National Cowboy Hall of Fame, Oklahoma City
1968	Life membership, Fort Griffin Fandangle Association, Albany, Texas
1971	Historical Preservation Award, Texas State Historical Survey Committee
	Longhorn Golden Chip Award for service to Albany and area, Junior Chamber of Commerce (Jaycees), Albany, Texas
1972	First American to export Hereford cattle to Hungary
1975	Wrangler Award, National Cowboy Hall of Fame, Oklahoma City
	Award for Contribution to Cattle Industry, Southwestern Exposition and Fat Stock Show, Fort Worth
1977	Honorary Membership, Philosophical Society of Texas
1978	Cornerstone Award for support of community and Ft. Griffin *Fandangle* production, Chamber of Commerce, Albany, Texas

1980	Invited, Board of Directors, National Cowboy Hall of Fame, Oklahoma City
1981	Gold Spur Award for preservation of western ranching heritage and promotion of the livestock industry, Ranching Heritage Association, Texas Tech University, Lubbock
	Recognition of fifty years' service on the board of directors, First National Bank, Albany, Texas
1982	Outstanding Soil Stewardship and Game Preservation Award, Soil Conservation Service, U.S. Department of Agriculture
	Man of the Year, Soil Conservation Service, U.S. Department of Agriculture
1983	Josia Wheat Award, Texas Historical Foundation
	Ruth Lester Achievement Award, Texas Historical Foundation
1984–85	Cultural Achievement Award, West Texas Chamber of Commerce
1987	Named one of twenty best Texas ranchers, Texas Ranchers
1989	Awarded honorary Doctor of Humanities degree, Hardin-Simmons University, Abilene
	Watt Matthews Day, City of Albany, Texas
	Watt's publication, *Watt Matthews of Lambshead,* by Laura Wilson, book awarded Wrangler Trophy Award, Western Heritage
1990	National Preservation Honor Award, National Trust for Historic Preservation, Washington, D.C.
	Inducted into Great Western Hall of Fame, National Cowboy Hall of Fame, Oklahoma City
	Named Resident Conservation Rancher of Texas, Soil Conservation Service, U.S. Department of Agriculture
	Elected member, Heritage Hall of Fame, State Fair of Texas, Dallas, Texas
	Publication, *Watkins Reynolds Matthews: Biography of a Texas Rancher,* by Laurence Clayton
1992	Named Man of the Year in Texas Agriculture, County Agricultural Agents Association
	Elected member, Heritage Hall of Fame, State Fair of Texas, Dallas
1994	Book signing with exhibition of Laura Wilson photos of Watt, Irving Heritage Society Art Center, Irving, Texas

1995 Charles Goodnight Award, sponsored by the *Fort Worth Star-Telegram,* with event benefitting the Ranch Management Program at Texas Christian University, Fort Worth

Honorary lifetime membership, American Hereford Association

Honorary lifetime membership, Texas Hereford Association

Honorary lifetime membership, National Cattlemen's Association

Honorary vice-president, Texas and Southwestern Cattle Raisers Association

Honorary vice-president, Southwestern Exposition and Fat Stock Show, Fort Worth

Honorary chair, Board of Overseers, Ranching Heritage Association, Texas Tech University, Lubbock

Director and president, Fort Griffin *Fandangle* Association, since 1958

Chair, Roundup, West Texas Rehabilitation Center, Abilene, Texas, for twenty-one years

Deacon, Matthews Memorial Presbyterian Church, Albany, Texas, for over fifty years

Appendix B

Watt R. Matthews's Preservation, Conservation, and Restoration Achievements

Wildlife Preservation and Land Conservation

1930s–70s	Original Lambshead Ranch wildlife is brought back and preservation programs are implemented.
1941	October, restoration of white-tailed deer to Lambshead is begun with the release of twenty animals. By 1995, these had multiplied to full carrying capacity.
1944	July 1, six-year research and management project for the native wild turkey is initiated between Lambshead Ranch and the Texas Parks and Wildlife Department. By 1995, these had multiplied to close to the ranch's carrying capacity; in addition one hundred or more wild turkeys had been supplied for experimental restocking of other ranches.
1950	Buffalo are brought back, given by Reynolds Cattle Company from their herd in the Davis Mountains on the Long X Ranch; Lambshead buffalo first appear in *Fandangle* production in the 1950s.
1972	April, Longhorn cattle are brought back to Lambshead from the herd in Fort Griffin State Park.
	April, Lambshead Longhorns first appear on the courthouse lawn in Albany during the *Fandangle* production.

1976	Longhorn bulls are first used with Hereford heifers to make a first calving easy and profitable.
1979	John Vandiver put in charge of management of range and wildlife.

Historical Restoration at Lambshead Ranch

1941	Watt R. Matthews purchases the forty acres of Reynolds Bend.
1943–83	Restorations of historic buildings on Lambshead are implemented.
1943	Barber Watkins Reynolds House at Reynolds Bend, built 1876, is restored by Watt R. Matthews
	The Matthews Family Cemetery, begun in 1881, receives care and supervision by Watt R. Matthews from this year onward.
1951	Nathan L. Bartholomew House at the Bend, built 1876, is restored by Lucile Brittingham, with her brother Watt R. Matthews, supervising.
1973	Schoolhouse at Reynolds Bend, built 1888, is replicated accurately upon the original foundation by Watt R. Matthews.
	The House Dugout, built 1890, is restored by Watt R. Matthews.
1976	The Butterfield Trail at Butterfield Gap and Relay Station at Old Clear Fork Crossing, both established in 1858, are marked with upright native limestone slabs by Watt R. Matthews.
1982	May, beginning of restoration by Watt R. Matthews, Old Stone Ranch in Stone Ranch Pasture, built in 1856 by Capt. Newton C. Givens stationed at Camp Cooper military post and occupied from April 1, 1866, to 1867 by Barber Watkins Reynolds's extended family, including Watt's mother as a child.
1983	Restoration Stone Ranch House, two very large corrals, and equally large pens. Dedicated by descendants of W. D. Reynolds.

Summary Statement as Presented by Shirley Caldwell to the National Trust for Historic Preservation:

Watt R. Matthews's Lifetime Commitment to Historical Preservation of the Built Environment

Preservation/Restoration Projects

REYNOLDS BEND COMPLEX:	Built	Restored
B. W. Reynolds House and Rock Fence	1876	1943
Barn	1846	
Rock Cabin	1852	
N. L. Bartholomew House and Rock Fence (supervised restoration for sister)	1876	1951
Rock Guest House	1955	
Cedar Bunkhouse	1966	
Schoolhouse at Reynolds Bend (rebuilt on original foundation)	1888	1973
Matthews-Reynolds Family Cemetery and Rock Fence	1881	Since 1943
The House Dugout	1890	1973

LAMBSHEAD RANCH COMPLEX	Built	Restored
Original Lambshead Camp Cabin (now maintained main headquarters house) and Rail Fence	1897	Maintained to present day
Additions	1906, 1919	
Bunkhouse	1897	Maintained
Red Barn	1907	Maintained
Four Guest Houses and Shop	1965–80	

OLD STONE RANCH COMPLEX:	Built	Restored
House	1856	1983
Sheep Shed	c. 1866	1984
Smokehouse	c. 1866	1984
Bunkhouse	c. 1866	1984
Rock Water Well	c. 1866	1984
Rock Corral and Fence	c. 1866	1984

All new buildings complement and blend with the historic structures.

Bibliography

UNPUBLISHED MATERIAL

Blanton, Matthews. Letter to Texas Water Development Board, August 10, 1966. Personal collection of Watt R. Matthews.

Brittingham, Lucile Matthews. Interviews with Frances M. Holden. Taped recordings, 1972, 1974, 1982, 1944.

Casey, Ethel Matthews. Interviews with Frances M. Holden. Taped recordings, 1972, 1974, 1982, 1994.

Craft, W. A. "The Change from Animal Husbandry to Animal Science." Presented to Animal Science Staff at Iowa State University, 1962.

Grant, Ben O. "The Early History of Shackleford County." Master's thesis, Hardin-Simmons University, 1936.

Heirman, Alan L., Soil Conservation Service, U.S. Department of Agriculture. Interview with Janet Neugebauer. Albany, Texas, September 14, 1992. Personal collection of Janet Neugebauer, Lubbock, Texas.

Judd, Sallie Reynolds Matthews. Interviews by Frances M. Holden. Taped recordings, 1972, 1974, 1982, 1994.

Lewter, Durward. Interview by David Murrah. June 13, 1973. Oral History Files, Southwest Collection, Texas Tech University, Lubbock, Texas.

Matthews, Joe B. Interviews with Frances M. Holden. Tape recordings, 1972, 1974, 1982, 1994.

Matthews, Watt R. Interviews with Frances M. Holden. Tape recordings, 1972, 1974, 1979, 1980, 1982, 1994, 1995, 1996.

———. Interview by Fred Carpenter. October 14, 1971. Oral History Files, Southwest Collection, Texas Tech University, Lubbock, Texas.

———. Interview by Thomas L. Charlton and Tom Z. Parrish. November 5, 1979. Transcript, Baylor University Institute for Oral History and Texas Collection, Baylor University, Waco, Texas.

———. Interviews by Janet Neugebauer. Lambshead Ranch, November 11, 1988; April 13, 1989; September 19, 1991. Personal collection of Janet Neugebauer, Lubbock, Texas.

Nance, Berta Hart. "Cattle," in Fort Griffin *Fandangle* program, 1985, p. 8.

Reynolds, Susan Matthews. Reference Files, Southwest Collection, Texas Tech University, Lubbock, Texas.

PUBLISHED WORKS

"Address by Ben H. Carpenter, President, Texas and Southwestern Cattle Raisers Association at Its Annual Membership Meeting, March 26, 1968." *Cattleman* 54, no. 12 (May, 1968): 28–29, 90, 92–94, 96, 98.

"AHA's Annual Meeting a Lengthy One." *American Hereford Journal* 57, no. 13 (November 1, 1966): 52, 168, 170–71.

"Albert K. Mitchell: National Golden Spur Award Goes to New Mexico Rancher." *Ranch Record* 7, no. 2 (September, 1978): 1.

Allred, B. W. *Practical Grassland Management.* Ed. H. M. Phillips. San Angelo, Tex.: Sheep and Goat Raiser Magazine, 1950.

"American National Meets in Colorado Springs." *Cattleman* 40, no. 9 (February, 1954): 26, 53–56.

"Analyzing the Cattle and Beef Industry." Part I, *Cattleman* 44, no. 11 (April, 1958): 28–31; Part II, *Cattleman* 44, no. 12 (May, 1958): 44–47.

Armstrong, John B. "The President's Message." *Cattleman* 66, no. 11 (April, 1980): 132, 168, 170, 172, 174.

Atherton, Lewis. *The Cattle Kings.* Bloomington: Indiana University Press, 1961.

Bailey, J. W. *Veterinary Handbook for Cattlemen.* 5th ed. Ed. Irving S. Rossoff. New York: Springer Publishing Company, 1980.

Ball, Charles E. *The Finishing Touch: A History of the Texas Cattle Feeders Association and Cattle Feeding in the Southwest.* Amarillo, Texas: Texas Cattle Feeders Association, 1992.

Beef Cattle Investigation in Texas, 1888–1950. Texas Agricultural Experiment Station Bulletin no. 724. College Station: Texas A&M College, 1950.

Berg, Roy T., and Rex M. Butterfield. *New Concepts of Cattle Growth.* New York: John Wiley and Sons, 1976.

Biederman, Henry. "Livestock Shows: Their Influence on the Development of the Livestock Industry." *Cattleman* 38, no. 8 (January, 1951): 18–19, 43.

"Big 'Yes' Vote for Joint Registration." *American Hereford Journal* 53, no. 13 (November 1, 1962): 28–29, 163.

Biggers, Don H. *Shackleford County Sketches*. Edited by Joan Farmer. Albany and Fort Griffin, Tex.: Clear Fork Press, 1974.

Blanton, Thomas Lindsay. *Pictorial Supplement to Interwoven: Centennial Memorial Commemorating the 100th Anniversary of the Birth of Judge John Alexander Matthews, March 2, 1853*. Albany, Tex.: Privately published, 1953.

Bomar, George W. *Texas Weather*. Austin: University of Texas Press, 1983.

Bonsma, Jan C. "Judging Cattle for Functional Efficiency." *Texas Hereford* 13, no. 11 (October, 1964): 14–15.

Burns, John H. "Summers at Lambshead." *Persimmon Hill* 13, no. 4 (winter, 1983): 24–35.

Cartwright, T. C. "Crossbreeding Beef Cattle for Hybrid Vigor." *Texas Agricultural Progress* 8, no. 5 (September–October, 1962): 25–26.

"Cattle Drive Reached Albany Wednesday: Bed Down for the Night." *Albany News*, August 3, 1972, p. 1.

"Cattlemen Display Optimism in Industry." *American Hereford Journal* 44, no. 19 (February 1, 1954): 100–102, 108, 110–11, 115, 118–20, 124–27.

"Cattlemen Support Rehabilitation Center That 'Thinks Like a Rancher.'" *Cattleman* 52, no. 4 (September, 1965): 104, 106.

"Centennial Convention Draws 2,478 Cattlemen to Cowtown." *Cattleman* 63, no. 12 (May, 1977): 21–23, 108–12.

"The Charles Goodnight Award, Watkins Reynolds 'Watt' Matthews." *Fort Worth Star-Telegram*, December 5, 1995, 1–4.

"CK Ranch" (advertisement). *American Hereford Journal* 46, no. 19 (February 1, 1956): 38–39.

Clarke, Mary Whatley. *A Century of Cow Business: The First Hundred Years of the Texas and Southwestern Cattle Raisers Association*. Fort Worth: Texas and Southwestern Cattle Raisers Association, 1976.

———. "Lambshead." *Cattleman* 55, no. 8 (January, 1969): 44, 46, 48, 50.

Clayton, Lawrence. *Chimney Creek Ranch*. Abilene, Texas: Privately published, 1992.

———. *Watkins Reynolds Matthews: Biography of a Texas Rancher*. Austin: Eakin Press, 1994.

Cochrane, W. W. *The Development of American Agriculture: A Historical Analysis*. Minneapolis: University of Minnesota Press, 1979.

Coe, Wilbur. *Ranch on the Ruidoso: The Story of a Pioneer Family in New Mexico, 1871–1968*. New York: Alfred A. Knopf, 1968.

Conkling, Roscoe P., and Margaret B. Conkling. *The Butterfield Overland Mail, 1857–1869*. 3 vols. Glendale, Calif.: Arthur H. Clark Company, 1947.

Connor, Seymour V. *The Peters Colony of Texas.* Austin: Texas State Historical Association, 1959.

"Control Powers Curbed." *American Cattle Producer* 33, no. 3 (August, 1951): 7.

DeGraff, Herrell. *Beef: Production and Distribution.* Norman: University of Oklahoma Press, 1960.

"Denver's 15,859 Feeders." *American Hereford Journal* 48, no. 19 (February 1, 1958): 202.

Diggins, Ronald V.; Clarence E. Bundy; and Virgil W. Christensen. *Beef Production.* 4th ed. Englewood Cliffs, N.J.: Prentice-Hall, 1984.

Dobie, J. Frank. *The Longhorns.* Boston: Little, Brown, 1941.

Douglas, C. L. *Cattle Kings of Texas.* Dallas: Book Craft, 1939.

Dyer, I. A., and C. C. O'Mary. *The Feedlot.* 2d ed. Philadelphia: Lea and Febiger, 1977.

Dykstra, R. R. *Animal Sanitation and Disease Control.* Danville, Ill.: Interstate Printers and Publishers, 1955.

Ensminger, M. E. *The Stockman's Handbook.* 6th ed. Danville, Ill.: Interstate Printers and Publishers, 1983.

Erickson, John R. *The Modern Cowboy.* Lincoln: University of Nebraska Press, 1981.

Evans, Joe M. *Bloys Cowboy Camp Meeting.* El Paso, Tex.: Guynes Printing Company, 1959.

Evans, Will F. *Border Skylines: Fifty Years of "Tallying Out" on the Bloys Roundup Ground.* Dallas, Tex.: Bloys Camp Meeting Association, 1940.

Farley, F. W. *Beef Cattle Husbandry.* Memphis, Tenn.: Stockman, 1947.

Farmer, Joan. "Fort Davis on the Clear Fork of the Brazos." *West Texas Historical Association Year Book* 33 (1957): 117–26.

———. "Sandstone Sentinels." *West Texas Historical Association Year Book* 34 (1958): 112–27.

Fatherree, A. P. "Revolution in Mississippi." *American Hereford Journal* 51, no. 17 (January 1, 1961): 132–34.

Faulkner, Lloyd C. "A Calf from Every Cow." *American Hereford Journal* 56, no. 5 (July 1, 1965): 152, 156, 161–62, 166, 824.

"Fort Worth Stocker-Feeders." *Texas Hereford* 6, no. 4 (November, 1956): 23.

"Four West Texas Cowmen Honored by Wichita Falls Ranch Roundup." *Livestock Weekly.* (August 20, 1987): 6.

Fowler, Steward H. *Beef Production in the South.* Rev. ed. Danville, Ill.: Interstate Printers and Publishers, 1979.

Freedgood, Seymour. "The Specter at Lambshead Ranch." *Fortune* 61, no. 4 (April, 1960): 123–30, 206, 210, 212, 215–16, 220, 222.

Fritz, George. "Fairs Cultivate the Customer." *American Hereford Journal* 55, no. 5 (July 1, 1964): 610–14.

"From the Water Plant War at Reynolds Bend." *Abilene Reporter-News*, August 6, 1966, p. 4A.

Fudge, J. F., and G. S. Fraps. *The Chemical Composition of Grasses of Northwest Texas as Related to Soils and to Requirements for Range Cattle.* Texas Agricultural Experiment Station Bulletin no. 669. College Station: Texas A&M College, 1945.

Garrett, Raymond G., and John L. Wilbur, Jr. "What Is the Brucellosis Situation?" *Cattleman* 46, no. 12 (May, 1960): 26–27, 38.

"Good Turnout for Denver Conference." *American Hereford Journal* 54, no. 7 (August 1, 1963): 28.

"Governor Connally Cites Need for Agricultural Mobilization." *Cattleman* 53, no. 11 (April, 1967): 32–33.

"Grass Fires Out After 100 Sections Burn." *Albany News*, January 25, 1951, p. 1.

Green, James Robert. "A Brief History of the Stone Ranch." N.p., 1984.

Green, Robert. "The Free Range Era of the Cattle Industry." *West Texas Historical Association Year Book* 46 (October, 1970): 204–10.

Greene, A. C. *A Personal Country*. College Station: Texas A&M University Press, 1979.

———. *900 Miles on the Butterfield Trail.* Denton: University of North Texas Press, 1994.

Haley, J. Evetts. *Charles Goodnight: Cowman and Plainsman.* Norman: University of Oklahoma Press, 1943.

"Hall of Famers Bring 'Wrangler' to Matthews." *Abilene Reporter-News*, May 5, 1975, p. 6B.

"Harmony the Keynote of AHA Meeting." *American Hereford Journal* 54, no. 13 (November 1, 1963): 24, 150–51.

Hatch, Stephan L., and Jennifer Pluhar. *Texas Range Plants.* College Station: Texas A&M University Press, 1993.

Hendrickson, Kenneth E., Jr. *The Waters of the Brazos: A History of the Brazos River Authority, 1929–1979.* Waco: Texian Press, 1981.

"Hereford Bull Sparks Electronic Brain." *American Hereford Journal* 51, no. 24 (April 15, 1961): 46.

"Hereford Journal to New Ownership." *American Hereford Journal* 51, no. 21 (March 1, 1961): 7.

"Hereford Progress Clinic Big Success." *Texas Hereford* 11, no. 8 (May, 1962): 147–48.

"Hereford Promotion Theme of Progress Clinics." *Texas Hereford* 10, no. 10 (July, 1961): 2–3.

"Herefords Dominate P1 Show's Carcass Contest with Four of Top Five Placings." *American Hereford Journal* 53, no. 23 (April 1, 1963): 58.

Holden, Frances Mayhugh. *Lambshead Before Interwoven: A Texas Range Chronicle, 1848–1878.* College Station: Texas A&M University Press, 1982.

Holden, William C. *Alkali Trails.* Dallas: Southwest Press, 1930.

Issel, William. *Social Change in the United States, 1945–1983.* New York: Schocken Books, 1985.

"It Was a Capitol Convention." *American Beef Producer* 51, no. 10 (March, 1970): 10–12.

"J. A. Matthews Ranch Co. Again Shows Herefords to Feeder Championship." *American Hereford Journal* 51, no. 20 (February 15, 1961): 101.

James, D. Clayton. *The Years of MacArthur: Triumph and Disaster.* Volume 3. Boston: Houghton Mifflin Company, 1985.

Jones, John W. "Total Performance Records." *Texas Hereford* 14, no. 7 (May, 1965): 19, 30–32.

———. "TPR Program Is Ready for You." *American Hereford Journal* 57, no. 5 (July 1, 1966): 564, 861.

Jones, Pat Lidia. "Ponderings by Pat." *Albany News,* February 5, 1987, p. 4A.

Jordan, T. G. *Trails to Texas, Southern Roots of Western Cattle Ranching.* Lincoln: University of Nebraska Press, 1981.

Kelton, Steve. *Renderbrook: A Century under the Spade Brand.* College Station: Texas A&M University Press, 1989.

Klingman, Glenn C. *Weed Control: As a Science.* New York: John Wiley and Sons, 1961.

Kurtz, Michael L. *Crime of the Century.* Knoxville: University of Tennessee Press, 1982.

Lackey, Carol. "Family Book Relates Area History." *Albany News,* 1987, pp. 3–5A.

Largent, Roy R. "Show Ring Competition Hailed as Inspiration to Breed Improvement and Type Stabilization." *Texas Hereford* 1, no. 11 (June, 1952): 7, 16.

Lasater, Laurence M. *The Lasater Philosophy of Cattle Raising.* El Paso: Texas Western Press, 1972.

Lasley, John F. *Beef Cattle Production.* Englewood Cliffs, N.J.: Prentice-Hall, 1981.

Lenamon, James F. "Watt Matthews and the Texas Tradition." *Persimmon Hill* 4, no. 4 (winter, 1974): 16–25.

"Leptospirosis Presents a Double Barrel Threat." *Cattleman* 47, no. 11 (April, 1961): 92.

Letz, Roger B. "Their Secret to Better Herefords." *Cattleman* 41, no. 3 (August, 1954): 38–39, 62–63.

"Lone Star Meeting." *American Cattle Producer* 33, no. 8 (January, 1952): 11–13.

"A Look at Some Proposed Changes in the Internal Revenue Code." *Cattleman* 49, no. 11 (April, 1963): 26.

Loughmiller, Campbell, and Lynn Loughmiller. *Texas Wildflowers: A Field Guide.* 4th ed. Austin: University of Texas Press, 1988.

Lucas, Donnie A. "Watt Matthews Given 2nd Award." *Albany News,* May 31, 1984, p. 1A.

McCann, L. P. *The Battle of Bull Runts: Overcoming Dwarfism.* Columbus, Oh.: Privately printed, 1974.

———. "Mission Accomplished." *American Hereford Journal* 52, no. 5 (July 1, 1961): 135, 138, 140, 142.

McConnell, Joseph Carroll. *The West Texas Frontier.* 2 vols. Palo Pinto, Tex.: Legal Bank and Book Company, 1939.

McCoy, Dorothy Abbott. *Texas Ranchmen: Twenty Texans Who Helped Build Today's Cattle Industry.* Austin: Eakin Press, 1987.

McNeely, J. G. "A New Market News Report." *Cattleman* 44, no. 5 (October, 1957): 22.

Maddox, Cynthia, "Watt Matthews, Rancher." *Texas Highways,* (April, 1991): 12–16.

Manchester, William. *American Caesar.* Boston: Little, Brown and Company, 1978.

"Matthews Receiving Award." *Albany News*, Febrary 14, 1985, p.1A.

Matthews, Sallie Reynolds. *Interwoven.* College Station: Texas A&M University Press, 1982.

———. *True Tales of the Frontier.* Arranged by Joseph EdwinBlanton. Albany, Tex.: Venture Press, 1961.

"Matthews To Receive KTB Award." *Albany News,* June 25, 1987, p. 3A.

"Men Walk on Moon." *New York Times,* July 21, 1969, p. 1.

Minish, Gary L. "The Showring Must Be Used as a Tool and Not a Toy." *Hereford Journal* 63, no. 4 (July, 1972): 276, 284.

Minish, Gary L., and Danny G. Fox. *Beef Production and Management.* 2d ed. Reston, Va.: Reston Publishing Company, 1982.

"Much in Agreement at Beef Symposium." *American Hereford Journal* 57, no. 2 (May 15, 1966): 16–17, 62.

"Mystery Spur . . . the OK." *Western Horseman* 33, no. 12 (December, 1968): 112–13.

Nail, Robert E., Jr. *The Fandangle: A People's Theater.* Albany, Tex.: Fort Griffin Fandangle Association, 1970.

National Live Stock and Meat Board. *Annual Report, 1971–1972: 50th Anniversary Edition.* Chicago: National Livestock and Meat Board, 1972.

Neighbors, Kenneth F. "Chapters from History of Texas Indian Reservations." *West Texas Historical Association Year Book* 33 (1957): 3–16.

———. "Indian Exodus out of Texas in 1859." *West Texas Historical Association Year Book* 36 (1960), 80–97.

———. *Robert Simpson Neighbors and the Texas Frontier, 1836–1859.* Waco: Texian Press, 1975.

"New Authority for TSCRA Strongly Supported." *Cattleman* 48, no. 5 (October, 1961): 28–32, 43.

"New Systemic Insecticides Kill Cattle Grubs." *Cattleman* 45, no. 3 (October, 1958): 94, 96.

"Ninety-sixth TSCRA Convention Sets Attendance Record." *Cattleman* 59, no. 11 (April, 1973): 21–23, 140.

Nordyke, Lewis. *Great Roundup: The Story of Texas and Southwestern Cowmen.* New York: William Morrow, 1955.

"Old West Comes Back to Life in the Amon Carter Museum of Western Art." *Cattleman* 48, no. 4 (September, 1961): 40–41.

Oppenheimer, Harold L. *Cowboy Arithmetic: Cattle as an Investment.* Danville, Ill.: Interstate Printers and Publishers, 1961.

Ormsby, Waterman L. *The Butterfield Overland Mail.* Ed. Lyle H. Wright and Josephine M. Bynum. San Marino, Calif.: Huntington Library, 1954.

Ornduff, Donald R. *The First Forty-Nine: Personalities in the Honor Gallery of the AHA's Hereford Heritage Hall.* Kansas City, Mo.: Lowell Press, 1981.

———. *The Hereford in America.* Kansas City, Mo.: Privately printed, 1957.

Pattie, Jane. *Cowboy Spurs and Their Makers.* College Station: Texas A&M University Press, 1991.

Perkins, Doug. "A Century of Ranching." *Cattleman* 69, no. 3 (August, 1982): 59–69.

———. "There's Gold in Those Hunting Leases." *Cattleman* 64, no. 2 (July, 1977): 42–44, 82–86.

"Plans for Clinic Programs Complete." *American Hereford Journal* 52, no. 3 (June 1, 1961): 10–11.

"Poage Fears Trouble from Low Farm Prices." *Cattleman* 53, no. 11 (April, 1967): 32–33.

"Portrait of a Frontier Family." *House Beautiful,* January, 1985, pp. 72–77, 115.

Putnam, P. A., and E. J. Warwick. "Beef Cattle Breeds." *USDA Farmer's Bulletin* no. 2228. Washington, D.C.: Government Printing Office, 1968.

"A Quick Look at Texas A&M Research." *Cattleman* 44, no. 5 (October, 1957): 18, 20, 22–24, 27, 74–76, 78.

Reagan, Danny. "Watt a guy, Watt a guy!" *Abilene Reporter-News,* May 12, 1988.

Reeves, Frank. "Cowmen Reaffirm Views at Fort Worth." *American Hereford Journal* 42, no. 18 (January 14, 1952): 14–15.

———. "Factory on the Hoof." *American Hereford Journal* 48, no. 17 (January 1, 1958): 28–30, 154.

———. "Texas Cowboy Reunion." *Cattleman* 46, no. 4 (September, 1959): 42–43, 70, 72, 74.

———. "West Texas Hereford Tour." *Cattleman* 42, no. 3 (August, 1955): 34–37.

"Research Frontier." *American Hereford Journal* 44, no. 18 (January 15, 1954): 136–37.

Rifkin, Jeremy. *Beyond Beef: The Rise and Fall of the Cattle Culture.* New York: Penguin Books, 1992.

Rister, Carl Coke. *Fort Griffin on the Texas Frontier.* Norman: University of Oklahoma Press, 1956.

"Ronald Reagan: On Free Enterprise." *Cattleman* 63, no. 12 (May, 1977): 70–82.

Rye, Edgar. *The Quirt and the Spur.* Chicago: W. B. Conkey Company, 1909.

Schacht, Henry. *The Long and Winding Trail: The History of the California Cattlemen's Association.* Sacramento: California Cattlemen's Association, 1991.

Schlebecker, John T. *Cattle Raising on the Plains, 1900–1961.* Lincoln: University of Nebraska Press, 1963.

Schulz, Ellen D., and Robert Runyon. *Texas Cacti.* San Antonio: Texas Academy of Science, 1930.

Scruggs, Charles G. *The Atom and the Deadly Fly.* Austin: Pemberton Press, 1975.

Seagraves, Dale. "Cowboy Reunion, Texas Style." *Cattleman* 67, no. 4 (September, 1980): 138–45.

Simms, Willard. "National Western Livestock Show." In "Livestock Shows," *Cattleman* 43, no. 8 (January, 1957): 34–36.

Siringo, Charles A. *A Lone Star Cowboy.* Santa Fe: Privately printed, 1919.

Skaggs, Jimmy M. *Prime Cut: Livestock Raising and Meatpacking in the United States, 1607–1983.* College Station: Texas A&M University Press, 1986.

"Soon—A Livestock Systemic." *Cattleman* 43, no. 8 (January, 1957): 60–62.

"Southwestern Exposition and Fat Stock Show." *Cattleman* 47, no. 10 (March, 1961): 74.

Spanier, John W. *The Truman-MacArthur Controversy and the Korean War.* Cambridge, Mass.: Belknap Press of Harvard University Press, 1959.

Swaffar, Paul. "What's Ahead for Purebred Herefords." *Cattleman* 45, no. 3 (August, 1958): 38, 62.

Texas Almanac, 1958–59. Dallas: A. H. Belo Corporation, 1957.

"Texas Hereford Round-up Conference Held." *Texas Hereford* 13, no. 9 (August, 1964): 2–3.

Texas in Review. Film Files, Southwest Collection, Texas Tech University, Lubbock, Texas.

Tharp, Benjamin Carroll. *Texas Range Grasses.* Austin: University of Texas Press, 1952.

"Tower Speaks on Defense," *Cattleman* 66, no. 11 (April, 1980): 133, 164, 166, 168.

Towne, C. W., and E. N. Wentworth. *Cattle and Men.* Norman: University of Oklahoma Press, 1955.

"Treat Early for Hornflies," *Weekly Livestock Reporter,* May 3, 1951, p.3.

"TSCRA to Continue Brand Inspection Service." *Cattleman* 48, no. 7 (December, 1961): 7.

Turque, Bill. "The War of the West." *Newsweek,* September 30, 1991, pp. 18–35.

U.S. Congress. House of Representatives. *Program for the Great Plains.* 84th Congress, 2d session, 1956, document 289.

U.S. Department of Agriculture. *Finishing Beef Cattle.* Farmer's Bulletin no. 2196. Washington, D.C.: U.S. Government Printing Office, 1964.

"U.S. Hereford Exports Boom as Hungary Purchases 445 Head." *American Hereford Journal* 63, no. 2 (June, 1972): 8–9.

Vay, Jane Montague. "Your Horse Will Load Himself." *Cattleman* 62, no. 4 (September, 1975): 92, 94.

"VEE Strikes Texas Horses." *Cattleman* 58, no. 3 (August, 1971): 22–23.

Watt, W. R. "Southwestern Exposition and Fat Stock Show." *Cattleman* 43, no. 8 (January, 1957): 34–36.

Wagnon, Kenneth A.; Reuben Albaugh; and George H. Hart. *Beef Cattle Production.* New York: Macmillan Company, 1960.

Webb, J. R. "Chapters from the Frontier Life of Phin W. Reynolds." *West Texas Historical Association Year Book* 3 (1927): 43–58.

Webb, Walter Prescott, and Bailey Carroll, eds. *Handbook of Texas.* 2 vols. Austin: The Texas State Historical Association, 1952.

Weber, Arthur D. "Showring Versus the Scales." *Texas Hereford* 6, no. 2, (September, 1956): 5–10, 17–22.

———. "The Traditions of America's Cattlemen and Their Significance to Our Nation's Beef Industry." *Aberdeen Angus Journal* 54, no. 12 (July, 1973): 112–13, 196–206.

"What Is a Corriente?" *West Texas Livestock Weekly,* April 18, 1963, p. 7.

"What the Texas Beef Council Is Doing for the Cowman." *Texas Hereford* 4, no. 9 (April, 1955): 7–9.

Whitaker, Bill. "Calf-Branding Is No Act for Watt Matthews." *Abilene Reporter-News,* December 2, 1984, p. 5E.

———. "Photo Exhibit Reveals Life in Albany." *Abilene Reporter-News,* December 2, 1984, p. 5E.

Willham, R. L. *The Legacy of the Stockman.* Ames: Department of Animal Science, Iowa State University, 1985.

———. "The Show Ring and Animal Breeding." *Aberdeen Angus Journal* 58, no. 7 (February, 1977): 132, 134, 136, 138, 140.

Wilson, Laura. *Watt Matthews of Lambshead.* Austin: Texas State Historical Association, 1989.

Winningham, Geoff. *Rites of Fall: High School Football in Texas.* Austin: University of Texas Press, 1979.

Wolff, Henry, Jr. "Cattle Roundup for Crippled Children." *Cattleman* 48, no. 4 (September, 1961): 136–38.

Wood, Charles L. *The Kansas Beef Industry.* Lawrence: Regents Press of Kansas, 1980.

Young, Vernon A.; C. E. Fisher; R. A. Darrow; W. G. McGully; and D. W. Young. *Recent Developments in the Chemical Control of Brush on Texas Ranges. Texas Agricultural Experiment Station Bulletin no. 721* (revised). College Station: Texas A&M College, 1951.

Index

Note: Pages with illustrations are indicated by italics.